NEW STUDIES IN BIBLICAL THEOLOGY 57

NOW AND NOT YET

NEW STUDIES IN BIBLICAL THEOLOGY 57

Series editor: D. A. Carson

NOW AND NOT YET

Theology and mission in Ezra–Nehemiah

Dean R. Ulrich

APOLLOS

IVP Academic
An imprint of InterVarsity Press
Downers Grove, Illinois

APOLLOS (an imprint of Inter-Varsity Press, England)
36 Causton Street, London SW1P 4ST, England
Website: www.ivpbooks.com
Email: ivp@ivpbooks.com

InterVarsity Press, USA
P.O. Box 1400, Downers Grove, IL 60515, USA
Website: www.ivpress.com
Email: email@ivpress.com

Inter-Varsity Press, England, publishes Christian books that are true to the Bible and that communicate the gospel, develop discipleship and strengthen the church for its mission in the world.

IVP originated within the Inter-Varsity Fellowship, now the Universities and Colleges Christian Fellowship, a student movement connecting Christian Unions in universities and colleges throughout Great Britain, and a member movement of the International Fellowship of Evangelical Students. That historic association is maintained, and all senior IVP staff and committee members subscribe to the UCCF Basis of Faith. Website: www.uccf.org.uk.

InterVarsity Press USA, is the book-publishing division of InterVarsity Christian Fellowship/USA and a member movement of the International Fellowship of Evangelical Students. Website: www.intervarsity.org.

First published 2021

Set in 10/13.25pt Minion Pro and Gill Sans Nova
Typeset in Great Britain by CRB Associates, Potterhanworth, Lincolnshire
Printed and bound in Great Britain by Ashford Colour Press Ltd, Gosport, Hampshire

Produced on paper from sustainable sources.

UK ISBN: 978-1-78974-346-3 (print)
UK ISBN: 978-1-78974-347-0 (digital)

US ISBN: 978-1-5140-0407-4 (print)
US ISBN: 978-1-5140-0408-1 (digital)

British Library Cataloguing-in-Publication Data
A catalogue record for this book is available from the British Library.

Library of Congress Cataloging-in-Publication Data
A catalog record for this book is available from the Library of Congress.

In memory of my parents
John Richard and Ann Lanicker Ulrich

And of my parents-in-law
Eric Gordon and Celia Turk Errickson

Now in the presence of the God of Ezra–Nehemiah
Not yet raised to life on the new earth

Contents

Series preface

New Studies in Biblical Theology is a series of monographs that address key issues in the discipline of biblical theology. Contributions to the series focus on one or more of three areas: (1) the nature and status of biblical theology, including its relations with other disciplines (e.g. historical theology, exegesis, systematic theology, historical criticism, narrative theology); (2) the articulation and exposition of the structure of thought of a particular biblical writer or corpus; and (3) the delineation of a biblical theme across all or part of the biblical corpora.

Above all, these monographs are creative attempts to help thinking Christians understand their Bibles better. The series aims simultaneously to instruct and to edify, to interact with the current literature, and to point the way ahead. In God's universe, mind and heart should not be divorced: in this series we will try not to separate what God has joined together. While the notes interact with the best of scholarly literature, the text is uncluttered with untransliterated Greek and Hebrew, and tries to avoid too much technical jargon. The volumes are written within the framework of confessional evangelicalism, but there is always an attempt at thoughtful engagement with the sweep of the relevant literature.

Nowadays it is a commonplace to speak of the running tension in the New Testament between the 'already' and the 'not yet'. For example, there are discussions of whether the eschatology in Hebrews is futurist or realized, and whether 'inaugurated eschatology' is a more appropriate label than 'realized eschatology'. This book deploys a somewhat similar bifurcation, 'now and not yet', but its subtitle signals what is novel about Dean Ulrich's approach: the focus is not on the New Testament but on the Old, specifically on Ezra–Nehemiah. Ulrich carefully traces out the rebuilding of the temple, the rebuilding of the people and the rebuilding of the wall, outlining the importance of each and celebrating the covenant renewal – and then he explores how badly in each case the 'now' degenerates into the 'not yet' that points to what is yet to come. Wisely read, the books of Ezra–Nehemiah thus become a paradigm of biblical eschatology that sheds light on how to read the entire Bible.

D. A. Carson
Trinity Evangelical Divinity School

Author's preface

The publication of this book would not have happened without the assistance of other people. I wish to acknowledge them here.

First, I thank the men and women whose works appear in the footnotes and bibliography. They have taught me much about Ezra–Nehemiah. Moreover, their insights have stimulated my thinking about this portion of the Christian Bible. Any contribution I have made simply adds to theirs.

Second, the following libraries enabled me to access this scholarship: John Bulow Campbell Library at Columbia Theological Seminary, Livingston Library at Shorter University, Memorial Library at Berry College and Pitts Theology Library at Emory University. I especially thank Hans van Deventer for allowing me to make use of the ATLA Religion Database through the library of North-West University in South Africa. I also owe a debt of gratitude to the interlibrary loan staff, especially Brian French, at the Rome-Floyd County Library.

Third, I thank Donald Carson for accepting this book into New Studies in Biblical Theology and for making editorial suggestions. This book is better because of his advice. I also thank Philip Duce (senior commissioning editor), Samantha Snedden (project editor), Eldo Barkhuizen (copy editor), Michelle Clark (proofreader) and others at Inter-Varsity Press for their oversight of the process that turned a manuscript into a monograph. Eldo, in particular, made some helpful suggestions regarding the arrangement of content. I am honoured to be a part of this fine series.

Fourth, Anita Errickson, my sister-in-law, and Susanah Hanson, librarian at Trinity School for Ministry, proofread the manuscript before the publisher's deadline. After I had read it so many times that I could no longer spot errors, they gave it a fresh reading. Their efforts have appreciably spared me some embarrassment. If they and I missed a mistake, I ask for the reader's forbearance.

Fifth, my mother died during the writing of this book. Meanwhile, the earthly lives of my father, father-in-law and mother-in-law had ended even earlier. My wife and I miss them. We are grateful for their sacrificial love, positive influence and good memories.

Dean R. Ulrich

Abbreviations

AB	Anchor Bible
AcT	*Acta theologica*
AD	Anno Domini
ANE	ancient Near East(ern)
ARAST	*Aramaic Studies*
BC	before Christ
BETL	Bibliotheca ephemeridum theologicarum lovaniensium
Bib	*Biblica*
BibInt	*Biblical Interpretation*
BSac	*Bibliotheca sacra*
BST	The Bible Speaks Today
BTCB	Brazos Theological Commentary on the Bible
BZAW	Beihefte zur Zeitschrift für die alttestamentliche Wissenschaft
CBQ	*Catholic Biblical Quarterly*
CTR	*Criswell Theological Review*
DSB	Daily Study Bible
EBS	Encountering Biblical Studies
ESV	English Standard Version
FAT	Forschungen zum Alten Testament
HB	Hebrew Bible
HBM	Hebrew Bible Monographs
HBT	*Horizons in Biblical Theology*
HTR	*Harvard Theological Review*
Int	*Interpretation*
ITC	International Theological Commentary
JBL	*Journal of Biblical Literature*
JBQ	*Jewish Bible Quarterly*
JETS	*Journal of the Evangelical Theological Society*
JHS	*Journal of Hebrew Scriptures*
JSOT	*Journal for the Study of the Old Testament*
JSS	*Journal of Semitic Studies*

JTISup	Journal of Theological Interpretation Supplements
kg	kilograms
km	kilometres
LNTS	Library of New Testament Studies
LSTS	Library of Second Temple Studies
m	metres
NAC	New American Commentary
NCB	New Century Bible
NICNT	New International Commentary on the New Testament
NICOT	New International Commentary on the Old Testament
NIV	New International Version
NIVAC	NIV Application Commentary
NovT	*Novum Testamentum*
NSBT	New Studies in Biblical Theology
OTL	Old Testament Library
OtSt	Oudtestamentische Studiën
PRSt	*Perspectives in Religious Studies*
PTMS	Princeton Theological Monograph Series
RTR	*Reformed Theological Review*
SBLAB	Society of Biblical Literature Academia Biblica
SBLDS	Society of Biblical Literature Dissertation Series
SBLEJL	Society of Biblical Literature Early Judaism and Its Literature
SBLMS	Society of Biblical Literature Monograph Series
SBLSS	Society of Biblical Literature Symposium Series
SHBC	Smyth & Helwys Bible Commentary
SJHC	Studies in Jewish History and Culture
ThTo	*Theology Today*
TJ	*Trinity Journal*
TOTC	Tyndale Old Testament Commentaries
TynB	*Tyndale Bulletin*
VT	*Vetus Testamentum*
VTSup	Supplements to Vetus Testamentum
WBC	Word Biblical Commentary
WTJ	*Westminster Theological Journal*
WUNT	Wissenschaftliche Untersuchungen zum Neuen Testament
ZAW	*Zeitschrift für die alttestamentliche Wissenschaft*

1
Introduction

Throughout the twentieth century, the book of Ezra–Nehemiah did not receive the same amount of scholarly attention as some other books of the Old Testament. When I began writing this book several years ago, a visit to Pitts Theology Library at Emory University in Atlanta revealed that there were noticeably fewer commentaries and monographs for Ezra–Nehemiah than there were for other books in the Old Testament. Meanwhile, the considerably shorter Ruth had about the same number of volumes on the shelf as did Ezra–Nehemiah. Why has Ezra–Nehemiah, at least until recently, suffered comparative neglect?

The first reason for less attention having been given to Ezra–Nehemiah is that this book seems to lack literary coherence. Both men, Ezra (Ezra 8:15 – 9:15) and Nehemiah (Neh. 1:1 – 7:5; 12:27–43; 13:6–31), speak in first-person singular, giving the book two first-person voices or what are often called 'memoirs'. Moreover, a third-person voice reports the first return from Babylon (Ezra 1 – 6), Ezra's return (Ezra 7:1 – 8:14), Ezra's handling of the problem of mixed marriages (Ezra 10), Ezra's reading of the law (Neh. 8), the priest's confession of sin (Neh. 9) and the people's repentance (Neh. 10). Aramaic sections, numerous lists and dischronologization in Ezra 4 add to the confusion and make it hard to get a sense of the whole. The person or people responsible for the final form of Ezra–Nehemiah might not have smoothed out the roughness of the compositional process, but a discernible message nevertheless runs through this book. That message will occupy the following pages.

Second, the lists of names make this book less appealing to the average reader.[1] In fact, they mean the boo kmay have a soporific effect.[2] The story of the post-exilic community is certainly compelling because of the

[1] Angel 2007: 143.
[2] Eskenazi (1988a: 48) refers to the 'tiresome specificity' of the lists.

obstacles encountered and the progress achieved. Even so, the numerous lists interrupt and slow the pace of the narrative. The reader who dutifully tries to look at each name may lose track of the narrative or simply become drowsy. While it is evident that the writer(s) of Ezra–Nehemiah meant to do more than compile the equivalent of a telephone book, the lists seem to work against his or their larger purpose, thereby preventing this account of post-exilic events from being a 'page-turner'. As will be seen, though, the lists convey rich meaning.

Third, biblical scholars have sometimes regarded the post-exilic era Ezra–Nehemiah describes as little more than an extension of the exile.[3] McEntire explains why:

> Ezra–Nehemiah is one of the most neglected books in the study of the Hebrew Bible/Old Testament. In the sub-field of Old Testament theology or biblical theology, this neglect is perhaps even more acute. It was easy enough to see why this was the case in the past, when historical approaches to biblical theology placed great emphasis on the 'mighty acts of God'. The God of Ezra–Nehemiah is not a mighty actor.[4]

In other words, Ezra–Nehemiah supposedly features no forward progress in God's plan of redemption. Nehemiah 9:10–15 may recall supernatural acts of Yahweh at the time of the exodus from Egypt, but Ezra–Nehemiah records nothing comparable during the returns from Babylon. No miracles occur in Ezra–Nehemiah. Moreover, although Nehemiah 9:22–25 mentions the stunning victories in the wilderness and in Canaan, Ezra 9:7, Nehemiah 9:32 and 9:36–37 speak only of current domination by foreign rulers. Hence, all of God's mighty deeds on behalf of his people seemingly occurred before the exile, but none in the years after. If, from a New Testament perspective, God's people must await the birth of Jesus for the next instalment in God's programme for history (Gal. 4:4–5), post-exilic believers apparently had little or no sense of the 'now' in their lifetime – just of the 'not yet'. According to this view, Ezra–Nehemiah has minimal spiritual vitality with which to encourage and challenge its readers. Perhaps, but Ezra 8:31 credits God with delivering Ezra's wave of returnees

---

[3] Levering 2007: 25, 32.
[4] McEntire 2012: 113 (see also 118–119, 123–124).

from trouble on the way from Persia to Judah. The Hebrew verb *way-yaṣṣîlēnû* is used of God's saving activity during the exodus from Egypt (Exod. 12:27; 18:8–10), wandering in the wilderness (Deut. 2:36), conquest of Canaan (Josh. 21:44; 24:11) and at other times (Neh. 9:28). Like other generations of God's people, the members of the post-exilic community thought that Yahweh was mightily active in their midst, and perceived typological parallels between their situation and that of their ancestors.[5]

Fourth, some people have considered Ezra–Nehemiah as more legalistic than gracious. For example, Noth thought that the role of the law underwent a change after the exile.[6] Before the exile, the law specified how the Israelites should live distinctively in covenant with Yahweh. Yahweh initiated the covenantal relationship and then gave the law for the purpose of instructing and guiding his people. The law did not create the relationship but enabled it to grow. After the exile, claimed Noth, the law became detached from the covenantal relationship and so lost its original purpose. If the Persian government used the law to maintain order on the western edge of the empire, the post-exilic community took the additional step of reversing the indicative and the imperative. Instead of God's initiative in the form of the exodus (the indicative) prompting human response in the form of obedience to the law (the imperative), human law-keeping was thought to be the basis of God's favour.[7] Noth's view, of course, is typical of Protestants who, having been influenced by Martin Luther's polarization of law and grace, consider Second Temple Judaism (Israelite belief and practice after the exile) a religion of works.[8] To this way of thinking, the post-exilic Ezra–Nehemiah with its interest in reading and practising the law of Moses fell short of Paul's declaration of freedom from the law.[9]

---

[5] Kissling 2014: 211–217.

[6] Noth 1967: 21–23, 76–79, 86–87, 95–96, 106–107.

[7] See also Eichrodt 1961: 342–349; Moore 1962: 9–13; von Rad 1962: 89–92; Koch 1974: 173–176; Childs 1979: 626; Bright 1981: 440–442; Blenkinsopp 1988: 35; Brueggemann and Linafelt 2012: 404; Saysell 2012: 3–4, 132–134; Wilson 2014: 53. For the effect of this alleged post-exilic turn towards legalism on NT scholarship, see Sanders 1977: 33–59.

[8] Consider the more balanced but still quite Lutheran approach in Steinmann 2010: 98–103.

[9] Moore 1962: 236. It is, of course, not unusual to encounter people who think that Israel's belief and practice before the exile were also works-based. For the contrast between the law of Judaism and the gospel of Christianity, see Wellhausen 1957: 3–4, 499–513 and Levenson's discussion (1993: 12–14) of Wellhausen. Wellhausen's discussion of Ezra and Nehemiah is found on pp. 405–410 and 495–498 of the *Prolegomena*. Wellhausen lived before Noth and so influenced his thinking about the OT (Blenkinsopp 2009: 2). The anti-Semitic background of Wellhausen's reconstruction of both Israelite history and the compositional history of the OT is discussed by Wilson (1989: 90–101) and Germar (2008: 23–94).

There is, however, another way to understand the relationship of law and gospel. Saysell, for example, observes:

> The recent trend is increasingly to defend EN [Ezra–Nehemiah] against an earlier charge of legalism in the Postexilic Period evident in the writings of such theologians as Eichrodt, Noth and von Rad. The strategy of those rejecting the alleged legalism in EN most often conceive [*sic*] of the Law as being in the context of the covenant following on from God's gracious deliverance of his people.[10]

Moreover, the Old Testament associates the law with God's mission for an already redeemed people (Exod. 19 – 23; Isa. 2:3; 51:4; Mic. 4:2). The remainder of this book will say more about the missional purpose of the law.[11]

Fifth, Ezra 9 – 10 and Nehemiah 13:23–27 mention the issue of mixed marriages in the post-exilic community. In both cases, Ezra and Nehemiah the men disapprove of these unions and react rather strongly to the news. Ezra even orders the Jewish men to separate from their non-Jewish wives and mongrel children. Nothing is said about support for these wives and children. Ezra and Nehemiah seem to display callousness, intolerance and xenophobia that contradict the concern of other parts of the Christian Bible for love and mission.[12] Regarding the 'exclusionary measures' of Ezra and Nehemiah the men, Laird says, 'While such tactics and their underlying motifs are no strangers to the human condition, it is disturbing to find them enshrined in what many deem to be sacred text.'[13] Pakkala represents the usual scholarly understanding of the seemingly harsh response to intermarriage in Ezra–Nehemiah:

> In the Ezra source [Ezra 7 – 10; Neh. 8], group identity is closely tied to the Law and Israel's obedience to it. The Israelites are expected to follow the Law, which separates them from other nations, but those who had remained in the land were unaware of it and had therefore

---

10 Saysell 2012: 141–142.
11 For now, see McConville 1985: 131.
12 LaSor, Hubbard and Bush 1996: 564–565; Satterthwaite and McConville 2007: 264; Harrington 2008: 100–101; Thiessen 2009: 63–79; Moffat 2013: 73; Wielenga 2013: 1; Redditt 2014: 192–193, 296.
13 Laird 2016: 1.

> taken foreign wives. The author wanted to demonstrate that ignoring the Law would lead the Israelites into the sin of intermarriage with other nations, which has the potential to threaten Israel's group identity and eventually its existence. Group identity and separation from the other is for this author essentially dependent on observing the Law, which lays down the precepts of Israel's exclusive religion.[14]

Pakkala, however, never mentions Ezra 6:21, which admittedly lies outside the Ezra source. To be sure, God's people were supposed to live distinctively, but for the purpose of modelling a redeemed community that might attract the nations. This attraction, according to Ezra 6:21, could lead to participating in the covenantal meal. It can be challenging, then, to identify any abiding relevance or redeeming value to the book of Ezra–Nehemiah. The challenge, though, is not insurmountable.

Sixth, the Hebrew Bible may treat Ezra and Nehemiah as one book, but modern translations of the Bible separate Ezra and Nehemiah. Preachers may then miss the themes that run through what is supposed to be a literary unit. If preachers tend to ignore Ezra, they often focus on Nehemiah as a manual for leadership.[15] When this happens, the book of Nehemiah is often approached moralistically in order to identify principles for motivating others to action. At this point, preachers may, in their estimation, be making the most of a book that does not seem to emphasize God's plan of redemption. Even so, Ezra–Nehemiah as a literary unit is also part of the Christian Bible that tells God's grand story of saving activity. God may be concerned about human conduct, but the moral imperatives of the Christian Bible appear in the larger context of God's acts and promises. However exemplary Ezra and Nehemiah the men may be, Ezra–Nehemiah the book is a unified work that focuses not so much on how to be an effective leader but on how to be a godly participant in God's story. More specifically, Ezra–Nehemiah has an interest in how God's people contribute to building the new (and New) Jerusalem, which is God's redeemed community that is bigger than any single person at any single moment. Mission – that is, participating in God's purpose for his world – factors into the message of these books.

---

14 Pakkala 2011: 82.

15 E.g. Getz 1995; Packer 1995; Swindoll 1998; Maciariello 2003: 400–407. For a list of other sources, see Schnittjer 2016: 34.

In the context of discussing the Old Testament as the Bible of the early church, Wilson asks, 'Would not seminary courses in homiletics be doing students a favor to require that at least one "evangelistic" sermon be preached in class using an Old Testament text?'[16] This NSBT volume assumes, in contrast to much previous scholarship, that such sermons can be preached from Ezra–Nehemiah. Perhaps, though, a better term than 'evangelistic' is 'missional'. God's people in both Testaments were supposed to have an evangelistic mindset of being a kingdom of priests (Exod. 19:6; 1 Peter 2:9) or a channel of redemptive blessing to the nations that, along with the Israelites, needed to experience the transforming grace of God. God, however, has more than individual regeneration and sanctification in mind. God's people have received God's law that tells them how to live as a redeemed community. Such a community has the corporate mission of modelling justice and compassion to outsiders. For this reason, God's law goes beyond personal piety to address matters of social interaction. Nothing short of the transformation of culture is in view. The New Testament, of course, presents Jesus as the redeemer because he – by virtue of his righteous life, atoning death and vindicating resurrection – is the unblemished lamb of God who takes away the sin of the world. Moreover, God's aim to make him pre-eminent over creation is the ultimate reason why God created anything at all (Rom. 8:29; Eph. 1:20–22; Col. 1:15–20). Consequently, living missionally as a kingdom of priests is how God's people advance his mission of exalting Jesus through the plan of redemption that encompasses every area of life.

So then, in view of these reasons for inattention to Ezra–Nehemiah, this book will avoid a moralistic approach that tries to salvage Ezra–Nehemiah by telling people to be like, or not to be like, Ezra and Nehemiah the men. Modern believers, no less than those who lived during the post-exilic period, are unable to live faithfully without the grace of God ultimately available in Jesus. It is, in fact, cruel to tell people to be faithful like Ezra or Nehemiah and not discuss the prerequisite for faithfulness; namely, faith in the promises of God that ultimately find fulfilment in the person and work of Jesus. This book, instead, will view the book of Ezra–Nehemiah as the record of the beginning of a new work of God among his

16 Wilson 1989: 112.

people after the exile (Isa. 43:16–21).[17] This new work that led eventually to the first coming of Jesus enables God's people to be restored presently in their relationship with God. Such restoration involves a combination of hope in God's promises and obedience to his instruction that has to do with mission. While each of this volume's chapters will discuss Christian living and so encourage readers to live for something bigger than themselves, the discussion will be rooted in what God has already done for his people and what he will yet do. This interpretive strategy for reading the Christian Bible is called 'biblical theology', which is the way the Christian Bible wants to be read.[18] This book on Ezra–Nehemiah is part of a series of studies about biblical theology. The next chapter will say more about this hermeneutic, especially as it relates to Ezra–Nehemiah.

[17] Referring to a new work of God after the exile does not deny the continuity of God's redemptive plan that runs throughout the Christian Bible. Rather, a new work means a post-exilic chapter in God's ongoing mission among and through his people.

[18] Stuhlmacher 1995: 1, 64–67, 80, 88; 2002: 189. Vanhoozer (2000: 54), similarly, says, 'The ultimate goal of biblical theology . . . is not to impose an alien framework onto Scripture but rather to let the Bible's own theological framework come to light.'

2
Biblical theology explained

In a Christian academic context, 'biblical theology' is a technical term that represents something different from, but complementary to, 'systematic theology'. Systematic theology is not necessarily less biblical than biblical theology, for it usually depends just as much on the Bible as biblical theology. The difference between the two has to do with method.

Biblical theology in relation to systematic theology

Systematic theology approaches the Christian Bible as a finished product that reveals God's plan for creation and redemption. Rather than focusing on the process by which the plan unfolded, systematic theology compiles the Bible's teaching on God, humanity and salvation. These doctrinal tenets move logically from one to the next. What the Bible says about God accounts for what it says about humanity, and what it says about humanity accounts for what it says about salvation. Hence, those who read the Bible can talk about the Bible's system of doctrine. Another name for systematic theology is 'topical Bible study'.[1]

The potential danger with systematic theology is that overemphasizing the system of doctrine can reduce the Christian faith to a set of propositions that ignores the redemptive-historical development of those propositions.[2] While Christianity includes propositions (e.g. God is triune), the Christian religion is not an abstraction derived from pure reason or even a divinely revealed statement of faith. The Christian religion is rooted in God's acts in history – hence all the narrative in the Bible. These acts show God to be great or omnipotent on the one hand

[1] Boda 2015: 24.
[2] Wilson 1989: 115, 153.

and good or gracious on the other. God is faithful to his promises because he has the means and the desire to keep his word. So then, the Christian's faith is not in a logical system but in a divine person who announces what he will do, does it and then explains what he has done. That said, systematic theology is possible and necessary because the God who acts and speaks does so with consistency. Stated differently, God has one plan of salvation throughout human history, and neither the plan nor the Planner change. What God has said about his acts that accomplish his plan can, therefore, be systematized into an abstract summary or confession.

Although biblical theology also affirms that the Bible is a finished book, it pays closer attention to the historical process by which God's plan unfolded. Because God did not reveal himself or his plan all at once, the Bible did not drop down out of heaven one day in completed form. Instead, God has acted progressively in history to save his people, and God's Word has been revealed progressively to explain his acts. Biblical theology focuses on the stages or the movement of redemption and revelation. More so than systematic theology, biblical theology wants to know why God revealed what he did to this group of people in this place at this time. If systematic theology focuses on what beliefs the biblical writers hold in common, biblical theology draws attention to their individual emphases for their original audiences.

Even so, Stuhlmacher says that biblical theology recognizes '*a continuity of God's activity in and through Christ, a continuity of salvation history*'.[3] What this means is that biblical theology reads all parts of the Bible 'in relation to God's final act of salvation in this Christ'. Of course, a final act assumes preceding acts that lay the groundwork for the final act. The final act does not occur without preparation; rather, it concludes the story that began in the first act. In fact, skilfully written acts foreshadow the conclusion, but the foreshadowing is often not appreciated until the end, when the observer can review the completed story and trace the developing artistry. At this point, the intentional foreshadowing is seen to be prophetic on the part of the author or playwright. He or she knew the outcome from the beginning.

Stuhlmacher summarizes the biblical story as follows:

[3] Stuhlmacher 1995: 5–6; emphasis original.

> This way [of God to humanity that biblical theology discusses] begins with the creation, runs through the complete history of Israel's election, reaches its apex in the sending, passion and resurrection of Jesus, and leads further to the kingdom of God, which the exalted Christ is to (and will) establish.[4]

Like any other story, the Bible's story unfolds progressively with the result that each part is related to all the other parts – those that come before and those that come after. From this point of view, the parts cannot be understood properly without taking into account their contribution to the whole. Stuhlmacher maintains that the message of the Bible finds its unity in God's work that climaxes in Jesus.

More specifically, the Christian Bible features the story of how God exalts his incarnate Son by redeeming his people and world from sin.[5] God introduced the plan of redemption in Genesis 3 and explained the plan throughout the Old Testament. Revelation accompanied each saving act in order to clarify the plan's significance.[6] From the perspective of the Christian Bible, the series of redemptive interventions reached its climax not at the end of the Old Testament but in Jesus the anointed one. By itself, the Old Testament is an incomplete story. Its promises and expectations remain unrealized until the fullness of time arrived in Jesus.[7] The earlier interventions typified and anticipated Jesus, who is the antitype or fulfilment of God's redemptive programme. Even so, all of the acts contribute to one plan of salvation. Likewise, the stages of revelation explain the advancement of the one plan of God to redeem a people for his name. Stated differently, the stages of revelation tell one story of how God implemented the plan. So then, God has acted progressively in history to save his people, and God's Word has been revealed progressively to explain his acts. Biblical theology focuses on this flowering character of redemption and revelation.

If redemption is progressive, it is also organic.[8] Each stage is a piece of the whole plan that develops gradually through time. Vos says:

---

4 Ibid. 81.

5 Vos 1948: 20; 1980: 8.

6 Vos 1948: 5–7; 1980: 9–10; Bright 1975: 130–131, 136, 159; Ridderbos 1982: 84; Gaffin 1988: 178–179; Goldingay 1994: 309.

7 Bright 1975: 138; Goldingay 1994: 48; Kuruvilla 2009: 110; Wright 2012: 66–67.

8 These terms are taken from Vos 1948: 7; 1980: 7, 10–11.

> The Gospel of Paradise is such a germ in which the Gospel of Paul [and the other New Testament writers] is potentially present; and the Gospel of Abraham, of Moses, of David, of Isaiah and Jeremiah, are all expansions of this original message of salvation, each pointing forward to the next stage of growth, and bringing the Gospel idea one step nearer to its full realization.[9]

God's redemptive acts and their revelatory interpretation resemble a small acorn and an immense oak tree. At first glance the two do not seem to be related, but the oak tree in reality grows out of the acorn. There is an organic relationship between seed and mature plant.[10] No other type of organism can grow from an acorn. The same is true for earlier acts of redemption and accompanying revelation on the one hand and later acts of redemption and accompanying revelation on the other. The latter grow out of the former. The seed of redemption that germinates throughout Old Testament history and revelation develops into a spreading shade tree to which Jesus likened the kingdom of God (Matt. 13:31–32; Mark 4:30–32; Luke 13:18–19).

Other comparisons are possible. For example, Greidanus uses the image of a river that undergoes change while moving downstream from its headwaters.[11] Wilson additionally likens the cumulative character of divine revelation to a snowball. He says, 'Throughout the Hebrew Bible, God gradually keeps building on earlier revelation by clarifying it, nuancing it, or illustrating its significance to a later generation in a new context.'[12] Bright also uses the analogies of a human that develops from an infant to an adult and of a play that has multiple acts.[13] Each of these images – tree, river, snowball, person and play – illustrates how the progressive and organic development of the Christian Bible's message involves continuity and surprise. Just as a tree has a different appearance from its seed, or the mouth of a river bears little resemblance to a trickling stream, or a rolling snowball may pick up debris in addition to snow, or a person may have brown hair in his twenties and grey hair in his fifties, or a play may have an unexpected twist, so a crucified and risen Saviour looked and looks different from much popular expectation.

---

9 Vos 1980: 11.
10 Beale (2011: 955) uses the image of an apple tree.
11 Greidanus 1999: 45.
12 Wilson 2014: 23, 29.
13 Bright 1975: 123–124, 202–203.

Even so, 'Christianity' says Bright, 'did spring, and in the form it took could only have sprung, from the soil of Israel. The Christ of the New Testament could have come only to this Israel.'[14] The reason, explains Bright, is not that the Old Testament gives law that condemns and the New Testament responds with grace that forgives. Rather, '[t]he two Testaments do indeed represent parts of a single redemptive history, and they stand to one another in a relationship of promise and fulfillment: the New Testament itself saw it so.'[15] So also does the Old Testament. Goldingay says:

> The theme of promise and fulfillment runs through the OT narrative from Genesis to Kings [or Genesis through Ezra–Nehemiah], as Yahweh keeps declaring his will and fulfilling it. Yet each such event makes Israel look the more to the future for this pattern of experience to continue, so that each fulfillment in the past becomes a promise for the future. The OT is thus a book of ever-increasing anticipation, a story moving towards a goal which lies beyond itself.[16]

Biblical theology, then, is not only read back into the Old Testament from the New Testament but also projected forward from the Old Testament into the New. Each Testament illumines the other.[17]

Biblical theology recognizes that God sovereignly rules over history to direct the course of human events to its foreordained denouement. One event leads to another and brings about the final result God decreed from before the creation. The consummation, however, does not render the beginning inferior or unnecessary. Earlier acts of God and their explanation in the Old Testament are not less efficacious and authoritative

---

[14] Ibid 188.

[15] Ibid. 193; see also 198–199. When Bright says, 'It [the OT] points beyond itself, beyond its own possibilities, toward a consummation it could neither see nor produce' (206), he correctly reflects the horizon of the human author (see 1 Peter 1:10–12) but not of the divine. God knows where his story of redemption is going.

[16] Goldingay 1990: 117–118. See also von Rad 1965: 319; Enns 2003: 277.

[17] Hays (2002: 405) says that '*the Gospels teach us how to read the OT, and – at the same time – the OT teaches us how to read the Gospels*'; emphasis original. Moberly (2000: 70) adds, 'Israel's scriptures not only prepare the way for Christ, not least by presenting an understanding of God and humanity in which Jesus' life, death, and resurrection become possible and intelligible in the form they take. There is also a retrospective movement from Jesus back to Israel's scriptures whereby they are recognized to be what they would not otherwise be recognized to be, that is Old Testament alongside the witness to God in Jesus Christ in the New Testament.'

than the later acts of God and their explanation in the New Testament. Rather, the earlier acts and explanation receive a fuller understanding from the person and work of Jesus the anointed one to whom they point in expectation by virtue of their inclusion in the chain of redemptive events. At the same time, these earlier acts of God that the Old Testament interprets also shape what comes later. Goldingay says about the Old Testament events and their explanation, 'It was this story that made Jesus the person he was. A different story would have produced a different Jesus.'[18] To return to Vos and Bright's botanical imagery, the seed determines what kind of plant grows. Given God's activity in history to redeem a people for his name for the exaltation of his Son, the whole Bible is a Christian book that narrates God's plan of salvation in Jesus.[19]

What God has done and is still doing in Jesus is what all parts of the Old Testament, including Ezra–Nehemiah, anticipate and foreshadow. God began to work out his plan of redemption in Old Testament times, but that work did not reach its climax until the first coming of Jesus. Even so, God continues to save his people and restore his creation until the second coming of Jesus. The same God implements and accomplishes his single plan of redemption in the Old Testament era (from Adam's sin to the first coming of Jesus) and in the New Testament era (from the first coming of Jesus to the second).[20] The first coming of Jesus is the middle and decisive point of redemptive history, when Jesus made the definitive sacrifice for sin and assumed his mediatorial rule over creation. Referring to the first coming of Jesus as the middle moment of redemptive history does not deny, but rather implies, that the person and work of Jesus were the means of salvation for Old Testament saints. Old Testament saints were saved no differently from New Testament saints: by grace through faith in Jesus. From a historical point of view, Old Testament saints were saved proleptically; i.e. before Jesus accomplished their salvation in time and space. Similarly, New Testament saints are saved retrospectively; i.e. after Jesus died, rose and ascended. In the mind of God, however, Jesus was slain before creation (2 Tim. 1:9; 1 Peter 1:20), and all saints receive

---

18 Goldingay 1990: 44.

19 Greidanus 1999: 44; Rosner 2000: 4–5, 10.

20 Von Rad (1963: 36) says, 'This renewed recognition of types in the Old Testament . . . is simply correspondent to the belief that the same God who revealed himself in Christ has also left his footprints in the history of the Old Testament covenant people – that we have to do with *one* divine discourse, here to the fathers through the prophets, there to us through Christ (Heb. 1:1)'; emphasis original.

the benefits of his work 'after the fact' of God's eternal decree. Consequently, Old Testament saints could (as Deut. 10:16 and 30:11–14 imply) proleptically experience new-covenant reality that only the grace of God in Jesus makes possible (John 1:17). The Spirit of God was at work in Old Testament times to apply the benefits of Jesus' active and passive obedience to those who believed what God said through his prophets. Old Testament saints could and did receive forgiveness of sins and undergo internal transformation that produced righteous conduct. Real change that owed its power to the future was available to them.[21] The first coming, however, is not the end point of redemptive history. Redemptive history runs until Jesus puts all his enemies under his feet and raises God's people (OT and NT saints) to their glorified inheritance (1 Cor. 15:20–28).

Nevertheless, saying that God's redemptive acts and their revelatory interpretation are progressive and organic does not ignore that the plan to reconcile God's fallen creation to his eternal purpose seems to unfold in fits and starts. So often God's people do not know what he is doing in history in general or in their lives in particular. Events often seem unrelated and arbitrary – even contrary to God's revealed will. Biblical theology does not eliminate divine mystery or human participation. Likewise, the Christian Bible (including the book of Ezra–Nehemiah in which the post-exilic community is not always the best practitioner of God's mission for his people) presents the story of redemption in its complexity and untidiness.[22] Still, the Christian Bible's teaching about God's sovereign and providential direction of world history as well as the personal histories of his people necessitates the use of the word 'organic' in any discussion of the progress of redemptive history. It is this inexorable movement from paradise lost to paradise restored that biblical theology traces. In so doing, biblical theology both assures God's people of God's faithfulness to his promises and challenges them to trust God enough to obey his commands in the situations of their lives – situations God has foreordained as parts of his grand story. The challenge for God's people

---

21 As seen in his comments on Jer. 31:33, Calvin (1981a: 131) recognized this truth. He said, 'the Fathers [OT saints], who were formerly regenerated, obtained this favor through Christ, so that we may say, that it was as it were transferred to them from another source. The power, then, to penetrate into the heart was not inherent in the law, but it was a benefit transferred to the law from the Gospel.'

22 Bauckham 2003: 92–94.

in their temporal and spatial contexts is to keep their eye on the bigger picture of God's plan for the whole world.

Jesus modelled this biblical-theological, redemptive-historical and Christ-centred hermeneutic in Luke 24 when he encountered the two men on the road to Emmaus and his disciples in Jerusalem. On the day of his resurrection, Jesus taught his followers how to read the Old Testament with reference to his person and work. He instructed his disciples to recognize that the chain of events before him and the accompanying revelation that explains those events progressively and organically led up to him and reached their fulfilment in him. This hermeneutics lesson is applied in Ezra–Nehemiah. As part of the Old Testament, Ezra–Nehemiah can also be read in view of the Christian Bible's story of redemption that finds its focus in Jesus. Ezra–Nehemiah is a stage in the growth of the tree or the flow of the river.

That said, biblical theology does not pre-empt grammatical-historical exegesis that has to do with understanding the Bible in its literary and temporal contexts.[23] According to Vos, 'Biblical theology, rightly defined, is nothing else than *the exhibition of the organic process of supernatural revelation in its historic continuity and multiformity*.'[24] History and genre cannot be ignored. By functioning as controls on the interpretation of an ancient text, they preserve both the human and divine authors' intended meaning. Stated more positively, attention to history and genre increases appreciation for the multifaceted performance and explanation of God's plan of redemption. To quote Vos again, 'Individual coloring, therefore, and a peculiar manner of representation are not only not detrimental to a full statement of the truth, but directly subservient to it.'[25] In the context, Vos has different literary genres in mind. So then, the timing of the event and the packaging of the explanation are integral to God's purpose for both. What Vos's hermeneutic means for this book is that the historical context and literary form of Ezra–Nehemiah must receive due consideration, for they reveal how this book should be read. If Ezra–Nehemiah can be read with the rest of the Old Testament as part of God's story that leads to the person and work of Jesus, it should also be read in view of its expressed concern for the post-exilic community. Ezra–Nehemiah is a

[23] Wilson 2014: 30.

[24] Vos 1980: 15; emphasis original. See also Rosner 2000: 4.

[25] Vos 1980: 14.

contextualized word from God to a specific audience in a particular place, but this word also has a far reach because of its contribution to the story of God's solution to his people's (and world's) need.

Ezra–Nehemiah in relation to biblical theology

Situating Ezra–Nehemiah in the development of biblical theology must begin with understanding how the literary form and historical context of this book contribute to its meaning. As already mentioned, the books of Ezra and Nehemiah in English Bibles are counted as one book in the Hebrew Bible. The Masoretic notes at the end of Nehemiah identify Nehemiah 3:32 as the centre of the book. Given that no notes follow Ezra 10, the book of Ezra evidently factors into the count for the book of Nehemiah. Moreover, the same list of names appears in Ezra 2 and Nehemiah 7:4–73a, and the names in this list appear in other chapters. As will be seen in the remainder of this chapter, that list functions as a structural device for the book of Ezra–Nehemiah. As uninviting as that list may be to the general reader, it is the key not only to the book's structure but also to its message.[26] From a literary point of view, repetition signals artistry and theme.[27] The point to be made now is that Ezra and Nehemiah are two chapters of a single story about the post-exilic community. Of course, Ezra–Nehemiah as a literary unit is part of the larger story (the metanarrative) of the Christian Bible.

If Ezra 2 and Nehemiah 7:4–73a have a structural function, they divide the book of Ezra–Nehemiah into three major sections: Ezra 1, Ezra 3:1–Nehemiah 7:3 and Nehemiah 7:73b–13:31.[28] Ezra 2 and Nehemiah 7:4–73a frame the middle section, which has three subsections. Each of the

[26] For additional arguments in favour of the literary unity of Ezra and Nehemiah, see Williamson 1985: xxi; 2008: 337–339; Eskenazi 1988a: 37, 1988b: 644–646; 2008: 315; Venema 2004: 159–160; Fried 2008: 75; 2015: 2–3; Harrington 2008: 98–116; Janzen 2008: 117–120; Karrer-Grube 2008: 136–137, 149; Min 2008: 160–175; Redditt 2014: 3–4, 30; Campbell 2017: 397–399. For a summary of the arguments for and against the unity of Ezra and Nehemiah, see Steinmann 2010: 12–21.

[27] Eskenazi 1988a: 89–93.

[28] A slightly misleading chapter division occurs after Neh. 7:73. Ezra 2:70 and Neh. 7:73a mark the end of the same list of names. The references to the seventh month in Ezra 3:1 and 3:6 on the one hand and in Neh. 7:73b and 8:2 on the other indicate that Neh. 7:73b belongs with the material in Neh. 8.

subsections involves a return of exiles under a named leader who encounters trouble.[29] The subsections receive further comment below. Throughout the book, some of the names in Ezra 2 and Nehemiah 7:4–73a appear in other contexts, such as the account of intermarriage in Ezra 10 and the pledge of repentance in Nehemiah 10. The names, then, unify the events that occur between the return from Babylon in 539 BC and the dedication of the wall in 445 BC. A near century's worth of descendants and events participated in a continuous effort to implement Cyrus' decree.[30] Several generations of descendants of those listed in Ezra 2 and Nehemiah 7:4–73b contributed to the grand project of rebuilding a new temple and city.

Ezra 4:6–23 and 6:14 add support to this generational understanding of the execution of Cyrus' decree. Ezra 4:6–23 falls between references to Darius in Ezra 4:5 and 4:24 and so seems to introduce historical confusion into the account of rebuilding the temple. Both Xerxes (Ahasuerus) and Artaxerxes reigned after Darius. A question arises about why the writer would interrupt the narrative about opposition to rebuilding the temple during Darius' reign in order to talk about events during the reigns of his two successors. Moreover, Ezra 6:15 reports the completion of the temple in the sixth year of Darius' reign. If the temple was completed before the reigns of Xerxes and Artaxerxes, one also wonders why the writer would introduce extraneous information about a later period. At first glance, then, Ezra 4:6–23 seems to be out of place in a section of the book that describes events towards the end of the sixth century BC and not events in the middle of the fifth century BC. Because Ezra 7–Nehemiah 13 deals with this later time period, Ezra 4:6–23 would seem to belong somewhere in that part of the book. Ezra 4:1–5, however, mentions the opposition to the reconstruction of Yahweh's house and city. Verses 6–23 may seem to be premature and intrusive, but make sense in view of Ezra 6:14. This verse understands that the implementation of Cyrus' decree, which is equated with God's decree, occurred over a span of time that went beyond the reign of Cyrus. In actuality, the post-exilic community rebuilt Yahweh's house and city during the reigns of Cyrus, Darius and Artaxerxes.[31] Over

---

[29] Throntveit 1992: 12, 58–59; Waltke and Yu 2007: 775. Venema (2004: 149) says that the three subsections 'contain common motifs, for instance the mission ordered by a Persian king, the written powers of attorney provided, and the resistance of the rulers around Jerusalem'.

[30] Williamson 1985: 376; Eskenazi 1988a: 45 and 1988b: 647, 655; Redditt 2014: 117–118.

[31] Eskenazi 1988a: 41–42, 188; Duggan 2001: 43; Venema 2004: 142–143; Nykolaishen 2008: 196. Except for a reference to a complaint (Ezra 4:6), Ezra–Nehemiah does not report any building activity during the reign of Xerxes, who ruled after Darius and before Artaxerxes.

the course of those three reigns, the post-exilic community faced not just the instance of adversity in Ezra 4:4–5 but other cases detailed in Ezra 4:6–23 and Nehemiah 4 – 6. It is as if the writer of Ezra–Nehemiah, knowing what will come later in the book, says in Ezra 4:6, 'While we are on the subject of opposition, let me suspend the narrative for a moment and give you some other examples of enmity. From start to finish, the whole project met with resistance and setbacks.'[32] Ezra 4:6–23 and 6:14 let the reader know that the completion of the temple during Darius' reign did not exhaust the intention of Cyrus' (or God's) decree. Rebuilding the temple constituted the first stage of a larger undertaking. More work still had to occur, and none of it would happen free of hardship.

To pursue this observation more, Ezra and Nehemiah lived and worked among a discouraged group of people. Isaiah 60 had announced a glorious restoration, and the initial return from exile seemed to mark the beginning of it. Moreover, the willingness of the Persian government to underwrite the cost of rebuilding the temple seemed to signify God's conversion of the Gentiles. The fulfilment of pre-exilic and exilic oracles of salvation was apparently at hand. God was in the process of performing a second exodus that would be accompanied by all the mighty displays of his power that attended the first exodus. If God had formerly humbled Pharaoh, the previously announced Messiah would soon appear and rule the nations. Such, however, was not the case. The situation of the post-exilic community was far from ideal because God's people had returned to a hard state of affairs. Their cities and homes lay in ruins, and difficulty came at them from every direction.

First, Haggai 1:3–11 mentions a food shortage that was caused by a divinely appointed drought. God withheld rain because work on the temple had stopped. Members of the post-exilic community struggled to demonstrate their belief in God's promises by obeying his command to rebuild the temple. They eventually abandoned work on the temple in order to look after their own needs. Until Haggai's theological explanation of the drought, members of the post-exilic community might not have made a connection between the unfinished temple and the wilting crops.[33]

---

[32] Kidner 1979: 48; Fensham 1982: 70; Williamson 1985: 57; Holmgren 1987: 30; Blenkinsopp 1988: 106; Throntveit 1992: 26; Fyall 2010: 73, 76; Goswell, 2010: 193; Fried 2015: 220–221.

[33] Japhet (2006: 219) says, 'The national sin of Israel, according to him [Haggai], is the failure to build the temple! It is this sin which is responsible for all the calamities, and a change in the people's fortune hinges entirely upon its correction.'

What they did know was that they did not have enough produce to sell or eat. Personal finances became an urgent matter.

Second, tension existed between those who returned from exile and those who never went away.[34] Both groups of Israelites thought they were the true remnant of God. In fact, the poorer Israelites who remained in the Promised Land (2 Kgs 25:12) might have thought that the richer Israelites who had gone into exile (2 Kgs 24:14) got what they deserved. After all, pre-exilic prophets in Israel (Amos 2:6–8; 5:10–13; Hos. 12:7) and Judah (Isa. 5:8; Mic. 2:1–2; Hab. 1:2–4) had condemned the 'haves' for exploiting the 'have nots'. When the descendants of the 'haves' came back from Babylon, the descendants of the 'have nots' had the superior social position.[35] According to the 'have nots', the God of the oppressed had finally turned the tables and vindicated those who could not defend themselves. The children and grandchildren of the formerly disfranchised would not allow life in the Promised Land to revert to pre-exilic inequity. Moreover, Gentiles who had moved into Palestine after Jerusalem's fall considered this land theirs and refused to recognize the former residents' right of ownership.[36]

The former residents and/or their descendants might have returned to their homeland, but no longer had control of it.[37] To add confusion, both groups could appeal to the words of Jeremiah, who is mentioned in Ezra 1:1. Those who returned from exile would favour Jeremiah 24:5–7 and 29:10–14. Those who remained in Judah would be drawn to Jeremiah 42:10–12. Consequently, the social situation was mixed and unstable.[38]

Third, the social situation had a political element. Before the Persian king Darius divided up his empire into provinces or satrapies, the land of Israel and Judah had fallen under Samaritan control. The Samaritans were the offspring of the Gentiles who had married the Israelites remaining in Palestine (2 Kgs 17:24–41; Ezra 4:1–5). While 2 Kings 17 draws attention to the problem of syncretism, Darius made Palestine a separate

34 Douglas 2002: 3–4; Johnson 2011: 36.

35 Bedford 2002: 161.

36 Fried 2015: 196–197.

37 Johnson 2011: 17.

38 Although the writer(s) of Ezra–Nehemiah is (are) often thought to be sympathetic to the repatriates, Ezra–Nehemiah's demonstrable interest in mission suggests that an absolute separation of these two groups (let alone a separation of the repatriates and peoples of the land) was not the goal of Ezra the man, Nehemiah the man or the writer(s) of Ezra–Nehemiah.

administrative district of the Persian Empire. This 'redistricting' meant that the Samaritans no longer controlled Palestine or its revenue. Ezra–Nehemiah describes how the Samaritans expressed their resentment.

This manifold hardship took its toll on the members of the post-exilic community. Dashed hopes influenced them to become self-absorbed. They put their wants ahead of God's will and pursued material goods rather than spiritual growth. In the process, they became apathetic towards civic responsibility and hypocritical in religious practice. In particular, work on the temple stopped between 535 and 520 BC. Because no descendant of David restored kingship in Israel and smashed Israel's foes, messianic dreams dimmed and people became practical atheists. They might speak orthodox words and perform prescribed rituals, but their hearts grew cold. It was into this state of hopelessness and apathy that Ezra and Nehemiah – along with Zerubbabel, Joshua and others – did their work.

Returning now to the structure of the book, the first section in Ezra 1 announces the theme as the carrying out of Cyrus' decree to rebuild the Jerusalem temple. This edict included not only the permission to rebuild but also the provision of supplies. Furthermore, Cyrus returned the sacred vessels Nebuchadnezzar had triumphantly removed from the first temple and Belshazzar had handled disrespectfully on the night of his death (Dan. 5). From a theological point of view, the execution of Cyrus' decree would remain incomplete without the restoration of these implements of worship. Ezra 1:9–10 gives an itemized list that represented not only continuity with the worship of pre-exilic Israel but also discontinuity from the shame of the exile. The return of the vessels to Yahweh's temple draws attention to his saving presence again in the midst of his people – a truth that was not so evident when these implements were in the temple of another god.[39] This material link to the past assured the post-exilic community that God's promises were still in effect. These promises, which had underlain Israel's praise and prayer before the exile, now gave hope for an open future to those returning from exile. Yahweh still cared about the returnees.

The second section of the book (Ezra 3:1–Nehemiah 7:73a) describes the performance of Cyrus' decree in three stages that encompass about a hundred years from the issue of the decree in 539 BC to the completion of

[39] Ackroyd 1987: 57–58; Fried 2003: 40.

the wall in 445 BC.[40] In each of these stages, a Persian king sends a Jewish leader back to Jerusalem. The leader faces opposition to executing Cyrus' decree, with the result that something unexpected happens. These unexpected developments enrich the message of the book.

During the first stage, the returnees under Sheshbazzar, Zerubbabel, Joshua, Haggai and Zechariah rebuilt the temple over the course of about twenty years and dedicated it in 516 BC. Ezra 3 – 6 describes this stage. One of the unexpected developments is the returnees' refusal of help from those already living in Judea. If Isaiah 60 anticipated the participation of the nations in a rebuilding effort, their exclusion would seem to miss a missional opportunity. Of course, the returnees, because of the absence of conflict in Isaiah 60 (esp. v. 18), might not have expected resistance to their effort to implement Cyrus' decree. So then, Ezra 4's record of antagonism from the people of the land and refusal of assistance from the returning Jews introduces tension missing from Isaiah 60.

Meanwhile, Haggai and Malachi's jarring criticism of the returnees' apathy (Hag. 1:2–11; Mal. 1:2 – 3:15) indicated that restored worship required more than a refurbished building. As seen in Ezra 7 – 10, the writer of Ezra–Nehemiah shared this conviction. So, for the second stage, Ezra returned in 458 BC to rebuild the people by instructing them in the law of Moses. If Solomon's temple had been defiled by all sorts of abominable practices (Ezek. 8), a new temple required a properly taught community that would singularly and fervently honour Yahweh with its worship and lifestyle. It is one thing to have a new building and another to have proper worship within the building.[41] Ezra 7 – 10 describes this stage, or at least the beginning of it. More instruction follows the third stage and is reported in Nehemiah 8. The surprising development during the second stage is the forced annulment of marriages between men who had returned to Judah and women who were born there. Intermarriage might have been a consequence of spiritual apathy. Still, if Yahweh hates divorce (Mal. 2:16) and allowed Israelite soldiers to marry female captives (Deut. 21:10–14), Ezra's approval of mass dissolution of marriages raises questions about his expert knowledge and application of the law.

---

40 Eskenazi 1988a: 39–49, 176.

41 Levering 2007: 34–35, 83. Green (1993: 207, 209–210) insightfully observes that two walls are built in Ezra–Nehemiah: Ezra's wall and Nehemiah's wall. Green refers to Ezra's teaching as an 'invisible, spiritual wall of obedience to the Law, by which Israel was to "separate themselves" from the unclean Gentiles'. Moreover, '"the house of God" will never be fully complete until a qualified people – separated from the foreign nations – is found to inhabit it'.

During the third stage, Nehemiah supervised the rebuilding of the wall, the purpose of which was not so much to keep foreign generals out of Yahweh's city as to protect the sanctity of the temple from spiritually unfit people, whether Jew or Gentile.[42] Past defilements of Solomon's temple were not supposed to happen to the post-exilic temple. According to Eskenazi, 'the building of the wall is an extension of building the temple', and the wall gives 'temple-like sanctity to the city as a whole'.[43] If the city is understood not only as a place but also as a people who worship at the temple, then the enlargement of holy space that Ezekiel 43:12 envisions makes sense.[44] No spiritually unfit person should ever rush into Yahweh's house again. Nehemiah 1 – 6 describes this third stage. What is unexpected is the apparent discrepancy between Nehemiah 1 – 6 and Zechariah 2:4–5. Zechariah, who lived before Nehemiah, had said that the rebuilt Jerusalem would not have walls because of the influx of so many people and because of God's protection of his city. Zechariah may complement the more historically situated account in Ezra–Nehemiah by drawing out the eschatological implications of post-exilic events. Even so, the person responsible for the final form of Ezra–Nehemiah knew about Zechariah's ministry but made no attempt to harmonize his walled Jerusalem with Zechariah's unwalled Jerusalem. The apparent contradiction is not insurmountable, but is, at first glance, somewhat confusing.

To review, then, the second section of Ezra–Nehemiah (Ezra 3:1 – Neh. 7:3) describes three stages to performing Cyrus' decree. These stages involve the temple, the people and the walls. Only when these three stages were complete had the generations of descendants of those listed in Ezra 2 and Nehemiah 7:4–73a fully carried out Cyrus' will.[45] Chapters 4–6 of this book will say more about these stages and the questions they raise.

Two sections of Ezra–Nehemiah have been introduced. The third section (Nehemiah 7:73b – 13:31) celebrates the completion of the building project. More teaching, confessing and repenting occur in preparation for inhabiting the new Jerusalem and worshipping Yahweh. The specific commitments of the people in Nehemiah 10:30–39 tailor repentance to

---

42 Grabbe 2001: 110; Oeming 2012: 142–143.

43 Eskenazi 1988a: 83, 86; see also Harrington 2008: 102–103.

44 For Ezekiel's influence on Ezra–Nehemiah, see Fried 2008: 75–97; 2015: 149–153; Blenkinsopp 2009: 129–159.

45 Williamson 1985: 376; Eskenazi 1988a: 86–87; Throntveit 1992: 116; Venema 2004: 163–164; Moffat 2013: 137.

the circumstances of the post-exilic community. After a listing of the residents of the new Jerusalem in Nehemiah 11, Nehemiah 12:1–26 identifies the religious personnel who ministered at the temple during the decades between Cyrus' decree and Nehemiah's labour. The names of Zerubbabel and Jeshua in verse 1 (see also Ezra 3:8–9) and Ezra and Nehemiah in verse 26 frame the multigenerational list. Like Ezra 2 and Nehemiah 7:4–73, Nehemiah 12 makes all the listed names participants in one work of restoration that climaxes in verses 27–47 with jubilant dedication of the finished project. The celebration of the temple's completion and installation of priests in Ezra 6:16–18 anticipates the installation and worship in Nehemiah 12.[46] The unexpected addition of Nehemiah 13, though, informs the reader that the execution of Cyrus' decree did not mark the full accomplishment of God's redemptive plan. The city of God may now be a viable entity, but the new Jerusalem of Ezra–Nehemiah did not fully match the New Jerusalem of Isaiah 60, 62, Zechariah 14 and Revelation 21 – 22. It was only a foretaste. Sin in Ezra–Nehemiah's Jerusalem indicates that more work is required to attain the ideal of these other prophecies as well as everything Yahweh had in mind when he stirred Cyrus' heart.[47]

Hebrews 11 reinforces this point. After verses 13–16 and verse 39 say that Abraham and his spiritual descendants (those who share his faith in the promises of God) are still waiting for a city God is preparing for them, verse 40 concludes the chapter with a promise that they will receive their inheritance along with Christians. Meanwhile, Hebrews 13:14 informs Christians that they have not yet received an enduring city but must wait for one that is coming. In other words, Christians are involved in the same work of building God's house and God's city. They can add their names to the lists in Ezra 2 and Nehemiah 7, for they participate in the grand project of a future Jerusalem where God dwells in unimpeded communion with his perfected people.

Summary

The rest of this book will read Ezra–Nehemiah as a unified piece of literature that recounts the effort of the post-exilic community to execute

[46] Eskenazi 1988a: 57; 1988b: 647.
[47] McConville 1985: 5.

Cyrus' decree to rebuild God's house. Ezra and Nehemiah the men certainly play important roles in that story, but the story does not focus exclusively on them as moral exemplars. Instead, the story highlights how God works through the ups and downs of ordinary people to advance his redemptive purpose in history. There may be a fair amount of 'already' and 'now' in Ezra–Nehemiah, but the book ends with the realization of just as much, if not more, 'not yet'. The reader knows there has to be more to the story. The movement of redemptive history that biblical theology traces beyond the days of Ezra and Nehemiah tells the rest of the story.

3
Return from exile

Ezra–Nehemiah opens on a hopeful note. The reference to the book of Jeremiah affirms God's faithfulness to his promises in the midst of circumstances that could be interpreted in more than one way. Jeremiah, who knew about the Assyrian deportation of the northern kingdom in the eighth century and the Babylonian deportation of the southern kingdom in the sixth, assured the exiles that Yahweh's future intention for them involved blessing. Yahweh would restore their fortune by bringing them back to the Promised Land (Jer. 29:10–14; 30:3). For many years the exiles had to take Jeremiah's word on faith. Beginning in 539 BC, Cyrus' decree that led to the return of the temple vessels and the first trek to Jerusalem made Jeremiah's expectation a reality. The writer of Ezra–Nehemiah perceived the hand of providence in these events. 'Providence', says Fyall, 'means that God has an ongoing relationship with his creation and directs his creatures and the whole created order ultimately to fulfill his purposes.'[1] According to Ezra 1, God's purpose in the post-exilic period was implementing his previously announced plan to give his people a future. This future would ultimately bring good to the rest of the world (Jer. 1:10; 29:6–7; 46:26; 48:47; 49:6; 49:39).[2] God had already said as much to Abraham (Gen. 12:2–3; 18:18), Isaac (Gen. 26:4) and Jacob (Gen. 28:14).

Cyrus' decree

Ezra–Nehemiah begins with a reference to a decree by Cyrus II, whose reign over Persia commenced in 559 BC. At the time, Persia was part of

---

[1] Fyall 2010: 30.

[2] See also Pss 22:27–28; 47:8–9; 96:1–10; Isa. 2:2–4; 19:19–25; 42:6–7; 49:6; 54:1–3; 56:6–8; Zech. 2:11.

the Median Kingdom that extended from the Caspian Sea to eastern Turkey. Cyrus' mother was the daughter of the last Median king, Astyages. In 550 BC, Cyrus led a successful revolt against his grandfather. Four years later he conquered eastern Turkey. Then in 539 BC, he invaded the city of Babylon and put an end to the Babylonian Empire. In 530 BC, Cyrus died in battle against nomads to the north-east of the Caspian Sea. He had conquered much territory, organized it under an efficient system of satrapies that were connected by a postal system and left his successors in a good position to expand.

Cyrus ruled differently from the Babylonians before him or the Assyrians before them. Instead of scattering subjects, he let them stay at home or return home. Rather than crush national sentiment or religious devotion, Cyrus and his successors tended to entrust responsibility to local princes. These could collect taxes from native residents, who remained productive in familiar surroundings and established careers. So in 539 BC, the Jews in Babylon were allowed to go back to Palestine, and Cyrus even encouraged the reconstruction of the temple.[3] Despite the reference in Ezra 1:2 to Yahweh, the covenant God of Israel, readers of Ezra–Nehemiah should not mistake Cyrus for a devout worshipper of Yahweh. For self-serving reasons, Cyrus did the same for other peoples.[4] He implemented religious tolerance with the hope that the gods of defeated peoples would bless him. The last part of the Cyrus Cylinder, discovered in the ruins of Babylon in 1879, reads as follows:

> May all the gods whom I settled in their sacred centers ask daily of Bel and Nabu that my days be long and may they intercede for my welfare. May they say to Marduk, my lord: 'As for Cyrus, the king who reveres you, and Cambyses, his son, [ ] a reign'. I settled all the lands in peaceful abodes.[5]

Cyrus might have thought that Yahweh would reward him for rebuilding the Jerusalem temple, but the appeal to other gods, including the chief

[3] Fried (2015: 31–32) observes that no one in the ANE would relocate to a remote place that did not have a temple for the local god. The Persians underwrote the cost of the Jerusalem temple because they wanted to repopulate Judea.

[4] Fyall (2010: 32) says, 'It may well be that Cyrus, astute politician as he was, would have in his civil service officials who were well skilled in spin-doctoring and could produce material targeted to specific audiences.'

[5] Cogan 2000: 315–316.

Babylonian god Marduk, indicates Cyrus' polytheistic orientation. He did not care which god favoured him. Like most politicians, he simply wanted the benefits of public order and increasing revenue (see Ezra 6:10; 7:23).[6]

In 539 BC, the Jews were losers in the ANE game of power politics. The relatively glorious days of David and Solomon were long over, and many Jews lived in exile because of their (or their ancestors') transgressions of God's covenant (2 Kgs 17:2–23; 21:10–16). Those Jews who remained in the Promised Land shared it with the descendants of transplanted foreigners (2 Kgs 17:24) who had similarly been defeated by the Assyrians towards the end of the eighth century. Even so, the post-exilic writers maintained that God still cared about the Jews. He had made promises to them and would keep his word.[7] Ezra 1:1 recalls what Jeremiah had said about restoration after seventy years of exile (Jer. 25:11–14; 29:10–14).[8] This reference to earlier prophecy draws attention to the hand of God in the decree of Cyrus. In 539 BC, God had not forgotten his promise to restore, nor had foreign kings (whether Assyrian, Babylonian or Persian) thwarted his intention. The execution of Cyrus' decree to rebuild Yahweh's temple was Yahweh's appointed means to restore the fortunes of his people (Jer. 30:1); that is, to revive their spiritual vitality after the shattering experience of the exile.

The Hebrew verb translated 'moved' (NIV) or 'stirred up' (ESV) in Ezra 1:1 further recalls Isaiah 41:2, 41:25 and 45:13 – verses that talk about Cyrus' unwitting contribution to God's plan for his people. As one moved by Yahweh, Cyrus would restore God's people to the Promised Land and

---

[6] Adams 2014: 141. According to Johnson (2011: 48), 'interactions between royalty and religious leaders frequently reflect intersections that had more economic than religious significance . . . Therefore, Isa. 45, which depicts Cyrus as the savior of the exiled Hebrew peoples, exemplifies a Yehudite response to such the Achaemenid ruling style [*sic*] and must be viewed guardedly . . . Whereas Isa. 45 seems to imply that Cyrus enjoyed a special relationship with Yhwh and Yhwh's worshipers, it is more likely that Cyrus manipulated the religious systems in Yehud and elsewhere throughout the empire to maximize cooperation from the local peoples. And his interest in the temple was more political than religious.'

[7] E.g. the book of Kings, in answer to questions about who failed (Yahweh or his people) and which deity was more powerful (Yahweh or Marduk), justifies the exile by documenting not only the unfaithfulness of the northern and southern kingdoms to the stipulations of the Mosaic covenant but also the faithfulness of Yahweh to the curses of that covenant. Even so, Kings also maintains that David's lamp, though burning dimly throughout the period of the monarchy, will never be extinguished (1 Kgs 11:36; 15:4; 2 Kgs 8:19).

[8] According to Karrer-Grube (2008: 155), the reference to Jeremiah in Ezra 1:1 'has in view no single quote from the book of Jeremiah, but summarizes the new fortune which is promised to Judah in the compilation of promises in Jeremiah 30–33 and 17.19–27'. Even though the book of Jeremiah says nothing about rebuilding the temple, which is the subject of Cyrus' decree and Ezra 3 - 6, Jer. 17:26 expects sacrifices at a temple in the future Jerusalem.

rebuild the Jerusalem temple (Isa. 44:28). Moreover, he would be used by Yahweh to promote the knowledge of Yahweh among the nations (Isa. 45:5–6). In other words, he would assist God's people in their mission to the world. Cyrus might have been the human agent that punished Babylon and liberated the Jews, but Yahweh was nevertheless working behind the scenes. Though a spectacular winner in the ANE game of power politics, Cyrus was, in reality, Yahweh's servant who did Yahweh's bidding. It is in this sense that Isaiah 45:1 calls him an 'anointed one' (a messiah). Yahweh, who had sent his people into exile by means of Assyrian and Babylonian deportations, was now restoring them by means of Persian policy. By giving the kingdoms of the earth to Cyrus (Ezra 1:3), Yahweh arranged the stage of history for another chapter of his redemptive story. The first readers of Ezra–Nehemiah would hardly have been unaware of how the book of Isaiah associates Cyrus' treatment of captured peoples with Yahweh's salvation of them. The reference to Cyrus in Ezra 1:1–2 recalls and advances what earlier prophecy had said about his contribution to the post-exilic stage of God's mission for his people.

Ezra 1:1 still speaks to God's people. They may not be exiles in Babylon, but they can feel like misfits among fellow humans who do not acknowledge the lordship of Jesus. In fact, 1 Peter 2:11 refers to God's people (believers in Jesus) as sojourners and exiles. First Peter 5:13 even seems to associate Rome (where Peter was writing) with Babylon (see Rev. 17 – 18).[9] There was, of course, no Babylonian Empire in the first century AD. Throughout the Bible, though, Babylon symbolizes the world in rebellion against its Maker. For Peter (and John) to liken Rome to Babylon was to say that Rome was the current embodiment of organized evil. Proud, idolatrous and oppressive, Rome considered its power absolute. People throughout the Mediterranean world might have been dazzled by Rome's splendour and been seduced by its propaganda, but soon realized that Rome, like Babylon, took more than it gave (Isa. 47:9, 12; Nah. 3:4). Tacitus wrote, 'To robbery, butchery, and rapine, they [the Romans] give the lying name of government. They create a desolation and call it peace.'[10] Rome promised the fruits of civilization but enslaved people instead. Human history, of course, did not end with the collapse of the Roman Empire. Other kingdoms have exploited their subjects and so matched the

---

[9] For a discussion of the provenance of 1 Peter, see Hagner 2012: 688–692, 699–700.
[10] Tacitus 1970: 81 §30.

arrogance, oppression and cruelty of Babylon and Rome. Whether in Babylon, Rome or some other empire, God's people have experienced disorientation and wondered what has become of his promises. Ezra 1:1 assures them that God has not forgotten.

Verses 2–4 identify the God of Ezra–Nehemiah as the God of heaven, the God of Israel and the God who is in Jerusalem. The second and third names may seem to restrict the God of Ezra–Nehemiah to the western edge of the Persian Empire. The first name, though, captures the universality of the God of Ezra–Nehemiah. He is not some minor deity in a remote corner of western Asia. Rather, he is the sovereign Lord of the universe – a big God for whom the nations, as Isaiah 40:12 says, are a speck of dust on a scale. This God who moved Cyrus as if he were a chess pawn is not, like other ANE gods, confined to the geographical borders of his people. He transcends the world he made and effortlessly uses any part of it for the advancement of his purpose. For the writer of Ezra–Nehemiah, the reference to God's being with his people (Ezra 1:3) combined his greatness and goodness. The sovereign Lord of the universe exerts his irresistible power on behalf of those whom he has chosen to love (see Jer. 30:18 – 31:6). He loves them not only to benefit them but also for the eventual blessing of their neighbours. The same Jeremiah who forecasted the geographical and spiritual restoration of the exiled Israelites also said that the nations would gather in Jerusalem to honour Yahweh (Jer. 3:17). He who will restore the fortune of his exiled people (Jer. 30:18; 32:44; 33:7, 11, 26) will also restore the fortune of the nations (Jer. 48:47; 49:6, 39). Cyrus might have been more concerned about his fortune than anything else, but the God of heaven gave him the kingdoms of the earth to advance a more enduring and beneficial outcome.

Some readers of Ezra 1 may wonder why God does not stir the heart of their ruler(s) to be benevolent to them. Throughout history, heads of state have often persecuted people of faith in an attempt to stamp out religious commitment and absolutize their subjects' loyalty to governmental authority. To those suffering at the time, a tyrant's heart may not seem to be in God's hand (Prov. 21:1), nor may a tyrant seem to perform God's pleasure (Isa. 44:28). While it is true that historical judgments often require patience, many people do not live long enough to witness the good that God meant to arise from evil. Even subsequent generations with the advantage of hindsight may wonder how an especially horrific event has any benefit for anyone. Ezra 1 may offer assurance that God was in control then, but it, like Romans 8:28, should not be cited flippantly about God's control of other situations. God's purpose for this or that happening can still exceed human comprehension. A humble willingness to say 'I don't know' remains an aspect of faith and empathy.

The same Hebrew verb in Ezra 1:1 also appears in 1:5 with reference to the Jews. God moved his people to act on Cyrus' decree and relocate to the Promised Land. The restoration, then, was not a case of opportunism or luck. Those Jews who returned did so because of divine leading. Ezra 1:5, however, does not explain how God aroused certain people (and not others) to 'pull up stakes' for a long journey to the western end of the Persian Empire. Perhaps God capitalized on one person's spirit of adventure or another individual's dissatisfaction with present circumstances. Someone else might have been eager to 'step out in faith' in order to see how God might use him or her for the advancement of his redemptive plan. There is mystery here about God's leading, but Ezra 1 asserts that God was in control of circumstances and people at the beginning of the post-exilic period. Whatever motive Cyrus or someone else might have had, or whatever setbacks might have occurred along the way, God was on the move to do something new in the aftermath of the exile. Given the fact that the exile had not eliminated sin or changed the human heart, God was not beyond employing a Gentile king or fickle Jews to implement his will. He sometimes uses unlikely candidates to get the job done.

Philippians 2:13 says that God 'works in you to will and to act in order to fulfil his good purpose' (NIV). The previous verse, however, tells God's people to work out their salvation. The Bible does not explain how God makes his people what he wants them to be and yet respects their volition. What it says is that God's people must choose to grow in likeness to Jesus and that God enables them to do so. Part of being a follower of Jesus is wanting to be like him. This transformation from what Paul elsewhere calls the old, unrighteous self to the new, righteous self (Col. 3:9–10) happens when someone asks God to conform him or her to the likeness of Jesus and then intentionally tries to act like Jesus. The Spirit of Jesus mysteriously empowers that person to obey God's commands in the situations of his or her life. Where observers formerly saw unrighteous conduct, they now see righteous conduct. God has moved within the praying and obeying believer to cause change. As part of the biblical story of redemption, Ezra 1 offers hope to anyone who is stuck in bad patterns of behaviour and wants to establish new ones. It does not say,

'Look within, find your inherent righteousness, and let it come to the surface.' Instead, it says, 'Ask the God who can make you righteous like Jesus to bless your desire to be like Jesus.' God puts that desire in those whom he regenerates, and he develops it in concert with sincere effort.

A second exodus

In view of Cyrus' decree, Ezra 1:4 and 1:6 present the return from exile as a second exodus. In both instances, God's people left a foreign land with the permission of its ruler and the wealth of its citizens (Exod. 3:21–22; 11:2–3; 12:35–36; Ps. 105:37).[11] If the first exodus resulted in the constitution of the Israelites as a kingdom of priests (Exod. 19:6) that was supposed to perform its mission according to the law of Moses (Exod. 20 – 23), the second exodus, similarly, led to a review of that same law, confession of disobedience and a pledge to obey (Ezra 9 – 10; Neh. 8 – 10). While Ezra-Nehemiah admittedly has a concern for holiness that has often been mistaken for xenophobia, Ezra 6:21 indicates that anyone who joined the covenantal community out of loyalty to Yahweh could partake of the covenantal meal.[12] This allowance maintained the original policy in Exodus 12:48–49. The God of Ezra-Nehemiah is no different from the God of Exodus. He welcomes any person who approaches him with faith in his promises and obedience to his commands. Far from being at odds with Exodus, Ezra-Nehemiah affirms both the sanctifying and missional purposes of the law of Moses. So then, the theme of a second exodus assured the post-exilic community that more than just a political favour accounted for their restoration to the Promised Land. As with pre-exilic Israel, God had brought his people to the Promised Land that was situated at the crossroads of the biblical world; that is, between Asia, Africa and Europe. He also considered post-exilic Israel to be his treasured

---

[11] Knowles (2004: 57–58) correctly points out that the neighbours in Exodus were Egyptians and that the neighbours in Ezra 1 were Jews who stayed in Babylon.

[12] Redditt (2014: 57–58, 63, 67, 153) claims that Ezra-Nehemiah, in contrast to Isa. 56:3–8, supports the exclusive right of the returnees to live in the rebuilt Jerusalem and worship at the second temple. Jews and others who were already in the land of Judah are called 'peoples of the lands' (Ezra 3:3; 4:4; 9:1, 2, 11; 10:2, 11; Neh. 10:28, 30, 31) and 'enemies' (Ezra 4:1; Neh. 4:11, 15). On p. 152, Redditt admits that Ezra 6:21 'recognizes the participation of at least some of those who had remained behind'. For more on the openness of Ezra-Nehemiah to the peoples of the land, see Fensham 1982: 96; McConville 1985: 43; Holmgren 1987: 16–17, 53–54; Japhet Blenkinsopp 1988: 133; 2009: 35; Lau 2009: 363–373; Fyall 2010: 94–95; Fried 2015: 286; 2006: 115.

possession (Exod. 19:5; Mal. 3:17) that would be a channel of redemptive blessing to the rest of the world.

This second exodus may seem to have been less spectacular than the first. If the first exodus involved ten plagues, the parting of the so-called Red Sea, the drowning of Pharaoh's soldiers, bread from heaven, water from a rock, two divinely engraved tablets and other unlikely events, the second exodus featured no supernatural displays of divine power, and the only new writing Ezra–Nehemiah mentions is the decrees of Persian kings. Moreover, the first exodus, after several hundred years, culminated in the kingdom of David and Solomon, but nothing comparable happened in the centuries after the second exodus. No Davidic descendant ruled in Jerusalem and maintained the Jews' possession of the Promised Land. Indeed, the second exodus was a small beginning by comparison (Zech. 4:10).

Even so, the post-exilic prophet Haggai announced that the glory of the second temple would exceed that of the first (Hag. 2:9), which Solomon had built. Haggai 2:3 indicates how unlikely the surpassing glory of the second temple seemed to the post-exilic community. This temple looked like a shed in comparison to Solomon's temple.[13] While Herod the Great's later renovation of the second temple might eventually have made it more outwardly splendid than Solomon's temple, there are two reasons to think that Haggai 2:9 looks forward to something more spiritually substantial than architectural ornamentation.

First, Haggai 2:9 recalls Ezekiel 9:3 and 10:4–18 on the one hand and 43:1–5 on the other. In these verses, Ezekiel sees God's glory or presence depart from the first temple (thus making it ready for the judgment threatened in Ezekiel's oracles of woe) and then return to the second temple (thus making possible the realization of Ezekiel's oracles of well-being). Nevertheless, Haggai and those Jews who lived between the post-exilic period (when the second temple was built) and the New Testament era (when the Romans destroyed the second temple) knew that God's glory never took up residence in the second temple. For this reason, Ezra–Nehemiah has no record of the return of God's glory to the second temple and therefore no equivalent to 1 Kings 8:10 or Exodus 40:34.[14] Haggai must have had some other manifestation of God's presence in mind.

---

[13] Calvin 1981b: 357.

[14] Wright 1992: 269; 1996: 621.

Second, Haggai 2:9 additionally promises the granting of peace, which goes beyond the aesthetic possibilities of brick and mortar to encompass reconciliation and well-being. In the absence of God's glory or presence there could be no peace with God or neighbour. Nevertheless, the Gospel of John, written hundreds of years after Haggai 2:9, clarifies the meaning of Haggai's words. John 1:14 says that God's glory appeared in Jesus at his first coming, and Jesus, when cleansing the second temple in John 2:13–22, distinguished between the second temple, where the glory of God is never said to reside, and the temple of his body, which the glory of God inhabited. As God incarnate, he is a greater temple than either Solomon or the post-exilic community could have built. Later in the Gospel of John, Jesus' body is crucified even though Pilate could find no fault with Jesus (John 19:4). John the Baptist, however, had anticipated this innocent death. In John 1:29, he called Jesus the Lamb of God who takes away the sin of the world. By means of his atoning death, Jesus made peace between God and repentant humans (John 14:6, 27; 20:19). Moreover, John 19:14 says that Jesus was crucified on the Day of Preparation for the Passover; that is, the day when the Passover lambs were slaughtered. In other words, Jesus as the Lamb of God died at the same time that the Passover lambs were being slaughtered for the Passover meal on the next day.[15] From a New Testament point of view, the saving efficacy of Jesus' death far surpassed, and therefore was more glorious than, the typological function of animal sacrifices. Jesus was the temple, the sacrifice made at the temple, and the priest who made the sacrifice at the temple.[16]

According to the writer of Ezra–Nehemiah, Cyrus' decree produced a second exodus. The return from Babylon might not have featured the supernatural acts that accompanied the first exodus, but God nonetheless brought his people back to the Promised Land after a lengthy absence. The implication of this migration is that the covenant God of Israel will resume the outworking of his plan of redemption through the

---

[15] According to Matt. 26:17 and Mark 14:12, Jesus died on the Day of Passover (Friday). According to John 19:14, 31–33, Jesus died on the Day of Preparation (Thursday) before the Day of Passover. For this reason, John has no record of the Last Supper. Given how the Gospel writers dischronologized other events of Jesus' life in order to emphasize their theological significance, these different presentations of his death should come as no surprise. For attempts at harmonization, see Miller 1983: 157–166; Smith 1991: 29–44.

[16] Wilson (1989: 55) says, 'Jesus subordinated many of the central symbols of Judaism to himself, and the New Testament writers continued that subordination. Thus, Jesus became the Temple (John 2:19–21) and the atoning sacrifice ("the Lamb of God, who takes away the sin of the world" - John 1:29).'

descendants of Abraham, to whom God announced the first exodus (Gen. 15:13–16; see also Isa. 11:11; 43:14–21; Hos. 2:14–15). Moreover, Ezra–Nehemiah may say next to nothing about future expectation (eschatology), but references to Jeremiah in Ezra 1:1 and to Haggai and Zechariah in Ezra 5:1 implicitly recall everything these prophets said about the restoration. What happened to the post-exilic community between 539 (Ezra 1:1) and 433 BC (Neh. 13:6) was only the beginning of what earlier and contemporary prophets expected after the exile. Ezra 1 presents a God who keeps his word.

That said, the second exodus seemed to be just as unlikely as the first. Although earlier prophets had announced a return from exile, who would have thought that a Persian king would allow defeated people to return to their homeland, pay for the reconstruction of their temple and encourage the worship of their God? Nevertheless, Cyrus did all of this. A few years earlier, during the reigns of Nabonidus and Belshazzar, the kings of Babylon, none of this would have seemed possible, but the God of Israel can make dreams come true (Ps. 126:1).[17] That God, according to the New Testament, is the God and Father of the Lord Jesus Christ. Through Jesus, this God has 'impossibly' remained just and yet justified those who were guilty of breaking his commandments (Rom. 3:26). What is more, this God says that no eye has seen or ear has heard what is still in store for those whom he has redeemed (1 Cor. 2:9; 1 John 3:2). Given what God has done and promised to do, the concerns of God's people today in the tension between the now and the not yet are nothing that God cannot handle for the glory of his name and the good of his people.[18]

The temple vessels

The first of many lists in Ezra–Nehemiah appears in Ezra 1:9–11, which inventories the temple vessels Nebuchadnezzar had plundered. The numbering of the temple vessels may seem pedantic to modern readers.[19] In reality, these vessels were theologically significant for a people who

---

[17] Belshazzar ruled on behalf of Nabonidus, who, for religious and perhaps economic reasons, spent much of his reign away from Babylon in Arabia.

[18] Hamilton 2014: 10–11.

[19] Modern readers know that the cumulative total of the individual tallies (2,499) in vv. 9–10 does not match the total (5,400) in v. 11. Fensham (1982: 46) concludes that the 'problem is probably due to textual corruption and appears to be insoluble'. For other explanations, see Segal 2002: 122–129.

returned to the Promised Land from exile. They represented continuity with pre-exilic Israel. If post-exilic Israel was using the same vessels as pre-exilic Israel to worship the same God, then the promises and mission of this God were still in effect. Post-exilic Israel inherited everything God had given to pre-exilic Israel. The inventory in Ezra 1 marked the vitality of God's relationship with the post-exilic descendants of pre-exilic Israel. He still cared about them and wanted to give them a future (Jer. 29:10–14). Moreover, he could give them a future. Nebuchadnezzar might have captured the vessels (2 Kgs 25:14; 2 Chr. 36:18; Jer. 52:18–19) and transported them to the temple of his god (the ANE proof of conquest), but was, according to Jeremiah 25:9 and 27:6, Yahweh's servant for a moment in redemptive history. His function, unknown to him, was to administer the final curse of the covenant – seventy years of exile (Deut. 28:15–68; Jer. 25:8–11).[20] Similarly, Belshazzar might have treated the vessels irreverently (Dan. 5:2–4) and thought that Yahweh was an impotent deity of a defeated people, but he was wrong. By 539 BC, Nebuchadnezzar had been dead for more than twenty years and Belshazzar for more than ten years. Meanwhile, the vessels were soon on their way back to a rebuilt temple in Jerusalem. God was alive and on the move to advance his saving purpose through the descendants of Abraham, Isaac and Jacob. He had not lost to Assyria, Babylon and Persia. These empires were simply his instruments of discipline that prepared his people and the rest of the world for a new chapter in the story of redemption (Isa. 10:5–27; 13:19 – 14:8; 43:14–21; 44:26 – 25:13; 47:5–7; Jer. 50:17–20; 51:1–10).

Even so, the first readers of Ezra–Nehemiah were a discouraged people. The enthusiasm created by Cyrus' decree (the already) had long since died down with the passage of time and the challenges of post-exilic life (the not yet). Here, then, was another instance of God's slow timetable. God's people may wish he sometimes worked faster at fulfilling his promises, but God has his reasons for taking his time from a human point of view. As seen throughout the post-exilic literature (Haggai, Zechariah, Malachi

[20] Because the commencement and conclusion of Jeremiah's seventy years are subject to multiple perspectives in the OT, seventy years of exile may be a more symbolic and less literal figure. Kugel (2007: 590) says, 'The number seventy is something of a conventional number in Hebrew and other Semitic languages, a bit like one hundred in English: it means "a lot".' In Ps. 90:10 and Isa. 23:15, seventy years represent the average span of a lifetime. Seventy years also seem to be used more technically in the ANE to convey a thorough enactment of judgment. See Fishbane 1985: 480; Applegate 1997: 93; Edelman 2005: 93; Miller and Hayes 2006: 464; Fried 2015: 49–50.

and Ezra–Nehemiah), this 'delay' took its toll on the post-exilic people. Their hopes faded and their complaints multiplied. They became indifferent towards godly living. For the eyes of faith, though, the exodus typology and temple vessels, which convey God's faithfulness through the years, could inspire hope and perseverance in the present. If God will have a people for his name, then obeying his commands demonstrates a desire to be included in the group.

The second temple and its vessels have, of course, disappeared (Jer. 3:16). Some archaeologist may yet unearth a portion of them, but such remains would no longer have a theological significance for God's people. According to the New Testament, continuity with the past and hope for the future are now guaranteed by the eternal priesthood of Jesus, which the temple and its vessels anticipated. Jesus alone atones for sin and reconciles sinners to God and one another. He alone embodies God's assurance of an eternal inheritance (Heb. 4:9 – 5:9; 1 Peter 1:3–4). Just as evidence of God's faithfulness in the form of returning the temple vessels to a rebuilt temple was supposed to inspire holy living in the post-exilic community, so the work of Jesus to save his people from their sins should lead them to love God and neighbour according to the revelation of God's will. This loving obedience expresses a heartfelt desire to be a part of building God's kingdom on earth.

That said, Christian readers of Ezra–Nehemiah can also be discouraged. If the first readers of this book lived at least a century after Cyrus' decree, Christians live between the two comings of Jesus, which have been separated, so far, by two millennia. Christians, understandably, can wonder what Jesus meant when he said that he would return soon (Rev. 22:20). They can also lose hope and question the sensibility of godly living in a long interim that has been full of ungodly conduct by Christians and non-Christians alike. Christians do not always sense the faithfulness of God in his apparent absence. If the exodus typology and temple vessels reminded the post-exilic Jews of what God had done and of what he had said he would yet do, the New Testament associates Jesus with the exodus by calling him 'our Passover' (1 Cor. 5:7). Moreover, the Lord's Supper was instituted during the Passover meal. After serving the cup, Jesus said he would not drink from the cup again until the coming of God's kingdom (Matt. 26:29; Mark 14:25; Luke 22:18). Jesus might have inaugurated God's kingdom and the Lord's Supper at his first coming, but the fullness of the kingdom awaits Jesus' second coming. At that time, he will appear in majesty and participate with his perfected bride in the wedding feast of the Lamb (Rev. 19:7). Until then, each observance of the Lord's Supper recalls what Jesus inaugurated at his first coming and anticipates what he will consummate at his second coming. Therefore, the biblical antidote to discouragement, which happens in the tension between the already and the not yet, is to look back at what Jesus has already done and look forward to what he will yet do. The former is a foretaste and guarantee of the latter.

The returnees

The relatively short inventory of temple vessels in Ezra 1 leads to a much longer, and perhaps more uninviting, list of people in Ezra 2. As already mentioned, this list reappears almost verbatim in Nehemiah 7 and so is integral to the structure of the book. The first occurrence of the list in Ezra 2 can now be discussed in terms of its relationship to Ezra 1. If Cyrus allowed the Babylonian exiles to go home, Ezra 2 reports that many Jews took the opportunity.

Ezra 2 looks like a membership roll of the post-exilic community. What is not so clear, though, is when these people left Babylon. The chapter opens with a list of those men who presumably led the first wave of returnees soon after Cyrus' decree in 539 BC, which was about seventy years before Ezra's arrival in 458 BC and almost eighty-five years before Nehemiah's arrival in 445 BC. If so, the Nehemiah in verse 2 is not the king's cupbearer in the book of Nehemiah, nor is Mordecai Esther's relative in the book of Esther. It is possible, though, that verse 2 lists the leaders of all the waves of returnees between Cyrus' decree in 539 BC and Nehemiah's first trip to Jerusalem in 445 BC.[21] In this case, Nehemiah could be the king's cupbearer in Nehemiah; Azariah, who is mentioned in Nehemiah 7:7 but not in Ezra 2:2, may be Ezra; and Mordecai could be Esther's cousin.[22] Such a diachronic list appears in Nehemiah 12:1–26, which names the priests and Levites throughout the post-exilic period. Perhaps the numerical tallies in Ezra 2 and Nehemiah 7 count multiple generations over the course of the post-exilic period and not just contemporaries at the beginning of it.

---

[21] Williamson 1985: 30–31; Knowles 2004: 65–66.
[22] Fried 2015: 93–95.

Ezra 2:64–65 reports that the post-exilic community had at least 49,897 residents. That figure comes from adding 42,360, 7,337 and 200. Ezra 2:3–60 subdivides the group of 42,360 into different categories with separate tallies. The individual tallies in verses 3–60 add up to 29,818 (31,089 in Nehemiah 7:8–62), which falls considerably short of 42,360. Ezra 2 offers no explicit explanation for the difference in the totals of verses 3–60 on the one hand and verse 64 on the other. Perhaps the higher total includes women and children.[23] Redditt suggests that the higher total in Ezra 2:64–65 includes everyone in the post-exilic community, regardless of commitment to implementing Cyrus' decree.[24] Meanwhile, the lower total of the individual tallies in verses 3–60 identifies the 'true Israel' that rebuilt the temple and the walls because of faithfulness to Yahweh's law. Using the figures in this chapter to distinguish between what theologians call the visible and invisible people of God seems to be too subtle, especially since Ezra 3:1 says that these people gathered as one man to begin work on the temple. Ezra–Nehemiah may appreciably be honest about the shortcomings of the returnees, but the list of names in Ezra 2 does not evaluate character or motive.

Verses 3–20 provide the family names of some of the laypeople who accompanied the leaders in verse 2. Parosh, Shephatiah, Arah and the others in verses 3–20 belonged to the generation that went into exile. Ezra 2:3–20 says that 15,604 of their descendants (16,817 according to Nehemiah 7:8–25) went back to Jerusalem after the exile. Verses 21–35 identify another 8,540 returnees (8,589 in Nehemiah 7:26–38) by the names of the towns in which their ancestors had lived before the exile. Why some people were counted by their ancestors and others by their towns is not known. God had promised progeny and land to Abraham, and Joshua 13 – 19 records the distribution of patrimonies to tribes and families. By preserving the pre-exilic interests in family and geography, Ezra 2 implicitly affirms the hope of inheritance for all of God's people.[25] The existence of the post-exilic community and its attention to these details establishes continuity between pre- and post-exilic Israel, thereby confirming God's remembrance of his promises to both groups.

Verses 36–58 list 5,022 (5,041 according to Nehemiah 7:39–60) temple personnel who consisted of priests, Levites, singers, gatekeepers and other

---

[23] Williamson 1985: 37–38; Wijk-Bos 1998: 11; Fyall 2010: 51; Steinmann 2010: 176.
[24] Redditt 2012: 224, 231–233, 236–238.
[25] Fyall 2010: 48.

servants. Because these individuals would not have been able to do their work in Babylon, relocating to Jerusalem presumably appealed to them. The seemingly low number of Levites in verse 40 may mean, more negatively, that most of them chose to stay in Babylon or, more positively, that most of them never went to Babylon. Meanwhile, the seemingly high number of priests (4,289) raises questions about how they stayed busy and how the rest of the post-exilic community supported them. The hundred garments in verse 69, unless shared by men working in rotation and in successive generations, would not seem to be enough vestments for so many priests. Later readers of Ezra 2 (and Neh. 7) may wish for more information, but the writer of Ezra–Nehemiah does not address these issues. Perhaps the original readers knew the explanation.

Verses 61–63 count at least 652 (642 in Neh. 7:62) people who could not prove their ancestry by family or town, thus bringing the total of returnees to at least 29,818 in Ezra 2 (31,089 in Neh. 7). This figure is 12,542 short of the grand total of 42,360 returnees in Ezra 2:64 (11,901 short of the same grand total in Neh. 7:66). Presumably, 12,542 (11,901 in Neh. 7) is the number of priests who, according to Ezra 2:61–63 (and Neh. 7:63–65), had no family records. If 652 and 12,542 are added together (642 and 11,901 in Neh. 7), then 13,194 returnees (12,543 in Neh. 7) could not prove their familial attachment to the covenantal community - an especially serious matter for someone claiming to be a priest. Improper handling of the sacred contents of the temple could result in death of the priest and defilement of the sacred precinct. The reference to the Urim and Thummim in Ezra 2:63 (Neh. 7:65) suggests that the loss of records did not permanently exclude undocumented people. Although little is known about this method of getting information from God, apparently it could be used to confirm a person's membership. Therefore, Redditt's conclusion that 40 per cent of the returnees were excluded from the post-exilic community seems to give an unnecessarily harsh assessment of Ezra–Nehemiah's portrayal of the restoration.[26]

The need for a pure people

All of this counting shows a concern for the purity of the belief and conduct of the visible people of God. God has standards that reflect his character, protect his people from syncretism and promote an accurate

[26] Redditt 2014: 78.

witness on his behalf. Like pre-exilic Israel, the post-exilic community was a holy nation with a priestly mission to the world. That mission involved being a channel of God's redeeming grace. Post-exilic Jews could perform this mission only by adhering to God's revealed will that defined a redeemed community. Any departure from the Law and the Prophets compromised the identity of the group and threatened the mission. God's standards can also lessen conflict. Those who agree to live by the standards tend to work together more harmoniously for the advancement of God's will.[27] Those who cannot agree to live by the standards should not receive the privilege of membership, which would grant them greater opportunity to disrupt the mission.

That said, standards that preserve the identity of a group and promote its mission do not necessarily make a group isolationist or unwelcoming. As already noted, Ezra 6:21, in keeping with Exodus 12:48–49, allowed others besides the documented returnees to partake of the Passover meal and so be counted as members of Yahweh's covenantal community. These so-called outsiders might have had to demonstrate commitment to God's standards in order to become insiders, but the point is that a way existed for them to be included. Moreover, just travelling from Babylon to Judah did not automatically make a person an insider. There had to be some evidence of commitment to the God of Israel. Where documentation was lacking, God could vouch for someone by means of the Urim and Thummim. So then, Redditt's claim that Ezra–Nehemiah was written to legitimize the returnees' possession of Judah and exclude those who had lived there during the exile misses the mark.[28] Anyone could express faith in Yahweh and receive a welcome into the covenantal community.

Churches today may not have access to the Urim and Thummim, nor do genealogies typically qualify a person for church membership or leadership. Nevertheless, measures exist to achieve a balance between being inclusive and protective. To become a member of a church and gain access to the Lord's Supper, a person may have to sit through a membership class, give a testimony, show a baptismal certificate (or undergo baptism)

---

27 Dray (2006a: 35) says, 'Only a united fellowship, striving together, is able to successfully face the tremendous demands which challenge its life and growth.'

28 Redditt 2014: 34–35. This denial of mission characterizes the scholarly literature on Ezra–Nehemiah. E.g. Wijk-Bos (1998: 27) says, 'The returned exiles are not interested in converts, in those who are outside the covenantal community; rather, they are fearful of mixing with them.' Southwood (2011: 53) adds, 'There is no possibility for conversion; one is simply within or without the Israelite *ethnos*.' See also Harrington 2011: 254.

and take vows. In the testimony, a person talks about his or her relationship with God; that is, how he or she came to faith in Jesus and how he or she is trying to grow in likeness to Jesus. By means of vows, a person promises to support the mission of the church. Full communicant membership, however, does not depend on a person's bloodline. Similarly, future ministers often have to receive special training, test their potential through internships and pass ordination exams. Growing up in a Christian home, though, is not a prerequisite for pastoral ministry, nor is being a 'preacher's kid'. People enter the ministry from all sorts of backgrounds. Other leaders such as elders and deacons may not have to prepare so formally, but their peers in the congregation will hardly nominate them for office without some evidence of orthodox belief and righteous conduct. Many churches, before allowing potential elders and deacons to stand for election, require them to complete in-house training in doctrine, polity and leadership. Still, no one checks the family tree. The only pedigree that matters is being in Christ. Christians may not be able to apply Ezra 2 directly to their lives, but the concern of this chapter for evident commitment to God and his mission pertains to all of God's people.

The reality of an ordinary people

Something else to notice is how many of the names in Ezra 2 are unfamiliar. Verse 36 mentions the high priest Jeshua (or Joshua), who appears elsewhere in Ezra–Nehemiah as well as in Haggai and Zechariah. Solomon in verse 55, of course, is none other than David's son and successor, but he died long before the post-exilic era. As for the rest of the names, almost nothing is known about them; nevertheless, these people will rebuild God's house and city.[29] Throughout redemptive history, not many of God's people have been superstars, and few have made the front page of the newspaper (1 Cor. 1:26). History may forget most of them, but they do not escape God's attention. Abraham Lincoln supposedly said, 'God must love the common man because he made so many of them.' As seen in Ezra–Nehemiah, God uses ordinary people to accomplish extraordinary results that advance his eternal purpose. The temple and city these people in Ezra 2 rebuild will later be visited by God himself in the person of Jesus. Moreover, Ezra 2:68–69 (see also Neh. 7:71–72) mentions the offerings of

---

[29] Eskenazi (1988a: 48) says, 'The people who will build the house of God [in contrast to prominent, heroic leaders] are the central focus of the book.'

the returnees. These average people contributed quite a sum to the Lord's work. This combined effort of commoners seems to be how God prefers to build his kingdom. Every once in a while there is a big donation. More often than not, the faithful giving of ordinary people supplies the need. No one may know in advance how God will build his city through humble servants, but he will build it.

If Ezra 2 and Nehemiah 7:4–73 frame the second section of the book, the intervening material reveals the shortcomings of the returnees. For example, some of the names in Ezra 2 are mentioned in Ezra 10 in connection with a problem of intermarriage, which will be discussed further in a later chapter. Meanwhile, Nehemiah 5 describes economic hardship due to usury, which will also be discussed later. While none of the names in Ezra 2 is singled out in Nehemiah 5, who else but the people in Ezra 2 could be the feuding Jews in Nehemiah 5? Some members of the post-exilic community were apparently taking financial advantage of other members. Nevertheless, God did not expel them from Jerusalem. Instead, he sent Ezra and Nehemiah to teach the law and call for repentance. God forgave them and moved forward with them. When Ezra 2 is read in view of the rest of the book, a prominent theme of Ezra–Nehemiah emerges: imperfect people live in God's city. Likewise, God's people today continue to fall short of God's will. They are no different from these people in Ezra–Nehemiah. Quite simply, perfect people do not live in God's city, enter his presence for worship or labour on behalf of his kingdom. Rather, redeemed sinners do. God has graciously forgiven all who believe in Jesus and made them productive citizens of his city. That is good news.

As a long list of names, Ezra 2 may not be anybody's favourite chapter in the Bible, but it is by no means an anomaly in the Old Testament. Other lists or genealogies, including the first nine chapters of 1 Chronicles, can be found. One function of the genealogies is to trace the covenantal line of Abraham's descendants. With an economy of words, these genealogies convey God's faithfulness across the generations. God said that he would create a people for his name, and the Old Testament genealogies, including the list of names in Ezra 2, indicate that he has. Moreover, God had told Jeremiah to purchase his uncle's field in expectation of the exiles' eventual return to the Promised Land (Jer. 32:6–15). If Ezra 1:1 sets the events of Ezra–Nehemiah in the context of Jeremiah's prophecies, Ezra 2 implies that Jeremiah, in the face of imminent invasion, had wisely kept his uncle's land in the family. Even the exile could not sabotage God's plan to give his people an inheritance on which they could model a redeemed community. By means of Cyrus' decree, God restored a remnant to the Promised Land from where he would continue saving the world.

Ezra 2 and the New Testament

Of course, the New Testament opens with a genealogy that briefly reviews Old Testament history from Abraham to Jesus. The first name, Abraham, recalls God's intention to use Abraham's family for the redemption of the world in Genesis 3:1 – 11:26 that sinned against God. The last name, Jesus, is the culmination of all the genealogies in the Old Testament. In Matthew 1:21, the angel that appears to Joseph instructs him to give the name Jesus to Mary's child. Jesus is the Greek form of Joshua, which means 'Yahweh saves'. The angel tells Joseph that Mary's child will save his people from their sins. Indeed, Matthew's genealogy recalls the imperfection of God's people in Old Testament times and God's repeated promise to forgive.

Matthew begins his genealogy with Abraham, Isaac and Jacob. Jewish readers of Matthew might have been proud of descending from these patriarchs whom God had elected and with whom he had made a covenant. These patriarchs, however, were hardly exemplars of sterling character traits. Abraham put his wife at risk by telling half-truths about her relationship to him. He also had another son from another woman in an effort to realize the promise God had made not only to him but also to his wife. Isaac and Rebekah played favourites with their sons, Esau and Jacob. Jacob tried to cheat Esau out of his birthright and later was not only partial to two of his sons who were born to his favourite wife but also indifferent towards his sons and daughter who were born to his other wife. As for Jacob's son Judah, what happens between him and Judah's daughter-in-law Tamar is not usually read in religious gatherings.[30] The patriarchal

[30] But see how Waltke and Fredricks (2001: 507–508, 515, 552, 558–559, 567) relate Gen. 38 to the importance of Judah in Gen. 37 – 50. In short, the uncaring Judah in Gen. 37 is later humbled by the Tamar incident in Gen. 38. Soon after that incident, Judah offers himself in place of Benjamin (Joseph's full brother and Rachel's second son) in whose sack Zaphenath-paneah's (Joseph's) silver cup was found. Judah trades places with Benjamin because he does not want their father (Jacob) to experience more grief (Gen. 44:34). Because of this sacrificial attitude, Judah, who is the real leader of the brothers, receives kingship as his inheritance from Jacob (Gen. 49:8–10). He had demonstrated the servant leadership that Jesus, his descendant, would later embody in an ultimate way. Meanwhile, Judah's father was able to pronounce a blessing on Pharaoh, a Gentile (Gen. 47:7, 10).

period was, by no means, a pristine era. Salvation for anybody seemed like the last thing that could come from this family.

If the first section gives the whole genealogy a shaky beginning, then surely the second section improves on the first. It begins with David, the man after God's heart. David took Israel from the dark days of the judges to the zenith of Israel's political influence in the ANE. As a psalmist, he was the Isaac Watts or Charles Wesley of Israelite worship. For some reason, though, Matthew mentions the adulterous and murderous incident with Bathsheba and spoils the reader's recollection of the glorious days of David. According to Kennedy, 'this ideal King David, at fourteenth position in the first section, becomes the David of reality in the second section'.[31] As for the other kings in the Davidic dynasty, there were a few godly ones, but most were disappointing. As a whole, they were an odd assortment of idolaters, murderers, power-seekers and self-indulgent types. If Matthew's genealogy builds in expectation from Abraham to David, it quickly declines until the second section concludes with the sad reference to the exile.[32] In four hundred years Israel went from glory to shame.

As for the third section that reviews the Second Temple period, Zerubbabel's name occurs in verse 13. He, of course, is mentioned in Ezra 3:2 and 5:2 as one of the earliest contributors to the reconstruction of the second temple. While most of the other names are unfamiliar, this section reviews the Second Temple period during which the Persians and Greeks, followed by the Ptolemies and Seleucids and then the Seleucids and Romans, fought for control of Judah. Meanwhile, many Jews, at the expense of religious fidelity, sought the favour of whatever king had the upper hand at the time. The so-called intertestamental period differed little from the patriarchal and monarchial periods.

This whole genealogy recalls sordid tales about Jesus' ancestors. What a way to begin the New Testament! Some readers may wish to ignore the first seventeen verses of the New Testament and start at Matthew 1:18. Surely Matthew should have avoided the infelicities of the Old Testament story. The story of Jesus, however, is not about a God who chooses the noble or the saintly and elevates them above the common and pagan. Ezra and Nehemiah would have been the first to acknowledge that there is no

31 Kennedy 2008: 93.
32 Ibid. 96–97, 218.

one with an unblemished record of devotion to God. Jesus the anointed one did not come to mingle with the beautiful people. He came to seek and save sinners in need of grace – the same people for whom Ezra prayed in Ezra 9:6–15 and for whom the Levites prayed in Nehemiah 9:5–38.

The people in Ezra 2 are the spiritual ancestors of Christians who, in Jesus, have become part of the biblical genealogies and biblical story. With the people in Ezra 2, Christians will inherit the New Jerusalem to which the post-exilic Jerusalem pointed in anticipation. The vicissitudes of world history and of the personal histories of Christians have not stopped God from fulfilling his promise to have a people for his name. Despite the problems of the post-exilic community and of God's people since, there is still a recognizable people of God at the end of Ezra–Nehemiah and nearly 2,500 years later. Nothing can thwart God's will.

Summary

The first two chapters of Ezra–Nehemiah establish God's intention to work through humans, both Jew and Gentile, in order to advance his redemptive plan after the exile. While the exile might have seemed to terminate this plan, the writer(s) of Ezra–Nehemiah insisted otherwise. God still cared about the descendants of those who went into exile. As seen in the opening reference to Jeremiah and the return of the temple vessels, the post-exilic community inherited the earlier promises of a restoration after the exile. Moreover, these people had support from Gentile rulers – this time, Persia. Taking into account the larger context of the Old Testament, God still shows favour to the descendants of Abraham so that they may be a blessing to the rest of the world. Much more may still have to be said about these Jews, but enough has already been said to indicate that they are not spiritual outcasts: God has these people where he wants them.

Christians today can learn at this point that they too are where they are for a providential reason. As believers in Jesus, the son of Abraham, Christians inherit God's promises to Abraham and become his spiritual descendants. God, similarly, remains faithful to Christians and meaningfully arranges the events of their lives for the advancement of his kingdom in their time and place. Recognizing God's direction of the situations of life offers comfort and perspective during those seasons that may seem to lack evidence of God's involvement or care. It also encourages perseverance at doing God's revealed will. If God is faithful to his people, they should be faithful in response, believing that he will bless their efforts on his behalf.

4
Rebuilding the temple

With its reference to the return of the temple vessels, Ezra 1 establishes continuity between the worship of pre- and post-exilic Israel. At the end of Ezra 2, however, the vessels may be back in Jerusalem, but there is no temple to house them. Solomon's temple, destroyed in 586 BC by the army of Nebuchadnezzar, had lain in ruins for nearly fifty years. If Ezra–Nehemiah opens with Cyrus' permission to rebuild the temple, Ezra 3 – 6 recounts the steps taken by the first waves of returnees under Sheshbazzar and Zerubbabel to raise up a new house of God on the site of the old. Ezra 3, in particular, describes the reconstruction of the altar of burnt sacrifice, the celebration of the Feast of Tabernacles, and the repair of the temple foundation. If Ezra 4 explains why work on the temple stopped for more than a decade, Ezra 5:1 – 6:15 gives details about the work's resumption and completion. Ezra 6:16–22 then records the dedication and celebration of the finished project.

Beginning efforts

Ezra 1:11 may credit Sheshbazzar with bringing the temple vessels back to Jerusalem, but Ezra 3 never mentions him in connection with the first effort to rebuild the temple. Instead, Zerubbabel is named, along with Jeshua. The relationship between Sheshbazzar and Zerubbabel is not clear.[1] Both are called 'governor' (Ezra 1:8; Hag. 1:1), and both are said to lead exiles back to Judah (Ezra 1:11; 2:1–2). Ezra 3 places Zerubbabel in Jerusalem during the second year after the return from Babylon (Ezra 3:8–9). Presumably this return occurred shortly after 539 BC during the reign of Cyrus. If so, Ezra 3:10 gives the impression that the first wave of

[1] For a more substantial discussion, see Kidner 1979: 139–142; Steinmann 2008: 513–522; Blenkinsopp 2013: 71–74; Redditt 2014: 95–97; Fried 2015: 80–82.

returnees, including Zerubbabel, promptly laid the temple's foundation. Ezra 5:16, however, says Sheshbazzar laid the foundation. Perhaps Sheshbazzar and Zerubbabel oversaw the repair of the foundation during Cyrus' reign about 535 BC. Then, about fifteen years later in 520 BC, Zerubbabel participated in the renewed effort to strengthen the foundation and build the superstructure.[2] Apparently Sheshbazzar was no longer involved with the project.

Only Ezra 1:8, 11, 5:14 and 16 mention Sheshbazzar. Called a 'leader' (*nāśî'*) and 'governor' (*peḥâ*), he might have been a Persian official who served as Cyrus' representative in Judah. His absence from the royal line after the exile in 1 Chronicles 3:17–24 suggests that he was not a descendant of David.[3] By identifying Sheshbazzar as a *nāśî'*, the writer of Ezra–Nehemiah might have wished to associate Sheshbazzar with Ezekiel's *nāśî'* (often translated 'prince'), who was a Davidic descendant. Ezekiel's prince would avoid the mistakes of earlier kings and promote proper worship among God's people. Meanwhile, 1 Chronicles 3:17–19, along with references in Haggai, Zechariah and Ezra–Nehemiah, establishes the Davidic ancestry of Zerubbabel. Apparently, he was the Davidic representative in the early years of the post-exilic community. Called a 'signet ring' in Haggai 2:23, Zerubbabel embodied Yahweh's signature that guaranteed his promises for the future, including the revival of Davidic kingship. The early years of the post-exilic era, however, featured plenty of contrary evidence that called the guarantee into question.

Worship as the antidote to fear

According to Ezra 3:1–6, the first group of returnees resumed the observance of sacrifices and feasts about twenty years before the second temple was finished in 516 BC (Ezra 6:15).[4] A rebuilt altar at the place where God had chosen to put his name (Deut. 12:5–7; 2 Sam. 7:13) was the first step towards worshipping God in accordance with Mosaic law, which was concerned with both the actions of the body and the attitude of the heart. At that altar in Jerusalem, the returnees could offer burnt sacrifices for

---

[2] This understanding of what happened eases the tension between Ezra 3:7 (the Phoenicians supply timber) and Hag. 1:8 (the returnees supply lumber).

[3] Shenazzar in 1 Chr. 3:18 may be a variant spelling of Sheshbazzar, but no independent confirmation exists.

[4] David similarly built an altar (2 Sam. 24:25) before Solomon erected the first temple (Laird 2016: 68).

atonement (Lev. 1:3–4) and thanksgiving (Lev. 3:1–5; 7:12), thereby '[casting] themselves daily upon the mercy of God and [reconsecrating] themselves to his glory'.[5] This concern for the law of Moses evidenced the faith and faithfulness of the post-exilic community. These returnees must have been aware of God's promise to Moses to grant his people a future beyond the exile (Deut. 30:1–10). This future, said Moses, would include sincere obedience to the law of Moses. Ezra 3:2 reports careful observance of what God had stipulated through Moses. Readers of Ezra 3 learn from the example of the post-exilic community that true worship emerges from interaction with God's Word, which tells God's people who God is, what he has done and how they should respond. Worship involves remembering what God has done, giving him proper (thankful) credit and declaring one's intention to trust and obey.

If Ezra 3:8 mentions the second month of the second year, the reference to the seventh month in Ezra 3:1 presumably refers to the first year back in Judah. During the seventh month, which was the religious high point of Israel's calendar, the Israelites celebrated three holy occasions: the Feast of Trumpets, the Day of Atonement and the Feast of Tabernacles. Ezra 3:4 mentions only the Feast of Tabernacles, which re-enacted the transience of the wilderness years. During the Feast of Tabernacles, God's people would live in huts for a week in order to remember their dependence on God and his sufficiency for their needs. This feast annually encouraged the Israelites to resist worry. The God who gave blessing in the past could and would provide in the present and future.

The reference to fear in Ezra 3:3 makes the Feast of Tabernacles especially relevant. From the start, the post-exilic community experienced hostility from those who had been living in Judah during the exile (Ezra 4:1–2).[6] According to 2 Kings 17:24–41, these so-called people of the land consisted of Israelites who never went to Babylon and Gentiles whom foreign kings transplanted in the former northern kingdom. Intermarriage occurred along with a syncretistic version of commitment to Yahweh. The fear was legitimate not only because of a concern for religious purity but also because of the outsider status of the returnees. While the ancestors of the returnees had formerly lived in Judah, the current occupants did

---

[5] Dray 2006a: 35.

[6] According to 1 Kgs 5:3, the opposition that David faced from his enemies similarly delayed construction of the first temple (Laird 2016: 67–68).

not recognize the right of the returnees (whether politically or theologically based) to take up residence. The current occupants were in no mood to give up or even share land and resources. Fried also draws attention to the rivalry among satraps that would put newcomers in a precarious position.[7]

Fear, however, does not have to cripple. As seen in Ezra 3, it drove the post-exilic community to worship and entreat the Lord. There is no shame in admitting fear and crying out for help. The psalms repeatedly call God a refuge for those who do so. In fact, crying out to God freed the returnees to persevere in carrying out Cyrus' decree. Moreover, verse 4 says that these people observed the Feast of Tabernacles, which recalled God's provision of needs during the wilderness wandering after the exodus. By re-enacting the temporary living arrangement of that time, successive generations of God's people were able to identify with the original event and make the theological lesson of that event applicable to new situations. In other words, they observed a pattern to God's behaviour; namely, that God takes care of his people.[8] By committing their situation to the God who had been the help of his people in previous generations, the returnees were able to turn their attention and energy from worry to work. If verses 8–9 describe a united effort to do what Cyrus had ordered, verse 10 reports the successful completion of the foundation. Cyrus' decree, which was also the will of Yahweh, may not yet have been fully implemented in Ezra 3, but the post-exilic community had made a good start (Ezra 3:8). God had kept them safe and blessed their effort. Their acknowledgment of fear in the context of worship enabled them to remember that their God was bigger than the humans of whom they were afraid. Because this God had already protected them, they could trust his promise to keep taking care of them.

Throughout the Bible, God tells his people not to be afraid of their circumstances. He does not say this because he expects his people to look inside themselves and find a hero. God never urges people to rely on their own strength – whether intellectual, financial, physical, rhetorical and so on. Many circumstances, God knows, arouse fear when people realize that they cannot handle them for one reason or another. Nevertheless, God calls people to trust him by obeying his commands regardless of how counterintuitive obedience may be. Moreover, he continually reminds his

[7] Fried 2015: 166–168.

[8] Hamilton 2014: 22.

people of what he has already done – hence all the history in the Bible. God's track record establishes his trustworthiness. Consequently, his people can commit themselves to him by using their intellects, finances, physical strength, rhetorical prowess and so on for his glory and the benefit of his world.

Not to be overlooked in this regard is the record of Cyrus' financial support (Ezra 3:7). He who had ordered the reconstruction of the temple also provided resources. Because of Cyrus' generosity, the post-exilic community could buy timber from Phoenicia (Tyre and Sidon). Of course, Solomon's temple had also been built with timber from King Hiram of Phoenicia (1 Kgs 5:8–9; 2 Chr. 2:16). Before Solomon, Egyptian gifts (Exod. 12:35–36) had made the tabernacle possible in the wilderness. Isaiah 60:5–14 speaks of the wealth of nations that flows into post-exilic Jerusalem and, especially, enhances the temple. Verse 10 specifically mentions the beneficence of kings. In the 530s BC, King Cyrus ruled much of the known world and controlled its assets. His contribution to the post-exilic temple replays a recurring theme in the Bible; namely, that Gentiles build God's house. In the New Testament, although believing Gentiles do not construct an actual building in Jerusalem, they are nevertheless said to be the living stones that form a spiritual house in which God's Spirit resides (1 Cor. 3:16–17; Eph. 2:19–22; 1 Peter 2:4–5). Their offerings helped Paul and others spread the gospel and build the church throughout the Roman world.

Ezra 3:11 recalls Jeremiah 33:10–11, which links God's goodness and faithfulness with hope for restoration after the exile. How unlikely Jeremiah's words seemed in 586 BC when the Promised Land, especially the temple in Jerusalem, was trampled by Babylonian soldiers. Now, more than fifty years later, God's people were singing at the dedication of the foundation of the second temple. No matter how bleak the situation, Yahweh can make his people sing again. This is one of the most important truths these texts can teach (see Pss 30:4–5; 133:4–6). Even so, the reference to the weeping of the old men in Ezra 3:12 reminds the reader of the tension between the now and the not yet. Similar to Zechariah 4:10, Ezra 3:12 affirms that God had begun a new work but had not yet finished it. The post-exilic temple did not match the size and splendour of Solomon's temple, and Jerusalem did not look like the city of a great king (Ps. 48:2). Zerubbabel the Davidic scion might have been present, but he was not ruling over an independent kingdom. Nor did surrounding monarchs envy his wisdom, wealth and influence. What earlier prophets had envisioned for the restoration was only barely evident. Much more still awaited realization.[9]

God does not always make a big splash. He often works in low-key, unimpressive people and places. Even Jesus, who has already received all authority in heaven and earth (Matt. 28:18), does not yet look like a potentate to whom everything is in subjection (Eph. 1:22; Heb. 2:8). For this reason, God's people must guard against becoming disappointed with little splashes. They must not give up too soon for something with more pizzazz. How many churches have fewer than a hundred members? Yet God is among them, blessing and using them. The God of Ezra–Nehemiah calls his people to be faithful, not necessarily big in numbers – genuine but not necessarily grand.

Ezra 3:1–7 mentions the resumption of worship in the form of daily sacrifices and annual feasts, especially the Feast of Tabernacles. God's people today may not observe this feast, but its theological significance still applies to them. Verses such as Matthew 6:25–32 and Philippians 4:19 assure followers of Jesus that God knows about their needs and will take care of them. For this reason, fear of circumstances need not paralyse them. Because God can handle any circumstances, his people can take the risk of committing themselves to the advancement of his kingdom. For post-exilic Jews, this risk involved building a temple in the midst of economic hardship and hostile neighbours. God's people today may encounter this risk in other settings, but they, like their spiritual ancestors, face it in the context of remembering what God has already done and awaiting what he will yet do.

Worship in the manner of David

Ezra 3:10 says that the first wave of returnees, after laying the foundation for the temple in partial accordance with Cyrus' decree (Ezra 1:2), worshipped in the manner of David described in 1 Chronicles 22 – 29. This foundation, of course, was in Jerusalem, which Ezra 3:15 calls the City of David. Along with Chronicles, Ezra–Nehemiah presents King David as the one who organized Israel's worship at the temple. That worship expressed hope for God to work out his redemptive plan through his chosen king in his chosen city. In other words, Davidic liturgy cannot be

[9] Koch 1974: 189, 196; McConville 1986: 213; Hamilton 2014: 27.

separated from Davidic theology.[10] Throughout Ezra–Nehemiah, including Ezra 3, no Davidic descendant reigns in Jerusalem. Nevertheless, rebuilding the temple in the City of David, where Yahweh chose to put his name, reminded the post-exilic community that their work in the absence of a Davidic king would be used of God to fulfil his promises that included a future for Davidic kingship. If salvation goes out from Jerusalem to bless the rest of the world, a Davidic king is both the instrument for and focus of that mission (Ps. 72:8–11). The post-exilic community has this hope in Ezra 3.[11] That said, the David in Ezra 3 (and later in Neh. 12) looks less like the warrior who finished the conquest of Canaan in the books of Samuel and more like the temple planner in Chronicles. Unlike Ezekiel 34:24, Ezra 3:10 may refer to David as 'king' (*melek*) instead of 'prince' (*nāśî'*), but the David of Ezra 3:10 resembles the royal supporter of temple worship and covenantal faithfulness in Ezekiel 37:24–28 and 45:7 - 46:18.[12]

As was the case with the company of worshippers at the opening of the first temple (2 Chr. 5:13), those who celebrated the laying of the second temple's foundation in Ezra 3:10–11 had a portion of 1 Chronicles 16:34 on their lips. This verse affirms:

> Give thanks to the LORD, for he is good;
> his love endures for ever.
> (NIV)

These words are part of a song David first gave to Asaph for the occasion of the ark's entrance into Jerusalem (1 Chr. 16:7).[13] David wrote '[H]e is

---

[10] Goswell (2012: 26–27, 30) argues that Ezra–Nehemiah presents David as a liturgist but not as a king (a messiah) who will rule righteously over God's people and world. David's liturgy, so far as it is known from other parts of the OT, does not separate Davidic theology from worship of Yahweh. See Ulrich 2016: 49–64.

[11] Not everyone agrees. Besides the reference to Goswell in the previous footnote, see Williamson 1982: 9–10; Eskenazi 1988a: 33, 36; Japhet 2006: 62; Karrer-Grube 2008: 155, 159; Klement 2011: 73–74.

[12] On Ezekiel's preference of *nāśî'* over *melek*, Block (2010: 212–213) suggests that *nāśî'* conveys the subordinate and supportive role that Israel's kings were supposed to play as Yahweh's vicegerent. Of course, the kings of Israel and Judah too often disregarded their covenantal responsibility to lead God's people in conformity to his law.

[13] David's song of thanksgiving in 1 Chr. 16:8–36 has content that appears in three psalms: 1 Chr. 16:8–22 // Ps. 105:1–15; 1 Chr. 16:23–33 // Ps. 96; 1 Chr. 16:34–36 // Ps. 106:1, 47–48. None of the psalms has a title that assigns authorship to David or anyone else. The song does not appear in the parallel account in 2 Sam. 6.

good; / his love endures for ever' about the covenant God of Israel, and God's people sang these words at three crucial moments in their history: the entrance of the ark into Jerusalem, the entrance of the ark into the first temple, and the completion of the foundation for the second temple. Each of these events represented advances in God's plan of redemption that is tied not only to the people of Israel but also to the house of David. David's transfer of the ark to Jerusalem with Yahweh's approval gave theological legitimacy to his kingship, as did Solomon's construction of the first temple. If David correctly understood that Yahweh had linked his redemptive programme with Davidic kingship (Ps. 89:19–29, 49), then these quoted words in Ezra 3:11 ('[H]e is good; / his love towards Israel endures for ever') cannot be separated from that redemptive-historical context. Moreover, there is no warrant for thinking that the singers in Ezra 3 recalled only David's composition of the words and not the theological context for which he composed them.

Whether or not the same person wrote Chronicles and Ezra–Nehemiah, Ezra 3:11 must surely be read in view of 1 Chronicles 16:34 and 2 Chronicles 5:13.[14] If the builders and priests in Ezra 3:10–11 did not sing in conscious recollection of David's song of thanksgiving in 1 Chronicles 16 or its echo in 2 Chronicles 5 – and their ignorance or forgetfulness seems unlikely – the writer of Ezra–Nehemiah makes the Davidic connection anyway for the reader. Moreover, Ezra 8:20 associates Ezra's journey to Jerusalem with David's organization of the Levites. This verse occurs in the so-called Ezra Memoir in which Ezra speaks in the first person. Not just the unnamed writer of Ezra–Nehemiah but Ezra himself considered his mission in Jerusalem to be in continuity with David's revision of worship. Ezra the priest followed the upgrades of David the king because Ezra the priest knew that David the king had received revelation from Yahweh. That revelation pertained to the Davidic covenant that Davidic worship celebrated. Ezra the priest travelled to Jerusalem with Artaxerxes' blessing in order to instruct God's people in the theology and worship of David the king. That theology grew out of the royal hope in God's covenants with Abraham (Gen. 17:6; 49:10) and Moses (Deut. 17:14–20). Not to be overlooked is how the royal hope in Moses' day

[14] This observation does not necessitate the composition of Chronicles before Ezra–Nehemiah. The singers and the writer of Ezra–Nehemiah could have known about the events in 1 Chr. 16 and 2 Chr. 5 from another source. Regarding common authorship of Chronicles and Ezra–Nehemiah, see Redditt 2008: 216–239.

received confirmation from Balaam's fourth oracle (Num. 24:17). Ezra the priest, of course, was well versed in the law of Moses (Ezra 7:6) and would have been able to make these connections between the Pentateuch and David's reign.

The reference to Jeremiah in Ezra 1:1 also comes into play at this point.[15] Looking ahead to the restoration of thank offerings at the Jerusalem temple (Ezra 3:11), Jeremiah 33:10–11 says that worshippers will give thanks to Yahweh because he whose love endures for ever is good. Nevertheless, worship that thanks God for his goodness is not the only thing that will be restored in Jerusalem. Jeremiah 33:15–17 also expects the revival of Davidic kingship. When God's people think about his goodness and love, the perpetuity of his promise to David inevitably comes to mind because Davidic kingship is the channel of God's goodness and love. The post-exilic community knew this even in the absence of a Davidic king.

Of course, Jeremiah 33 also mentions the priests. If Jeremiah 33:17 says that David will always have a descendant on the throne of Israel, the next verse speaks of the perpetuity of the priesthood. Together, Davidic kingship and Levitical priesthood were the means Yahweh established to aid his people in being fit for their mission as a royal priesthood. The descendants of Levi (both priests and Levites) were supposed to teach the law of Moses to the rest of the tribes, and the priests had the added responsibility of making atonement for infractions of that law. Meanwhile, kings were supposed to model Torah piety and promote it through righteous rulings. Too often, priests and kings failed to perform these responsibilities, and God's people as a whole followed the bad example of their leaders. Jeremiah, who had much to say against priests and kings, also anticipated a day when they would perform their duties and so be the blessing to God's people that Yahweh had originally intended.

Although Zerubbabel and Joshua are said to be present at this celebration in Ezra 3, the ministry of priests admittedly features more prominently in Ezra–Nehemiah than does the contribution of the descendants of David. Why Ezra or the writer of Ezra–Nehemiah did not say more about Davidic theology in Ezra 3 or elsewhere is not so easy to explain. Obviously, no Davidic descendant ruled as king in Jerusalem, and

---

[15] Eskenazi (1988a: 44) says, 'Jeremiah's word in Ezra–Nehemiah is open-ended, inviting the reader to ponder what precisely will be completed.' As already noted, she does not think that Ezra–Nehemiah shares Jeremiah's hope for David.

the writer of Ezra–Nehemiah did not try to deny political reality. The weeping in Ezra 3:12 may have to do not only with the reduced splendour of the post-exilic temple (Hag. 2:3) but also with the absence of a politically independent descendant of David for the dedication (1 Kgs 8:22; 2 Chr. 6:12). Perhaps the returnees muted their royal hope so as not to arouse Persian suspicion.[16] This practical concern, however, does not indicate a total lack of interest in God's promises to David. It simply means that the post-exilic community did not try to implement the royal eschatology of earlier prophets. It accepted the political situation at the time and focused on other pastoral issues about which something could be done immediately.[17] With or without a Davidic king in Jerusalem, this community recognized its present need to restore its relationship with God and took concrete steps, especially after receiving instruction from Ezra and the Levites, to do so. So then, concluding that Ezra or the writer of Ezra–Nehemiah had no interest in Davidic theology goes beyond the evidence. David is mentioned, and his words that were sung (the liturgy) at the completion of the foundation had a history to them. They had accompanied God's redemptive activity through David and his descendants, and they hold out hope for fuller fulfilment in the future.

ANE people, including the Israelites, believed that kings on earth represented deities in heaven. An empty throne might suggest a weak god, but post-exilic Jews resisted this conclusion. The writer of Ezra 1:1 expresses a belief in Yahweh's power over Cyrus. Ezra and Nehemiah express a similar conviction about Artaxerxes in Ezra 7:27–28 and Nehemiah 1:5, 11. Moreover, Ezra 3:11 recalls 1 Chronicles 16:34, which occurs in the context of David's thanksgiving at the arrival of the ark of the covenant in Jerusalem. This thanksgiving includes affirmations of Yahweh's wonderful acts (1 Chr. 16:9), miracles (1 Chr. 16:12) and marvellous works (1 Chr. 16:24). Moreover, Yahweh is said to judge the whole earth (1 Chr. 16:14), and the various parts of this earth are thought to react to his deeds (1 Chr. 16:30–32). If the first wave of returnees recalled David's words in 1 Chronicles 16, then these people believed that a big and powerful God was being good and loving to them at the laying of the second temple's

[16] Perhaps, but Haggai did not seem to be afraid of discussing his messianic expectation. Hag. 2:23 likens Zerubbabel, the Davidic scion, to a signet ring, which was used to seal official documents. Like a signature, it guaranteed the authenticity of the contents. So then, Zerubbabel was God's signature, guaranteeing a future for the house of David and the people of God.

[17] Brueggemann 1991: 134–136; Satterthwaite and McConville 2007: 256.

foundation. An empty throne in Jerusalem did not tell the whole story: there was more to come.

The New Testament echoes this hope for the followers of Jesus, the heir of David's throne, who died ignominiously during his first coming. Nevertheless, the writers of the New Testament recounted his resurrection and ascension. They also preserved Jesus' announcement of his second coming in all of his rightful majesty. Moreover, the writer of Hebrews observed that Jesus was a more effective priest than Levi and his descendants. Ezra–Nehemiah, then, displays a characteristic of other sections of the Christian Bible. It knows that the post-exilic era is part of a long process of a great work of redemption. God's people at any point in redemptive history must keep in mind that not all of God's promises come to fruition at once.

Senior tears

Ezra 3:12 contrasts the joy of the younger with the sorrow of the older generation. Here is the possibility of further tension. Because the younger generation had grown up outside the Promised Land, they had never seen a temple dedicated to the worship of Yahweh. Nor had they ever participated in building one. The events of Ezra 3 were new and exciting to them. A foundation anticipated a superstructure, furnishings and activities. The younger generation could hardly wait for the finished product. Meanwhile, older people who had seen Solomon's temple knew that this current effort could never match what once was. Their tears betrayed their regret over what had been lost. If the two groups were not careful, their perspectives could work against each other and create friction. The older people could discourage or belittle the younger generation, thus driving them away. The younger generation could fail to learn from the older people and repeat past mistakes.

Proverbs 20:29 says:

> The glory of young men is their strength,
>   grey hair is the splendour of the old.
> (NIV)

This verse teaches that the generations need each other. In Ezra 3, the young men had the vigour to build a temple, but they needed the wisdom, symbolized by the grey hair, of the seasoned citizens. That mature judgment could curb raw, untaught enthusiasm and prevent mistakes. The seasoned citizens, however, might have possessed the insight that comes with experience but still needed the energy of youth. Otherwise, the building project might prove to be too physically demanding. Ezra 3 draws attention to the so-called generation gap and thereby demonstrates that God's people of all ages need one another's contributions. No one has all of the answers or all of the ability.

Opposition

Starting in Ezra 4, the writer of Ezra–Nehemiah indicates that the effort to execute Cyrus' decree encountered opposition. Ezra 4:1 mentions adversaries of Judah and Benjamin, and Ezra 4:4 further identifies these adversaries as the people of the land. After many residents of the southern kingdom went into exile between 605 BC (Dan. 1:1) and 581 BC (Jer. 52:30), the Promised Land was not vacant.[18] Some Israelites remained (2 Kgs 24:14; Jer. 40:7–12), as did Gentiles whom Assyrian and Babylonian rulers had moved to western Asia from other parts of their empires (2 Kgs 17:24). Ezra 4:2 refers specifically to a scattering by Esarhaddon who ruled Assyria from 681 to 669 BC. These relocated people and their descendants – whether Gentile, Jew or mixed – lived in Judah during the exile and met the returnees when they arrived from Babylon.

Their offer to assist in the reconstruction of the temple in Ezra 4:2 seems friendly and ecumenical, and later readers might wonder why Zerubbabel, Jeshua and others would turn away willing hands. Religious organizations always seem to need volunteers and often view volunteer help as a low-pressure way to introduce outsiders to the group's mission. In other words, welcoming volunteers can be a form of evangelism. Moreover, Cyrus' decree mentioned the support of the surrounding people (Ezra 1:4) and so, in its canonical context, recalls the generosity of the Egyptians at the exodus (Exod. 12:35–36). A fair question to ask, then, is could the post-exilic leaders have excluded people wrongfully? Perhaps Yahweh wanted them to be included so that they could learn more about him.

What should be kept in mind, however, is that the writer of Ezra–Nehemiah lived after this incident and knew how this situation played out. Ezra 4:4–5 summarizes the more immediate hostility during the

[18] Much of the northern kingdom had gone into exile in 722 BC.

reigns of Cyrus and Cambyses in the sixth century, and Ezra 4:6–23 interrupts the narrative to describe additional opposition during the reign of Artaxerxes in the fifth century. Verse 24 brings the reader back to the time of the events in verses 1–5; specifically, the reign of Darius I after the reigns of Cyrus and Cambyses and before the reigns of Xerxes and Artaxerxes. In other words, the passage of time brought out the true colours of these people of the land – hence, their identification as adversaries in Ezra 4:1. They did not want to worship Yahweh with appropriate commitment, humility and inclusiveness (mission). Otherwise, they would have refrained from lies and accusations. They wanted to control the newcomers, whose royal support threatened the local power structure.[19] The new house of worship was simply the flashpoint, and the post-exilic leaders knew it.

If Ezra 4:5 mentions the enemies' bribery of Persian officials in the sixth century, verses 13–14 illustrate the enemies' use of false accusation in the fifth century. The enemies argued that Judah's disloyalty towards Babylon at the end of the seventh and beginning of the sixth centuries (2 Kgs 24:1, 20; Jer. 41:1–3) guaranteed rebellion against Persia in the middle of the fifth century. What goes unmentioned is the different set of circumstances of the post-exilic community in the middle of the fifth century. If these Jews could even have fielded an army (which is unlikely), they were making no effort at insurrection and liberation. They were merely acting on Cyrus' order to rebuild the temple (Ezra 5:13–15). Contrary to the fearmongering of the enemies, Artaxerxes was in no danger of losing the western end of his empire to Jewish rebels (Ezra 4:16). Still, he might not have known about Cyrus' edict or been up to date on the state of the western edge of his empire, which was nearly 1,000 miles (1,609 km) away. Like any other ANE king, Artaxerxes took the rumour seriously enough to confirm its veracity. Moreover, the revolts of Inarus in Egypt about 460 BC and of Megabyzus in Syria about 449 BC would have made Artaxerxes especially reactive to any hint of suspicious activity in Judea.[20] For this reason, he stopped work on the city until he had full knowledge

---

19 Hamilton 2014: 38.

20 Johnson (2011: 42) says that 'Yehud's [Judah's] strategic location in the semi-periphery of the Empire rendered it very important to the well-being of the Achaemenid Empire. Yehud's geographic location in relationship to Egypt and the Mediterranean Sea, as well as to Ashkelon, Samaria, Syria, and Phoenicia, thrust Yehud into the centre of important military and economic functions pertinent to the Persian Empire's continued success.'

of the situation, but did not destroy what had been done. In fact, the words 'until I so order' in Ezra 4:21 (NIV) leave open the possibility of a later resumption of work.

The people of the land might have claimed to worship Yahweh, but 2 Kings 17:24–41 describes what that worship looked like. It involved polytheism (worshipping other gods along with Yahweh) and syncretism (mixing religious ideas and practices). 'What is being proposed here', says Fyall, 'is a multi-faith act of cooperation.'[21] Consequently, Yahweh was treated as one god among many – a denial of his holiness that the leaders of the post-exilic community could not condone. As mentioned earlier, the book of Kings was written during the exile in order to justify the exile. In answer to the question 'Why are we in Babylon?' the book of Kings documents the failure of Israel and Judah's leaders to promote faithful worship of Yahweh. Most of the southern kings are condemned for allowing rival worship centres in the hills or high places outside Jerusalem. In other words, they did not enforce the law of centralized worship in Deuteronomy 12. Promoting adherence to God's law, however, was their primary responsibility as rulers of God's people (Deut. 17:18–20).

In the case of the northern kings, the book of Kings additionally condemns them for repeating the sin of Jeroboam I, who intentionally established rival worship centres in Dan (the northern limit of the northern kingdom) and Bethel (the southern limit of the northern kingdom). He did this in order to prevent his subjects from travelling to Jerusalem and being reminded of God's promises to David (1 Kgs 12:27). Worried about defections for theological reasons, Jeroboam I and his northern successors made religion the servant of politics. This concern about royal legitimacy was unnecessary because God had already promised to establish Jeroboam I's throne (1 Kgs 11:38). Jeroboam I, however, would not trust God's word through his prophet. Instead, he promoted civil religion, the god of which is never the self-revealing God of the Bible but, rather, a human projection and construction that wants what its worshippers (often the ruling class) want. The god of civil religion exists to secure the worshippers' future by granting prosperity and social order. Politicians who promote civil religion do not care who this god is or what he/she/it says. Rather, they are trying to provide

[21] Fyall 2010: 74.

theological sanction for their vision or platform. Whether or not Jeroboam I ever concluded a speech by saying 'May God bless Israel' (as opposed to Judah), he traded the worship of Yahweh for the worship of his own political goals.

The post-exilic leaders in Ezra 4 would probably have known about the theological interpretation of the monarchy in the book of Kings and rightly heeded the warning about compromised (false) worship. They knew Yahweh was a different kind of deity who did not play the game of religion by the same rules as the ANE gods. The reason had to do with the ontological contrast between him and the other so-called gods. The gods of the nations, from a biblical point of view, existed only in the minds of their adherents, and so their being and power were derived from the trust people invested in them. They did not have independent being and power. Moreover, ANE people considered their gods personifications of the forces of nature. In other words, the gods did not transcend the natural world. Instead, they had births and deaths and so were locked into the cycles of nature.[22] In short, they were not holy or different, which contrasted with the Old Testament claims that Yahweh is holy: he is separate or distinct from all he has made. Yahweh is different from everything else, including humans, because he is self-existent and eternal. He depends on nothing outside himself. Everything else is created by, derived from and dependent on him. Stated differently, everything else, including other gods, has limits. The post-exilic leaders did not want to repeat the mistake of earlier generations that had compromised Yahweh's holiness by allowing false worship at Jeroboam I's rival altars, at the high places (e.g. 1 Kgs 14:23), at a temple of Baal (1 Kgs 16:32) and even at the Jerusalem temple (2 Kgs 16:10–18; Ezek. 8). Such false worship had precipitated the exile. The post-exilic leaders wanted to stay in Judah and wanted Yahweh in their midst. Therefore, they said 'No' to interfaith cooperation that would dilute their witness to Yahweh's uniqueness.

Holmgren says:

> It is difficult at this late date to decide whether the leaders of the early Jewish returnees were too exclusive in their relationships to

[22] Walton 2006: 87–92, 97–99. See the discussion of continuity in the ANE world view and transcendence in the biblical world view by Oswalt (2009: 47–84). See also the discussion of idolatry by Wright (2006: 136–188).

> other groups in the land. From our viewpoint they seem to have been so. In terms of preserving a tradition and creating a future, however, they may have done what needed to be done.[23]

By 'our viewpoint' Holmgren seems to refer to the pluralist mindset that characterizes democratic societies. God's people, of course, have benefited from living in democracies that grant them access to the marketplace of ideas where they can respectfully present the biblical world view alongside others, making a case for their understanding of reality. 'Our viewpoint' could also refer to the perceived need 'to win friends and influence people' by 'going along to get along'. Behind this give-to-get strategy, of course, is a belief (or a fear) that other humans ultimately control one's destiny. Even so, avoiding ideological compromise and syncretism does not necessarily qualify as being narrow and intolerant. Being exclusive in one's ultimate commitments is the demand of faithfulness to a holy God. Holmgren additionally observes, '*But the community that does not say no to ruinous people* (who set themselves against that which gives life to the group) *cannot hope to exist for long.*'[24] The God of the Christian Bible explains how his people should relate to him. Ignoring this instruction brings deleterious consequences of which the post-exilic leaders were all too aware (Ezra 5:11–12).

What are those consequences? In other words, why is the Old Testament so concerned about false religion; that is, other religions? The answer has to do with the distinction between the Creator and the creature. In biblical thinking, as already noted, God is self-existent and independent. Everything else derives its existence from him and is accountable to him. When evil entered God's creation, it attacked the authority of the Creator. The serpent promised Adam and Eve that they could be like God (Gen. 3:6) and, further, said that they would be able to distinguish good from evil. The serpent was not saying that Adam and Eve could recognize the difference between good and evil. Ethical living that glorifies God requires humans to recognize this difference and then choose the good. Rather, the serpent suggested that Adam and Eve could define good and evil. What the serpent said, of course, was a pernicious lie. Humans live in God's world, and he alone

[23] Holmgren 1987: 35.

[24] Ibid. 34–35; emphases original. See also Bright 1981: 378–379, 444.

has the right to make the rules. The creature has no right to usurp the Creator's prerogative. Moreover, the Creator will not allow the creature to steal what belongs to him. Still, Adam and Eve fell for the lie, and their descendants have followed suit by seeking to live without reference to the God of the Christian Bible. Acting like gods, of course, does not make humans divine. Indeed, devastating consequences follow from the effort.

Eliminating the Creator–creature distinction undermines ethics. Any objective reference point for moral discrimination becomes impossible. When people ignore Yahweh and focus on themselves, they do whatever seems right in their own eyes (otherwise known as chaos), and injustice results (see Judg. 2:10–23; 17 – 21). Other people become tools to be used for the self's agenda, and there is no objective standard of moral good beyond the self's wants. Each individual defines what is right for him or her, and other people either cooperate or get in the way. Because humans quickly grow frightened of chaos, they soon trade autonomy for tyranny. Humans foolishly think that false religion sets them free. Instead, it enslaves them to insatiable passions and then to an opportunistic dictator. Having learned from past mistakes (Ezra 5:11–12), the post-exilic leaders wisely stuck to the mission Yahweh through Cyrus had given them. They refused at this point to be distracted by compromising situations that could have jeopardized their witness to the nations. Because of their stance, those outside the covenantal community would learn who Yahweh is.

What happens next in Ezra 4 seems to overturn the affirmation of divine providence in Ezra 1:1. If Yahweh had stirred Cyrus to order reconstruction, why did he not prevent the so-called enemies from bribing officials or Artaxerxes from stopping reconstruction?[25] There is no easy explanation except to say that faithfulness to God's Word does not always win the approval of others. It often meets hostility (John 15:18–19; 1 John 3:13) in the form of lies, ridicule and violence. Ezra 4:4 reports that the enemies succeeded in discouraging the post-exilic Jews and making them fearful.[26] God's people lost their will to persevere in the mission God through Cyrus had given them. As seen in Haggai 1:2–11, discouragement

[25] Throntveit 1992: 28.

[26] Fyall (2010: 80) says that Ezra 4 describes 'a war of attrition where people's nerves are worn down'.

led to practical atheism that denied Yahweh's intervention in human affairs. Where once there was affirmation of God's enduring love and goodness (Ezra 3:10), now there was a preoccupation with personal pursuits. For this reason, Ezra 4:24 reports the stoppage of work on the temple for about fifteen years. This delay was not caused by a subsequent edict from Cyrus, Cambyses or Darius in the sixth century. It also was not caused by Artaxerxes' edict in the fifth century (Ezra 4:7–23). Rather, the post-exilic Jews in the sixth century allowed their circumstances to become more real than God's promises. They were walking by sight instead of by faith.

Meanwhile, Ezra 4:21–22 places responsibility for the fifth-century stoppage of work on Artaxerxes, and Nehemiah 2:8 reports that Artaxerxes later permitted Nehemiah to resume work. This verse further attributes the king's change of heart to the gracious intervention of God. The point is that the writer of Ezra–Nehemiah distinguished between human and divine causation of events. The humans acted as they did for their reasons, but God mysteriously worked behind the scenes to teach all involved lessons about him and them. At no time were events out of his control. Given this truth, Ezra 4:4–5, 5:1–2 and 6:6–7 imply that the post-exilic Jews in the sixth century should have continued to build the temple. The Persian kings, whose decisions were promoting Yahweh's will, had not told these Jews to do otherwise.

God's people can become confused in the situations of their lives. Numerous voices simultaneously shout competing messages, and all the noise is distracting. So also is the pressure to make snap decisions that affect other people. God's people can forget what God wants and what they in their heart of hearts also want. They can be so overwhelmed by circumstances that they are unable to see how any good could come out of the present. Perhaps the memory of poor choices in the past compounds the discouragement with guilt. A person can reach the point of doubting that even God can sort things out and make them right. It is at this point that God's people, like the post-exilic Jews, need to hear Haggai, Zechariah and the other writers of the Bible (Ezra 5:1). God's Word offers a perspective that transcends momentary circumstances. It assures readers that God remains in control for the good of his people and world. It tells readers what they should do in order to make their circumstances the scene of God's redemptive activity. Reading God's Word is a necessary step to overcoming discouragement.

Ezra 4 takes its place among many other parts of the Bible that describe opposition to God's work.[27] The unified witness of these passages is that serving God rarely seems to be easy. Some form of resistance within or beyond God's people inevitably accompanies efforts at doing God's will, and these challenges can frustrate even the most pious of saints – not to mention slow a ministry or even shut it down. God's people are not immune to hardship and disappointment. No one, however, can upbraid God for not giving advanced warning about the cost of being associated with him. God's Word honestly tells people what is in store and urges them to get involved anyway. They have God's assurance here and in other sections of the Bible that ultimately nothing can thwart his plan. Somehow or other he will redeem labour that is done for his honour.

At the same time, recalling the challenges to building the first temple indirectly offered encouragement to those who built the second temple. The book of 1 Kings attributes to David's wars the slow progress on the first temple (1 Kgs 5:3). Surely, also, the effects of David's sin against Bathsheba and Uriah (2 Sam. 12 – 18) distracted him and others. Even so, the first temple was eventually completed, and it stood for many years. Thousands of people visited it to worship Yahweh, receive forgiveness of sins and renew hope for the future. Similarly, God would bless the labour on the second temple. God finishes what he starts, and people receive the benefits of his faithfulness.

Christian readers of Ezra–Nehemiah cannot ignore the similarity between the experience of the post-exilic community and the life of Jesus. He too encountered adversity that eventually succeeded in killing him. So then, God does not ask his people to do what he in Jesus has not done. Of course, the suffering of Jesus was redemptive in a way that the suffering of God's people is not. His death expiated human sin and propitiated divine wrath. No other suffering has been so salvifically efficacious. The point to be made now, though, is that God uses suffering, and not just Jesus' suffering, to advance his good purpose. As was the case with Job's suffering, the one suffering may not fully understand what God is doing,

[27] Even work on the first temple is said to have been slowed by the enemies of David (1 Kgs 5:3). According to Laird (2011: 101–102), 'Setbacks to the fulfillment of the divine wish are a common feature in temple reports, and conflict over the project provides this element of uncertainty regarding the temple's completion . . . For both temples, adversaries surrounding the builders impede the project and, except for the altar and temple foundation, construction is deferred until the next generation . . . Overcoming opposition from surrounding peoples becomes a necessary condition for the construction of both temples.'

but Job still found himself in a position to intercede for his friends (Job 42:8). In Ezra–Nehemiah, much of the suffering happens because of the hostility of enemies, but Nehemiah 5, which will be discussed later, attributes some suffering to greed among members of the Jewish community. With regard to outside hostility, God demonstrated his power with the result that the outsiders acknowledged his involvement (Neh. 6:16). With regard to inside injustice, God brought about repentance and restitution (Neh. 5:7–13). Although hard to acknowledge because of the pain involved, the truth is that God does not waste suffering: he makes it an instrument of sanctification and mission.

Of course, the death of Jesus by itself, tragically, would have marked victory for his adversaries. If Jesus' ministry had ended in the grave, he would have been remembered, at best, as a would-be reformer whom the religious establishment 'chewed up and spat out'. The resurrection was necessary to vindicate Jesus. By raising Jesus from the dead, God declared his satisfaction with Jesus' righteous life and atoning death. Even the schemes of God's enemies could not thwart God; rather, they became the vehicle by which God accomplished his will. The ultimate futility of the opposition in Ezra 4 (and later in Nehemiah) anticipates the irony of the cross in the Gospels. God always wins in the end. For this reason, Fyall can quip, 'When we come to an apparent graveyard of our hopes, we need to renew our trust in a God who knows his way out of the grave.'[28] Whatever form that hostility or frustration may take and however endless it may seem, God's steadfast love, according to Ezra 3:11, lasts even longer. That love brings good to those who trustingly wait on God and do what they know to be his will at the time. Just as God's love for his Son eventually delivered him from the grave, so his love for those who are in Christ will raise them on the last day.

Resumption and completion

Cyrus died in 530 BC and was succeeded by his son, Cambyses (530–522 BC), who spent much of his reign in Egypt. Cambyses conquered Egypt in 525 BC, but a coup in 522 BC forced him to return to Susa. He died on the way home. Darius I, who was not the legitimate heir, put down the coup and then spent two years consolidating his power. During this

[28] Fyall 2010: 81.

time, the Jews resumed work on the temple. Ezra 5:1 says that the prophets Haggai and Zechariah encouraged the people to go back to work. This verse does not say why these prophets urged the resumption of reconstruction at this time.

The books of Haggai and Zechariah give the impression that these prophets wanted to arouse the post-exilic community from its spiritual apathy to recommit itself to participating in God's mission to the world – the same mission that pre-exilic Israel had (Gen. 12:3; 18:18; 22:18; 26:4; 28:14; 1 Kgs 8:41–43; Ps. 67; Isa. 2:3; Hag. 2:7; Zech. 2:11; 14:16). Rebuilding the place of worship from which the message of salvation would go forth was the most obvious way for post-exilic Jews to reidentify with this mission. Moreover, those living at the beginning of Darius' reign did not know how the political tumult would turn out. It is conceivable that members of the post-exilic community were anxious about their future in an unstable empire. Haggai and Zechariah, who represented the God of Israel (Ezra 5:1) and the God of heaven (Ezra 5:11), reminded them of a higher authority that transcended the Persian Empire and could act within it. Haggai assured discouraged people that Yahweh was with them and that he would fill the rebuilt temple with glory (Hag. 1:13; 2:4; 2:7). Zechariah added that Yahweh was jealous for Jerusalem (Zech. 1:14) and would live there for the comfort of his people (Zech. 1:17; 2:10). As a result, many nations would live there too (Zech. 2:11), a promise that recalls the missional outlook of God's covenant with Abraham (Gen. 12:3; 18:18).[29] Whatever was happening in Susa (or anywhere else), the God of Israel remained the sovereign Lord who works out his redemptive plan in the vicissitudes of world history.

Here again is the importance of God's revealed and preached word. It provides necessary perspective and impetus during the tension between the now (what God has begun) and the not yet (what God must still do). It reminds people of who, ultimately, is in control and why daring to take the risk of serving him is reasonable. Consequently, God's people do well to persevere at performing his will and trusting him to bless their effort on his behalf. Rulers come and go and often fail to realize their agendas. God, however, never fails. Those who remember his word and do it can overcome anxiety about uncertain circumstances – what Zechariah 4:10 calls a day of 'small things'.

[29] Wilson (2014: 85) goes so far as to identify Abraham as the world's first missionary.

According to Ezra 5:3, the Persian officials who oversaw land to the west of the Euphrates River wondered about the motive of the Jews in Jerusalem. They had an understandable concern. Given the recent coup and resulting instability, the Jews on the western end of the empire might be making a play for independence. Even so, the Jews were not rebelling. As they explained to the Persian officials, they were trying to finish what Cyrus had ordered (Ezra 5:13). The unrest in the eastern regions of the empire was none of their concern. Moreover, Ezra 5:12 presents the humility of the returnees. They admitted the sins of the past and then indirectly expressed appreciation of Cyrus for giving them an opportunity to set matters right (Ezra 5:13–14). Ezra 5:5 remarkably reports that the Persian officials never forced the Jews to stop rebuilding. This verse further attributes the non-interference to the providence of God. Eyes of faith could detect his superintendence behind the scenes. If the post-exilic community was trying under the leadership of Haggai and Zechariah to reconcile with the God of Israel, this God was blessing their effort. Ezra 5 reinforces a point made throughout the synoptic accounts of the monarchy (Samuel–Kings and Chronicles); namely, that listening to God's prophets brings God's blessing. The New Testament further encourages paying heed to the revelation of God's will through prophets (1 Thess. 5:20).

Darius' reply to the officials (Ezra 6:6–12) shows the unpredictable greatness of God. Who would have thought that Darius would respond so favourably by telling the critics to back off? He even recognizes that the God of the Jews can handle those who would try to thwart his purpose (Ezra 6:12). Such a statement on the lips of a pagan king shows discernment that members of the post-exilic community had lacked for the last decade. Through this king's affirmation of Yahweh's power, God's people learned that 'sometimes [their] own fears may get the best of [them]'.[30] God can turn around the most hopeless of situations. Rather than being restricted by humans, he works through them (Ezra 6:14). In this instance, opposition had the opposite effect, of obtaining more royal funding for the Jerusalem temple. As if Cyrus' decree were not enough, the Jews now had Darius'. Full support had been pledged again with the result that the project was completed four years later. The God of the post-exilic community is a generous God for whom nothing is impossible. He can meet any need and sometimes chooses to do so through the unlikeliest of

[30] Berman 2007: 170.

means.[31] He also seems to like doing far more than people can imagine (Eph. 3:20).

Of course, the opposition that begins in Ezra 4 intensifies throughout Ezra–Nehemiah. If the eye of God (Ezra 5:5) continually watches the people of God and the enemies of God, the result is not always protection of God's people and defeat of God's enemies in this lifetime. Sometimes God comes to the aid of his people, and sometimes he does not. Ezra–Nehemiah may not try to resolve this mystery, but nonetheless it affirms God's activity in history. At the beginning of Darius' reign, the gracious involvement of Israel's God was evident as God granted the wish of this Gentile king, of all people (Ezra 6:12). The enemies in Ezra 4:1 failed to prevent the timely completion of the temple that Ezra 6:15 reports.

The New Testament, similarly, reports opposition to the ministry of Jesus. The Gospels make no effort to hide the antagonism of the Jewish leaders. According to Acts 2:23 and 4:27, Jews and Gentiles conspired together to put Jesus to death. Nevertheless, they served God's larger purpose, which was to use the death of Jesus as the payment of the penalty for human sin. What seemed to be the bleakest event in human history became God's finest moment. He unexpectedly used human sin as a means of redemption from sin. Paul an apostle of Jesus could also say that his hardships were used by God to advance his proclamation of the gospel (Phil. 1:12–18). To this day, God sovereignly works behind the scenes in the best and worst of circumstances to accomplish his purpose. He silently moves, rearranges and changes. Therefore, it would be a mistake to think that a silent God is a distant or uncaring God. God is not asleep, out of touch or impotent. He is always aware of the intentions of the human participants in a situation, yet incorporates them into his good pleasure and will.

Celebration

In language reminiscent of 1 Kings 8:62–63 and 2 Chronicles 7:4–7, Ezra 6:16–18 describes the jubilant dedication of the post-exilic temple. What had seemed impossible a few years before became a reality by the confluence of Yahweh's providence, Persian enlightened self-interest, prophetic encouragement and Jewish labour. The post-exilic community is

31 Nykolaishen 2008: 184–188.

said to have offered 712 animals. While the number of slain animals falls considerably short of the total of 142,000 animals for the dedication of Solomon's temple, what was offered attests to the commitment of God's people to God's purpose for the temple. At God's house, his people expressed through costly sacrifices their trust in him to provide for their needs. Moreover, the sin offering for each tribe represented repentance for past neglect of the mission. The post-exilic community acknowledged corporate failure and expressed its intention to do better.

Observance of the Passover reinforced this commitment by both Jew and Gentile alike. For the first Passover, the Israelites in Egypt had to smear the blood of the Passover lamb on their doorposts. Exodus 12:13 calls this blood a sign that God would see. As a sign, the blood had to do with the Israelites' response to God's word through Moses. God said that he would pass through Egypt and distinguish between those who were for him and against him. The blood on the doorpost was a simple test of faith and commitment. If a person identified with God and believed his promises, that person would smear the blood. This act of obedience would signify a person's desire to be a part of God's plan for his world. That plan featured the fulfilment of God's earlier promises to Abraham, Isaac and Jacob (Exod. 6:8). The person who sided with the God of the patriarchs of old declared that this God was more real to him or her than Pharaoh in all his present pomp and power. Meanwhile, a person who disbelieved God and feared Pharaoh would have a clean doorpost. By doing nothing to the doorpost, that person renounced any share in God's redemptive activity. So then, Passover involved a declaration of ultimate loyalty to God as well as faith in the blood of the lamb. God might have brought his people out of Egypt with overwhelming displays of power, but his people consisted of those who believed his word through Moses and obeyed it at Passover. The blood of the lamb on the doorpost was the external evidence of an internal commitment to God. Centuries later the post-exilic community might not have smeared blood on their doorposts, but killing the Passover lamb and eating it, similarly, involved their identification with God's ongoing purpose for Abraham's descendants. They affirmed their belief in the faithfulness of the God of the exodus.

They also identified with God's missional desire for his house: that the nations would gather there for forgiveness and worship, in no small part because of the witness of the distinct lifestyle (holiness) of his people. Ezra 6:21 presents the other side of Ezra 4:3. The post-exilic Jews, like the pre-exilic Israelites, could be a kingdom of priests that welcomed outsiders.[32] The outsiders, though, had to identify exclusively with Yahweh and submit to his law (instruction) for his people.[33] No mixed loyalty or ulterior motive was allowed. Inviting outsiders to become insiders at the Passover meal represented another down payment on the much larger incursion of the nations that is envisioned in Isaiah 60 and Zechariah 2.

Paul in 1 Corinthians 5:7 refers to Jesus as the Christian's Passover lamb. In the context, he is responding to news of sexual immorality in the Corinthian church. He tells these Christians not to boast about their tolerance of incest. Permissiveness in this instance will gradually lead to corruption of the offending individual and the supporting group. Instead, the group should avoid evil on the one hand and show concern for purity on the other. Stated differently, the members of the Corinthian church should act like the redeemed people they already are and confront sin in their midst. This response will keep them from relapsing into their former way of life that leads to spiritual death (separation from God's favourable presence). It might also bring about the repentance of the incestuous couple. While giving this instruction, Paul mentions the observance of a feast, which is presumably the Lord's Supper. Like the Passover meal, the Lord's Supper challenges God's people to be committed to God above all else. The supper, by reminding redeemed sinners of what God in Jesus has already done for them, assures them of an open future in which they can dare to act on behalf of God's revealed will. God will not punish those who act in faith in his promises; rather, he will bless what is done for his honour.

Meanwhile, the observance of the Feast of Unleavened Bread recalled the haste with which the Israelites had to eat the first Passover meal and prepare to leave Egypt. For the post-exilic community, time might have seemed to crawl during the twenty years or so between the return from Babylon and the dedication of the second temple. Nevertheless, God can act quickly and decisively when he chooses to do so. In fact, he always acts on time according to his schedule. The Feast of Unleavened Bread teaches God's people to hold their possessions lightly and not put down roots too

---

32 Blenkinsopp 1988: 133.

33 Moffat (2013: 70) says, 'People needed either to be returned exiles or to accept the cultic standards of the *golah* (exilic) community in order to be regarded as the people of Israel.'

deeply. God has a way, in his time, of moving his people from one opportunity to another. Moreover, earthly circumstances do not hinder him. By referring to the Persian king as the king of Assyria (Ezra 6:22), the author of Ezra–Nehemiah recalled how Yahweh had used the fierce leaders of an earlier empire for his disciplinary purpose in the eighth century (Isa. 10:5).[34] Now, two centuries later, the Persian leaders were no less imperialistic, but were just as subject to Yahweh's design. The God of Israel does what he wants when he wants and with whomever he wants.

Not to be overlooked is the emphasis on joy, which is a deep-seated feeling of satisfaction. Ezra 6:16 reports that the post-exilic Jews dedicated the finished temple with joy. Then they, according to verse 22, kept the Feast of Unleavened Bread (and the Passover meal before that) with joy. They did this because Yahweh had made them joyful by performing a second exodus and settlement. As the Jews celebrated the completion of the temple, they could not help but see the hand of God in this effort. Verse 14 may appropriately give credit to the Persian rulers, who authorized the project, but verse 22 curiously refers to these rulers, especially Darius, as the king of Assyria. Assyrian kings did not assist conquered people with building projects; rather, they harshly deported the survivors of a ruined city away from their sacred sites. Then they mocked the gods that could not protect and preserve those sites (2 Kgs 19:10–12). The post-exilic Jews who rebuilt the temple marvelled not only at the recapitulation of sacred history but also at the reversal of secular policy. Both seemed equally unlikely in the Assyrian and Persian empires.[35] As verse 14 also indicates, ultimately, the Jews attributed these happy, yet unexpected, developments to the providential intervention of God. God's undeniable involvement in their lives produced joy. His inclusion of them in the reconstruction of the temple, which was a stage in the outworking of his long-standing redemptive plan, yielded a rewarding sense of participation in something bigger than the struggle to survive. So then, God's faithfulness to his promise of a covenantal relationship is the source of joy. God's people can rejoice because God does not give up on them.

---

[34] Breneman (1993: 122) adds, 'Some think the designation "king of Assyria" a mistake. The author, however, must have been thinking in terms of a continuation of virtually the same empire from the time of the Assyrians through that of the Persians.'

[35] Of course, the Babylonian Empire arose between the zeniths of the Assyrian and Persian empires and, similarly, crushed the hopes of God's people (see Lamentations).

Summary

Ezra 3 – 6 describes the effort of the post-exilic community to rebuild the temple in Jerusalem. The reconstruction of the temple Cyrus approved in Ezra 1:3 is said to be finished in Ezra 6:22. If the Babylonian army had destroyed Solomon's temple in 586 BC, the second temple opened in 516 BC – seventy years later. In fulfilment of earlier prophecy, God's people had returned to the Promised Land, Gentiles had assisted the renovation of the temple and the worship of Yahweh had resumed in Jerusalem. Here was evidence that God was now restoring his relationship with his people and his mission for them. The book of Ezra–Nehemiah, however, does not end at Ezra 6:22.[36] The following chapters recount Ezra's ministry to prepare people to worship at the temple, and Nehemiah's reconstruction of the wall that protected the sanctity of the temple. These later developments further contributed to the execution of Cyrus' decree in Ezra 1:2–4. They are part of the 'not yet' of God's word to the post-exilic community.

---

[36] Eskenazi 1988a: 56–57.

5
Rebuilding the people

Ezra 3 – 6 describes the first stage of implementing Cyrus' edict, and Ezra 6:14 reports the completion of the second temple in 516 BC. This stage of Cyrus' project took about twenty years, and much of the work was done in the last four years. Ezra 6 ends with a reference to the celebration and renewal of temple worship at that time. The typical reader might reasonably expect Ezra 7 to discuss what happened next, but Ezra 7 moves to the reign of Artaxerxes I, who succeeded Xerxes I in 464 BC. Xerxes had succeeded Darius in 486 BC. According to Ezra 7:8, Ezra arrived in Jerusalem during the seventh year of Artaxerxes' reign; that is, 458 BC. Fifty-eight years had elapsed since the completion of the temple in 516 BC.

No Old Testament book explicitly addresses these decades between the completion of the temple and the arrival of Ezra.[1] Some scholars think that Malachi ministered during this interval.[2] If so, the book that bears his name describes an apathetic community that had lost sense of its mission to the world (Mal. 1:11–14). Whether Malachi ministered before, with or after Ezra, the books of Ezra–Nehemiah and Malachi address similar conditions in the post-exilic community after the completion of the temple in 516 BC (Mal. 1:10). Both books mention marriage to foreign women (Ezra 9 – 10; Neh. 13:23–27; Mal. 2:11–15), neglect of tithes (Neh. 13:10–14; Mal. 3:8–10), unfaithfulness among priests (Ezra 10:18–24; Neh. 13:7–8; Mal. 1:6 – 2:9) and instances of social injustice (Neh. 5:1–5; Mal. 3:5). Clearly, Ezra had to do much work of reformation and revitalization.

In the larger world of King Darius, Greeks in western Turkey rebelled in 499 BC with Athenian aid. Darius suppressed the revolt in 494 BC,

---

1 Esther may discuss events during the first half of the fifth century, but the setting of the narrative is in Susa instead of Jerusalem.

2 E.g. Dumbrell 1976: 43, 51; Kidner 1979: 26; Verhoef 1987: 157–158; Hill 1998: 82–84; Longman and Dillard 2006: 498; Arnold and Beyer 2008: 470; Fyall 2010: 96.

moved against Athens and lost at Marathon in 490 BC. Egypt rebelled late in Darius' reign but was defeated by Xerxes, the son of Darius, in 485 BC. Xerxes put down two revolts in Babylon and then turned to Greece. His losses in Greece forced him to return home, during which time Esther is said to have become queen (Esth. 2:16). Artaxerxes followed Xerxes in 465 BC and reigned until 424 BC. When rebellion broke out again in Egypt in 460 BC, Artaxerxes might have sent Ezra to Palestine to maintain Jewish loyalty on the western edge of the Persian Empire.[3] A political mission for the Persian authorities also had a spiritual function for the God of Israel. He used Ezra to restore his depressed people to covenantal faithfulness. The political authority Artaxerxes granted Ezra (Ezra 7:25–26) promoted observance of the law of Yahweh, to which Ezra had already devoted much of his life.

Ezra 7 – 10 discusses the second stage of implementing Cyrus' edict. If the first stage involved rebuilding Yahweh's temple in Jerusalem, the second stage concerns the sanctity of the community that worshipped at the temple.[4] Some scholars, as mentioned earlier, think that Malachi addresses the condition of the post-exilic community before Ezra's arrival; that is, during the fifty years between Ezra 6:21 and 7:1. If so, then a recently restored temple was in danger of being defiled by covenantal unfaithfulness, which had earlier been responsible for the desecration of the pre-exilic temple. After the exile, disobedience originated in the disappointment and apathy of returnees who had expected different circumstances in the Promised Land.[5] A skilled teacher such as Ezra was needed in this situation to form worshippers who were committed to knowing God's Word and doing it, regardless of the circumstances.

Ezra 7:10 says that Ezra's expertise as a teacher came from committed study and the practice of God's Word. Whereas the first wave of returnees who rebuilt the temple had the prophets Haggai and Zechariah in their midst, Ezra's generation is never said to receive new revelation. Instead, a learned priest applied previous revelation to new situations.[6] Ezra spent

---

3 Holmgren 1987: 55–56; Throntveit 1992: 41–42.

4 Eskenazi (1988a: 62, 68) says, 'Holiness thus is no longer a matter only for priests and Levites but for the larger community. Becoming a holy people (Exod. 19:6) is at stake.' Exod. 19:6 further refers to the holy people as a kingdom of priests. Though recalling Exod. 19:6, Eskenazi does not associate becoming a holy people with the mission that a kingdom of priests was supposed to have among its neighbours.

5 Japhet 2006: 228.

6 Steinmann (2010: 279) observes that Ezra 'is unique in the Scriptures, since he is the only person who is described as seeking God in his Word'.

much of his life reading God's Word and saturating his mind with its language and concepts. He thought in terms of the world view of Moses and the prophets. He knew the themes that united the biblical writers as well as the individual emphases pertinent for different situations. He had mastered God's Word, which simultaneously had the effect of mastering him. Constant reading with the eyes led to internalization of Scripture in the heart. God wrote his Word on Ezra's heart with the result that God's Word changed Ezra from the inside out. Ezra first thought God's thoughts and then did God's commandments. In other words, he acted as God would act. Such integrity made Ezra an effective teacher because his listeners could observe him practising what he had learnt.[7]

As a teacher, Ezra engaged in mission. His scholarship not only enriched his personal relationship with God, as important as that might have been, but Ezra additionally dedicated his life to studying God's Word so that he could help others to understand it. Those whom he taught could then undergo the same transformation from the inside out. One man's teaching in word and deed had a ripple effect throughout a community. That community, in turn, could model a redeemed lifestyle to outsiders.

Ezra's teaching

Ezra 7:1–10 says nothing specific about why Ezra wanted to go to Jerusalem. Verse 6, however, alludes to a request Ezra made of Artaxerxes. It seems as if Ezra's study of the law had aroused a concern about the conformity of the post-exilic community to that law. As Nehemiah would later do, Ezra asked Artaxerxes for permission to go to Jerusalem. What Ezra wanted to do in Jerusalem, presumably, is reflected in Artaxerxes' letter to Ezra.[8] As suggested by Ezra 7:14, Ezra wanted to learn more about the spiritual state of Judah; and Ezra 7:15–23 gives the impression that Ezra was especially concerned about the quality of worship at the rebuilt temple. In other words, Ezra had doubts about the priorities of the post-exilic community. Ezra 7:25 then implies that Ezra wanted to teach those

[7] See Wilson 2014: 263–265 for more on the relationship between knowing and doing.

[8] Eskenazi 1988a: 65; Breneman 1993: 128; Steinmann 2010: 286, 289. Laird (2016: 291) comments, 'Indeed, if one compares Ezra's purpose for the return (7:10) with the royal letter, the king appears to have clearer reasons for the return than Ezra – including lavish provisions for the temple!' Of course, Ezra 7:10 describes Ezra's preparation before going to Judea and so does not claim to summarize Ezra's conversation with the king in v. 6.

who had an inadequate understanding of God's will for his people. The king's letter and resources indicated that he shared Ezra's concern (though for political reasons only) and authorized him to make necessary reforms on the basis of the law of Moses.[9] Not to be missed is Ezra's interest in mission, and therefore Ezra–Nehemiah's interest in mission. According to Ezra 7:25, not just Jerusalem or Judea but the whole province or satrapy to the west of the Euphrates River was supposed to learn the law of Ezra's God. If Artaxerxes' letter reflects Ezra's request, then Ezra wanted Jerusalem again to become the centre from which knowledge of the law of God would spread to other nations. Ezra shared the vision of Zechariah 2:11–12 and Malachi 1:11.

Ezra 7 has three references to the hand of God that allowed Ezra to travel to Judea (vv. 6, 9, 28), but it also presents an active Ezra who made plans to go. Both God and Ezra wanted to address the spiritual needs of the post-exilic community, and both wanted to advance God's will (mission) for the post-exilic community. Even so, Ezra did not merely wait passively for God to stir his people to action (Ezra 1:5), but recognized how he could be of service to the divine king and approached the human king who could help. Ezra wanted what God wanted and took appropriate steps, in the context of the Persian Empire, to get it.

Ezra promoted personal and communal holiness by providing instruction for life, worship and even mission. Ezra 7:8 – 8:36 emphasizes that worship and mission flow from instruction. According to Ezra 7:8–10, Ezra arrived in Jerusalem and then devoted himself to studying, practising and teaching God's law in Israel. Meanwhile, Ezra 7:11 – 8:36 presents Artaxerxes' letter of permission and the details of the return to Jerusalem. Although Ezra's return would have happened before any teaching in Jerusalem, Ezra might have had opportunities to teach in Babylon. Artaxerxes' authorization of Ezra's trip to Jerusalem might have given Ezra 'teachable moments' in both places where God's people needed instruction about what Yahweh was doing in history and how they could participate.

A Persian king might not have known about the description of the restoration in Isaiah 2:2–5 and 60:1–22, but Ezra surely recognized a parallel between Isaiah's prophecies and Artaxerxes' letter. Both assume a return from exile and mention Gentile financing of the reconstruction of the temple, the resumption of worship and instruction from God's law.

---

[9] Wijk-Bos 1998: 36–37.

Moreover, the verb *p'r* (to glorify, adorn, beautify) that is used with reference to the post-exilic temple in Isaiah 60:7 and 60:13 appears in Ezra's praise in Ezra 7:27. Ezra evidently saw a fulfilment of Isaiah's prophecy in Artaxerxes' authorization of this work in Jerusalem. Though probably operating from a purely political motive, Artaxerxes nevertheless advanced the mission of God's people to promote knowledge of God's Word, worship of God's name and trust in the atoning efficacy of God's prescribed sacrifices. More specifically, Artaxerxes wanted Ezra to teach anyone who did not know God's law (Ezra 7:25). By allowing God's people to advance God's interests alongside Persia's, Artaxerxes' letter unwittingly revived Israel's longstanding mission to the world. It was this missional emphasis of God's law (whether the Pentateuch or the Pentateuch plus other parts of the Old Testament) that Ezra had to teach.

Ezra did not miss the opportunity. Ezra 7:28 reports how he put together a team of exiles to join him in the implementation of Artaxerxes' letter. Meanwhile, Ezra saw the hand of God at work in this preparation. By praising Yahweh, the God of 'our' fathers, Ezra affirmed that the God who had made covenants in the past was on the move among his people and through the policies of Persian kings to advance his redemptive programme for all people. Properly taught descendants of 'our' fathers could model a redeemed community that contrasted with the business-as-usual of the ANE and even the covenantal infidelity of previous generations of Israelites. In this way, the post-exilic Jews could be a light to the Gentiles.

In Ezra 7:25, Artaxerxes associates the law of God with the wisdom of God. Artaxerxes hardly had the covenantal understanding of wisdom that is found in Proverbs 1:7 and 9:10. He would not have thought that a relationship with Yahweh, the covenant-making God of Israel, was the prerequisite for being wise. Nor would he have thought, on the basis of Proverbs 8:22–36, that wisdom, ultimately, has to do with understanding God's purpose for creation and identifying with that purpose. From an Old Testament perspective, God created a world that could declare his praise. From a New Testament perspective, God created everything for the honour of Jesus. In both cases, the law tells people how to contribute to God's purpose. It makes them wise; that is, able to understand and willing to promote God's reason for creating anything at all (Deut. 4:5–6). If Artaxerxes knew nothing about biblical wisdom, he would have thought of wisdom as a skill for living in such a way as to maintain a deity's favour. This favour and social calmness that was expected to ensue were the real interests behind Artaxerxes' benevolent letter. Even so, Jewish and Christian readers can consider the possibility that Artaxerxes wrote better than he knew and that a man like Ezra could read the biblical understanding of wisdom into Artaxerxes' reference to a more secular type of wisdom. Ezra's benediction in Ezra 7:27–28 indicates that he saw deeper significance in Artaxerxes' letter.

Ezra's journey

Ezra 8, because it contains numerous names as well as details about finances, may seem like nothing more than a mundane description of Ezra's journey. One point to be made is that true spirituality pays attention to details. Ezra did not go about the Lord's work in a sloppy manner. Because only the Levites could transport the sacred furniture and vessels of God's house, Ezra made sure that he had adequate personnel. Understandably, he would not want a repetition of David's mistake in 2 Samuel 6:6–7. Ezra 8 also informs the reader that Ezra's handling of Persian finances was transparent. He gave no opportunity for suspicion or question. The point is that God (or Artaxerxes) does not entrust responsibility to just anybody. Far from being a novice priest, Ezra was a man of proven integrity who could be trusted with responsibility. Likewise, God's people today should be equally attentive to detail. God cares about balanced budgets, matching curtains, sound systems and so on (Matt. 25:21). The church should be as professional as possible in these matters. Professionalism may not be an end in itself, but it can protect against suspicion and unnecessary offence.

Even so, Ezra 8 has more to offer. It records another wave of returnees to the Promised Land. Ezra would not have been alive at the time of the first wave about 538 BC. For whatever reason, his parents and grandparents stayed back in Babylon. Neither Ezra nor the person responsible for the final form of Ezra–Nehemiah offers an explanation or a judgment. Instead, the providential hand of God is emphasized. God prepared Ezra to lead a later caravan of members of the same families mentioned in Ezra 2. God does not watch the clock to see who comes late (Matt. 20:1–16). What matters is that people come. In Ezra 8, God even works behind the scenes to make sure that Ezra's group arrives. Here is another example of divine grace.

Moreover, Ezra's refusal to ask the king for protection indicates a concern for mission. According to Ezra 8:22, Ezra had already told

Artaxerxes about how the God of Israel provides for his people and protects them from his and their enemies. Now the time had come for Ezra to live out that belief in a dangerous situation. Ezra could hardly profess a special relationship with Yahweh and then depend on a pagan king for safe passage. His claims about Yahweh would ring hollow, and Artaxerxes would remain unimpressed. But to transport about 28 tons (28,000 kg) of silver and 4 tons (4,000 kg) of gold over a stretch of 1,000 miles (1,609 km) without the ANE equivalent of an armoured vehicle with police escort would get the attention of a Persian king. Constantly surrounded by sycophantic advisers, Artaxerxes would know that Ezra was different because he had the courage of conviction. He lived by what he preached; namely, that Yahweh could make a difference in the real world of corruption and crime. If Ezra's caravan travelled safely to Jerusalem, then Artaxerxes might realize that Ezra's God was worthy of trust. Artaxerxes would have witnessed how belief in this God affected the daily lives of those who worshipped him, with the result that they sometimes acted in peculiar, even self-denying, ways.[10] There was little chance Artaxerxes would visit the Jerusalem temple he helped to refurbish. Instead, he met Yahweh through Ezra.

The same is true today. If, as polls report, fewer people in the West are attending church, then they are less likely to learn about Jesus and come to faith in the context of a Sunday morning service. Where, then, will they meet Jesus? Ezra embodies the answer. When those who do not know God observe the transforming effects of the Gospel in God's people, they meet Jesus in those who love him, imitate him and trust him. At such times, God may give birth to faith in them. That developing faith will then seek out the nourishing environment of the covenantal community, the church.

Reactions to intermarriage

Ezra 9 begins with a reference to the events in Ezra 7 and 8. If Ezra 7 and 8 focus on the sanctity of the people who would worship at the temple, Ezra 9 alerts the reader to a problem. Members of the post-exilic

[10] McConville (1985: 57–58) says, 'The act of dependence on God would prove his faithfulness both to the king and to the people themselves. The king would see that these Yahweh worshipers took their God seriously, and were no mere nationalists.' He adds, 'It is well to *affirm* faith, as many Christians do regularly in the creeds. Yet it is salutary to ask whether anything that one ever does actually *requires* faith'; emphases original.

community at the time of Ezra's arrival were not ready for worship. Moreover, they had compromised their mission to the world. The priests who travelled with Ezra had been set apart for their service (Ezra 8:24), but priests and laity already in Jerusalem were not behaving as if they were set apart (Ezra 9:1). Instead, they had entered into unholy relationships with those to whom they were supposed to present a distinct witness. More than casual or commercial contact was in view.[11] The problem had to do with mixed marriages, and the issue was not so much racial or consanguineous (mixing blood through marriage) as religious or theological (mixing ideas through marriage).[12] In other words, the daughters of the peoples of the lands (Ezra 9:2) did not put their faith in Yahweh or obey his commandments.[13] Consequently, they could not worship Yahweh sincerely, nor were they committed to Yahweh's mission for his people. The Jewish men who married these women would probably grow lax in faithfulness to God's law (Deut. 7:3–4) and thereby lose the distinct witness a kingdom of priests and a holy nation/seed (Exod. 19:6; Deut. 7:6; Ezra 9:2) were supposed to have.[14]

What made God's people, including the post-exilic generations, holy? They were not in themselves superior in any way to other people. God had told the children of the exodus generation that they were not entering the Promised Land because they were more righteous than the Canaanites. They were not more righteous (Deut. 9:4–24). Rather, God had graciously set them apart for his glory and mission. To perform this mission, they

---

[11] Commerce, which required access to land now in the hands of others, may explain why Jewish returnees who did not have land married the daughters of Gentile men who did (Johnson 2011: 18, 50).

[12] Because Shekaniah tells Ezra that he and others have 'sat' or 'lived' (*wanniše̊b*) with foreign women (Ezra 10:2), Laird (2016: 312–313) suggests that *marriage* may not be the best word to describe these relationships. Nevertheless, the expected verb for 'to marry' (*nāśʾû*, which means 'they took women as wives') appears in Ezra 9:2.

[13] For a discussion of the options for identifying the peoples of the land, see Brown 2005: 439–445; Usue 2012: 159–160; Moffat 2013: 77–79. Blenkinsopp (2009: 64) says that 'the women in question were not primarily, and certainly not exclusively, Gentiles'. 2 Kgs 25:12 and Jer. 40:4–12 indicate that not all Israelites (citizens of the northern and southern kingdoms) went into exile. Moreover, 2 Kgs 17:24 mentions Gentiles whom the king of Assyria deported from their homelands into Israel (the former northern kingdom). Just as the transplanted Gentiles mixed the worship of their gods with the worship of Yahweh (2 Kgs 17:41), so the remaining Israelites probably engaged in syncretism (Jer. 44). Their children and grandchildren, whether the product of Jewish marriage or intermarriage, might not have had a covenantally orthodox upbringing.

[14] Saysell 2012: 44–45. McConville (1985: 60) says, 'Chapter 9 is central to the whole book because of the sharp contrast which it draws between the people of God as it ought to be and as it actually is.'

had to remain theologically and behaviourally distinct. Their relationship with God had to take precedence over all others, and every decision had to be made with this primary relationship in mind. Nothing, not even marriage, could be allowed to distract from a holy calling.[15] It was this calling that set them apart. This sense of mission is where the tension between the now and not yet came to individual lives. Though back in the Promised Land, formerly exiled Jews discovered that a change of place did not automatically bring a change of character and behaviour. A new location did not make the mission easier. Temptations to assimilate in Babylon took new forms in Judea. A holy seed or family might have a special calling from God, but individuals within that family daily had to make choices to be who they were. Otherwise, they would compromise their identity and neglect their calling.

Ezra and others 'who trembled at the words of the God of Israel' (Ezra 9:4) were emotionally disturbed by and gravely concerned about the gradual assimilation that could be expected to happen when marriage partners with different world views made concessions.[16] In the case of the Israelites/Jews who had a mission to the world, assimilation would lead to an increasingly diluted witness, and it is this unacceptable prospect that prompted the comparison of the peoples of the lands in Ezra's day with the inhabitants of the Promised Land (Canaanites, Hittites, Perizzites, Jebusites, Ammonites, Moabites, Egyptians and Amorites) in Moses' day. Ezra and the tremblers saw a similarity between the situations after the

[15] Johnson (2011: 68) says that 'the foreign woman is depicted [in the prophets] as a great threat to the covenantal relationship between Yhwh and the people of God.' Why? She adds, 'Foreign women were feared because of their perceived ability to seduce and lure Yehudite men to foreign gods' (69). In other words, they could do mission in reverse. Nevertheless, the relationship between Yahweh and his people, even in Ezra–Nehemiah, included mission. Johnson minimizes this theme (see 69–70, 88). Curiously, Ezra 6:21 or 7:6 (with 7:25) is never mentioned, despite Johnson's stated aim (2–7, 80, 109–111) to offer an alternative reading to the racist, sexist and xenophobic interpretations that have, in her estimation, characterized historical-critical readings of Ezra–Nehemiah. Johnson appreciably draws attention to misreadings of Ezra 9 – 10 but, regrettably, does not advance the discussion by reading these chapters in view of the missional interest of Ezra–Nehemiah.

[16] Moffat (2013: 87) says that the tremblers were committed to God's law as interpreted by Ezra. His additional suggestion that they 'prioritized God's word over temple service' seems to miss the missional purpose of Ezra's teaching, which was to prepare people, both Jews and Gentiles, to worship at the temple. Meanwhile, some scholars (Wellhausen 1957: 406; Bright 1981: 393; Duggan 2001: 2–6; Grabbe 2001: 94–97; Fried 2008: 77–78; Karrer-Grube 2008: 140–141; Pakkala 2008: 202–203; Reinmuth 2008: 242–243, 251–256) wonder why Ezra waited thirteen years to teach the law in Neh. 8 (cf. Ezra 7:7 with Neh. 2:1; 6:15; 8:2). The reference to the tremblers in Ezra 9 gives the impression that Ezra did not wait. Neh. 8 records a separate instance of teaching.

first exodus from Egypt and the second from Babylon/Persia.[17] Names and faces might have changed over the centuries, but the temptation to syncretize and apostatize remained the same. Within an intimate relationship like marriage, choosing to think like the peoples of the land (adopting their world view) would result in imitating their behaviour, and thus the opportunity to model a redeemed alternative would be lost. Ezra 9:1, 11 and 14 call both their thinking and behaving an abomination.

The Hebrew word for 'abominations' (*tôʿēbôt*) may refer to idols or false gods (Deut. 7:25–26; 17:3–4; 32:16; 2 Kgs 23:13; Isa. 41:24; 44:19; Jer. 44:4). It can also describe child sacrifice (Deut. 12:31; 18:9–10), divination (Deut. 18:9–12), cultic prostitution (1 Kgs 14:24), homosexuality (Lev. 18:22), adultery (Ezek. 22:11) and cheating (Deut. 25:13–16; Prov. 11:1). Jeremiah 7:9–10 adds stealing, lying and murder to the list of abominations. In fact, 'abomination' can describe any violation of God's revealed will. Specifically in the case of sexual deviancy, Leviticus 18:26–28 associates such abomination with the people groups who lived in the Promised Land before the Israelites. Imitating their behaviour would result in failure to model a redeemed community and disqualification to stay in a holy place (Ezra 9:14). Yahweh had chosen this place as the centre from which his plan of redemption would go out to the ends of the earth. Those not committed to that plan could not remain there.

It is in this sense that verse 12 recalls the prophetic (Mosaic) prohibition to seek the peace and prosperity of Canaan's inhabitants. Yahweh might have wanted to bless the nations through Abraham's descendants (Gen. 12:2–3), but he had also told Abraham that the sin of the Amorites (the current occupants of Canaan) had not yet reached full measure (Gen. 15:16). Consequently, Abraham's descendants could not inherit the Promised Land for several generations. When the Amorite cup of iniquity filled

17 Moffat (2013: 193) says, 'The Exodus grand narrative was a root paradigm for significant sections of the Persian-era community in Yehud. The significance of the Exodus paradigm has long been understood to shape the writer's presentation of the events in the book of Ezra. However, the influence of the paradigm goes much deeper. The *golah* [exilic] community's self-understanding was founded in the Exodus grand narrative. That is not just the view of the community as presented by the writer, but reflects the social situation of the writer and his readers. The community understood itself as a covenant people who were holy, separate from others and required to maintain that holiness and separation. They were the recipients of Yahweh's benevolence, rescued from foreign slavery and given a land. They saw those in the land who did not conform to their views on Yahwism in the same light as the pre-conquest inhabitants of Canaan.' What is missing here is a reference to mission, which Exod. 19:6 and Deut. 4:6–8 associate with holiness. Holiness (a distinct lifestyle based on Yahweh's law) was the means of mission.

up and spilled over, then Yahweh would use Abraham's family as a judicial instrument to mete out punishment on impenitent sinners and confirm them in the consequences of their moral choices. Individuals such as Rahab, though, could still repent and find a home within God's covenantal community. From Ezra's point of view, previous and current residents of the Promised Land (whether Jew or Gentile) should not, and ultimately cannot, experience well-being as long as they persist in their abominable ways. Ezra prays that Yahweh will forgive his fellow Jews for not acting distinctively as God's people.

Ezra's prayer of confession does not shirk responsibility or mince words. It multiplies terms that are part of the Old Testament's vocabulary of sin. Ezra says in verse 6 that he is 'ashamed' (*bōštî*) because of 'our iniquities' (*'áwōnōtênû*) and 'our guilt' (*'ašmātēnû*). Moreover, he includes himself in the larger group that has 'forsaken your commandments' (*'āzabnû miṣwōtêkā* [Ezra 9:10]) and performed 'evil deeds' (*ma'ásênû hārā'îm* [Ezra 9:13]). As a result of this 'abominable behaviour' (*tô'ēbôt* [Ezra 9:11]), post-exilic Jews have imitated the pre-exilic Canaanites and post-exilic peoples of the land by making the Promised Land 'impure' (*niddâ* [Ezra 9:11]) and 'unclean' (*ṭum'â* [Ezra 9:11]). The rhetorical effect indisputably establishes the contrast between the God of Israel who has shown 'steadfast love' (*ḥesed* [Ezra 9:9]) and the post-exilic Jews who have 'acted unfaithfully' (*ma'al* [Ezra 9:4]). The vocabulary of sin assumes a standard of right conduct; namely, Yahweh's revelation through his prophets (Ezra 9:11). Ezra leaves no doubt about what the standard for his confession is. The post-exilic community has disregarded God's spokesmen and, therefore, God himself. One of those spokesmen, of course, was Moses. He may not be mentioned specifically, but the citation in verses 11–12 summarizes the requirement of holiness or religious separation in the law of Moses (Exod. 34:15–16; Lev. 18:24–30; Deut. 7:3; 18:9; 23:6).

When Yahweh made the Sinaitic covenant with his newly constituted kingdom of priests that recently had been rescued from Egypt, he gave specific instruction through Moses about how a redeemed people should live and thereby perform their mission to the nations. Throughout the wilderness years, the exodus generation had Moses in their midst to give additional instructions. Near the end of his life, Moses told the children of the exodus generation how they would hear the word of God in his absence. They would not learn the will of God through divination as their neighbours did but through Yahweh's individually sent prophets (Deut. 18:9–22). Prophets would remind God's people of his covenant and God's mission and, if necessary, call them back to obedience. One source of instruction (Moses) was not more authoritative than another (prophets), and Israel would ignore either to its detriment. Ezra's chosen words and phrases for violations of God's revelation offer a rather complete picture of the covenantal negligence of the post-exilic community. Much like previous generations of Israelites, post-exilic Jews had failed to keep their part of the relationship with Yahweh, and these instances of disobedience added up to insurrection against the Lawgiver. Israel acted treacherously by betraying their promise to do God's will for the promotion of his redemptive mission among the nations. Ezra prayed so bluntly not because of careless oversight but because of deliberate rebellion. The post-exilic community had not been a holy nation and a kingdom of priests. Moreover, those leaders charged with modelling and encouraging covenantal faithfulness had, to the community's peril, disregarded God's messengers. They had led God's people away from their mission (Ezra 9:2). Ezra's prayer admitted that Israel had received their due recompense and deserved no favour (Ezra 9:7). Meanwhile, Yahweh had faithfully adhered to the terms of the covenant, even in the enactment of the curses (Ezra 9:13).

Like Israel's unfaithfulness before the exile, Jewish disregard of the prophets after the exile brought shame on the post-exilic community, for Yahweh had done so much on behalf of his people only to be treated with such ingratitude. As his covenant name Yahweh still implied, God had graciously chosen his people out of all nations, provided for their sustenance and protection, reiterated laws that would distinguish them as a just and compassionate nation, made them participants in a mission that involved nothing less than reconciling all creation to his eternal plan and returned them to a land that was a foretaste of Eden restored. These privileges and blessings belonged to God's people, but they, as Ezra candidly admits, did not cherish them and so spurned the One who lovingly bestowed them.

Similar to the book of Kings (2 Kgs 21:15), Ezra has a cumulative view of retribution. God's people had disregarded his commandments from the beginning of their history (Ezra 9:7). Consequently, sin is more than what individuals think and do at any given moment. By spreading horizontally within society (government, temple, work, school and home) and vertically through generations, sin can become endemic and institutionalized. People are born into sinful patterns that affect society (how they treat one another), economics (how they do business) and government (how they administer justice). They may not fully understand these patterns or think that they have power to change them. Certain forms of evil are accepted with a shrug, almost as if normal. 'That's just the way things are' is often the sigh of the helpless onlooker. The onlooker, however, is not so helpless. Boda says, 'There is . . . solidarity between the generations that necessitates intergenerational confession.'[18] Ezra understood that later generations can use penitential prayer to begin the process of setting matters right. No, the sins of the past cannot be undone as if they never happened. Nevertheless, acknowledging solidarity and thereby taking responsibility for ongoing consequences can be the catalyst for change, including mission, in the future.

Although Ezra's prayer of confession does not explicitly plead for mercy, it does say that the post-exilic community, identified as a remnant (Ezra 9:8, 13), has already experienced divine 'mercy' (*tĕḥinâ*) and 'love' (*ḥesed*). This favour has established the returnees (literally, given them a tent peg) within God's holy place (Ezra 9:8), which initially might seem to refer to God's temple. Perhaps, though, 'holy place' more broadly has the Promised Land in view. Verses 8 and 9 speak of 'reviving' (*miḥyâ*). In verse 8, the reviving occurs in the holy place. In verse 9, the reviving in the holy place allows for the restoration of the temple. The holy place, then, seems to be a bigger entity in which the temple is located. Ezra's point is that God's people back in Judah have enjoyed his goodness that has, despite the occasion of this prayer, promoted their spiritual revitalization. The rebuilt temple was tangible proof of God's favour. It represented God's intention to give his people a future that included fulfilment of all his promises.

If this holy place was the scene of a revival in the midst of continuing servitude to the Persian Empire, then more reviving would seem to be expected in the future.[19] Indeed, the remnant theology of the prophets included more than a rebuilt temple. For example, Micah 5:5 likens the remnant to a lion that dominates other creatures – something that could

[18] Boda 2015: 155. Bautch (2003: 72) says, 'The change [from first-person singular to first-person plural], in Ezra 9:7, is intended to show that a solidarity of guilt binds together the speaker and all of his contemporaries while it reaches back to their ancestors.'

[19] Koch 1974: 188–189.

not be said of the post-exilic community in the fifth century. Ezra in his prayer even admits that members of the post-exilic community, though back in the Promised Land, are still slaves (Ezra 9:8). God had begun a good work in the events of the post-exilic restoration, but not everything promised to the remnant had yet come to fruition. Moreover, Jeremiah 31:7–9 says that the remnant will not stumble, and Zephaniah 3:13 adds that the remnant will do no wrong. These verses, written more than a hundred years before Ezra's ministry, do not describe the people among whom Ezra ministered. God might, in response to Ezra's prayer, have forgiven their sins, but the sins of the remnant could still be identified in the fifth century. Jeremiah 50:20 looks ahead to a time when sin cannot be found among the remnant of Israel and Judah. It would seem, then, that Ezra–Nehemiah describes a partial realization of what the rest of the Old Testament expects for the remnant.[20]

Still, Ezra acknowledged God's favour to an undeserving people. Any more goodness in the future would also be unwarranted. Such is the God of the Bible, though. More often than not, he does not treat people justly (giving them what their sins deserve: judgment) but graciously (giving them what their sins do not deserve: forgiveness). In fact, Ezra 9:15 says guilty people have escaped, and are escaping, the full extent of divine judgment because, or though, God is *ṣaddîq* (righteous, just). More precisely, this verse says that God is righteous because, or though, his people remain a remnant of survivors. The conjunction *kî* can be translated causally ('You are righteous *because* we remain an escaped remnant') or concessively ('You are righteous *though* we remain an escaped remnant').[21] The concessive option may fit the immediate context better because it contrasts God's righteousness with the returnees' unrighteousness that has elicited Ezra's prayer. The causal option, however, accounts for Ezra's implied plea for grace. It conveys that God cannot have a people for his name unless he does for them what they cannot do for themselves. In other words, grace in the form of Yahweh's faithfulness to his covenantal promise to have a people for his name must trump justice in the form of Yahweh's enactment of covenantal curses for disobedience. God's faithfulness to the covenant in either form constitutes righteousness.[22] Ezra did not fully understand

20 Werline 1998: 52.
21 See the discussion in Byun 2019: 467–473.
22 Boda 2003: 54–56; 2006: 43.

how this trumping could happen, but it is the unstated request of the prayer.[23] The New Testament, of course, explains how, paradoxically, God can be both just and gracious; that is, faithful to the covenantal threats and promises. By means of Jesus' active and passive obedience, God satisfied his justice and extended grace to sinners. After living a righteous life (active obedience), Jesus at his death willingly expiated the sins of his people and propitiated God's just wrath (passive obedience). Meanwhile, God imputed Jesus' righteousness to those unrighteous people for whom he died. Grace and mercy for the sinner came at great cost to Jesus.

In the book of Ezra, the reality of incomplete sanctification is seen in the marriages of post-exilic men to the daughters of the people of the land. If Ezra 9 – 10 is read in view of Israel's calling as a kingdom of priests to the nations (and Ezra 1:1 indicates that Ezra should be read in continuity with Jeremiah who, according to Jeremiah 1:10, was a prophet to the nations), then the nationality of the women by itself had no bearing on their status in the post-exilic community. The dismissed women, like Solomon's wives in 1 Kings 11:1, are called *nāšîm nokrîyôt* (alien women). This term occurs nine times in Ezra–Nehemiah (Ezra 10:2, 10–11, 14, 17–18, 44; Neh. 13:26–27) but only one other time (1 Kgs 11:1) in the Hebrew Bible. In that context, the *nāšîm nokrîyôt* clearly influenced an Israelite king (Solomon) to depart from his covenantal responsibility of leading God's people in faithfulness to God's law (Deut. 17:14–20). It seems evident, then, that the *nāšîm nokrîyôt* in Ezra–Nehemiah neither shared the covenantal community's faith in Yahweh nor showed interest in embracing that faith.[24] Their unbelief adversely affected a holy community, presumably by leading the husbands astray as the idolatry of Solomon's wives had done to him (Neh. 13:26).[25] Religion, not race, was the concern.[26] 'Beneath the surface of the intermarriage issue', observes Johnson, 'lurks idolatry as a force of contamination to the religious and cultural norms of Yehudites according to Ezra.'[27] The idol was economic

---

23 Boda (2003: 55) says that 'the great emphasis in these [penitential] prayers is on the grace of God, which provides hope that the request will be heard, and [on] the might of God, which provides hope that the request can be fulfilled'.

24 Brown 2005: 449–450, 457 n. 65; Glover 2009: 308; Steinmann 2010: 96; Saysell 2012: 45–49, 219–220; Moffat 2013: 110–111, 149, 152; Wielenga 2013: 5.

25 Fensham 1982: 124, 135; Throntveit 1992: 57; Becking 2011: 44–45, 59–61; Harrington 2011: 256; Moffat 2013: 181–184.

26 Fensham 1982: 125; Throntveit 1992: 57; Bautch 2003: 70–71; Eskenazi 2006: 522; Japhet 2006: 113; Johnson, 2011: 22, 98–99; Moffat 2013: 81–82; Kissling 2014: 216.

27 Johnson 2011: 23.

security that marriage to the daughters of pagan landowners afforded.[28] Nevertheless, such marriages had the potential to do more economic harm than good. Extended families could lose property because of a foreign wife's inheritance at the death of her husband.[29] In this event, the covenantal community would lose portions of the covenantal land, which was the stage on which it was supposed to perform its mission.

The husbands had to make a guilt offering because they, out of religious indifference, had married women for the wrong reason and compromised the distinct identity and mission of God's people.[30] That mission, of course, was to model a redeemed community by keeping Yahweh's law. Such obedience not only thanked Yahweh for his saving deeds (thereby expressing trust for continued provision of needs) but also invited the nations to experience the riches of his grace that come from doing his will. Evidently, God had used Ezra's teaching to convict these men of their covenantal (missional) apathy and lead them to repentance (Ezra 10:3).

Perhaps some of the foreign women also embraced Ezra's teaching, became part of the covenantal community and remained married to their husbands as insiders by faith. The committee of officials that took three months to examine each case (Ezra 10:14–17) might have heard sincere professions of faith from some women.[31] Ezra 9 – 10 may not explicitly discuss this possibility, but the God of the Old Testament, as seen in the examples of Rahab and Ruth, does not turn away anyone who believes in him.[32] Moreover, Ezra 6:21 and Nehemiah 10:28 (HB 10:29), in accordance with Exodus 12:43–49, make allowance for the conversion of foreigners and their participation in the covenantal community.[33] It seems unjustified, then, to say that Ezra and the writer of Ezra–Nehemiah wished to exclude Gentiles as such from the covenantal community.[34] If Ezra 9 – 10

[28] Ibid. 23, 25, 28, 64. Further, Johnson (2011: 24) says, 'Economic viability was a catalyst for Yehudite men to seek alternative marital arrangements.'

[29] Adams 2014: 27.

[30] Williamson 1985: 161.

[31] Ezra 9:1 indicates that men and women shed tears. Perhaps the conviction of Jewish husbands was used of God's Spirit to convict Gentile wives.

[32] Beckwith 2001: 187–188; Hamilton 2014: 91.

[33] Japhet 2006: 115; Lau 2009: 365–366; Schnittjer 2016: 44–45.

[34] Harrington 2008: 115–116; Conczorowski 2011: 105–106; Johnson 2011: 87–92. Hayes (1999: 6) maintains that Ezra's ban on intermarriage modified the law of Moses by prohibiting all intermarriage. The intention of this more stringent policy was to eliminate any chance of religious profanation from outsiders. Hayes never interacts with Ezra 6:21 and Neh. 10:28–29 (HB 10:29–30), which indicate a continuation of the missional openness in the law of Moses. Similarly, Lubeck (2010) argues that Zerubbabel, Ezra and Nehemiah exceeded God's law and

is read in the context of Ezra 6:21, Nehemiah 10:28 (HB 10:29) and the rest of the Old Testament, racial purity is not the concern. A holy people and racial purity are not the same thing. As an anointed priest, Ezra tried to balance Israel's calling as a kingdom of priests to be both distinct and missional.

Marriage between Israelites/Jews and Gentiles was sometimes permitted and even beneficial: for example, the marriages of Joseph (Gen. 41:45), Moses (Exod. 2:21), Machlon (Ruth 4:10), Boaz (Ruth 4:13) and various Israelite soldiers (Deut. 21:10–14). The implication in these cases is that the Gentile women shared their husbands' commitment to Yahweh. No syncretism or apostasy (no abomination) occurred.[35] Meanwhile, other instances of intermarriage became the avenue for theological compromise and shipwrecked lives (Gen. 28:6–9; Judg. 14:1–3; 1 Kgs 11:1–8; 16:31). In these instances, the Israelite men and Gentile women had weak or no faith in Yahweh. What happens in Ezra 9 – 10 should be read in view of the positive and negative possibilities of intermarriage. Given Ezra's prayer of confession, the emphasis of these chapters, of course, is on preventing the mistakes of the past in the current situation.

Modern readers of Ezra 10 may wince at the decision to send the foreign wives and mixed children away.[36] The author says nothing about any provision for their care.[37] Given the recollection of the earlier extermination of the Canaanites, Saysell and Moberly suggest that the post-exilic community reinterpreted the *ḥerem* (devotion to destruction) law in Deuteronomy 7:1–5.[38] Rather than kill the unholy women of the land, the returned exiles excluded them from participation with God's people. Similarly, any Jewish man who refused to send his foreign wife away would lose his share of the Promised Land and thus forfeit membership in the covenantal community.[39] He would not die, though. These measures

---

Persian directives by refusing help for the temple, breaking up marriages and building a wall. These leaders might have succeeded in their building projects but not in community relations (mission). Lubeck also never discusses Ezra 6:21 or Neh. 10:28–29 (HB 10:29–30).

[35] These permissible instances of intermarriage balance Duggan's (2006: 180) contention that 'the traditional legislation . . . prohibits mixed marriages (Deut 7:3)' between Jews and Gentiles, regardless of the latter's loyalty to Yahweh.

[36] Williamson 1985: 161; Holmgren 1987: 84; Throntveit 1992: 48, 56; Wijk-Bos 1998: 43–48; Redditt 2014: 204.

[37] Laird (2016: 318) says, 'For today's reader the account ends on a note of poignancy that remains unresolved.'

[38] Saysell 2012: 74, 77; Moberly 2013: 69, 72.

[39] Johnson 2011: 89; Saysell 2012: 78; Moffat 2013: 188.

may seem harsh, but the identity and mission of God's people after the exile were at stake. Any religious community that does not take steps to preserve its distinctiveness will not last long.[40] It will eventually transmute into something quite different from the original vision of the founder(s). For the post-exilic community, the original vision belonged to God, who had spoken through Moses and the prophets. The marriages with unbelievers violated God's law by compromising the religious purity of God's people and threatening their mission to model a redeemed community. Sending the wives and children away must have been hard for everyone, but the marriages should never have occurred in most cases. Faithfulness to Yahweh and a commitment to his mission for his people should have taken precedence over whatever attracted a Jewish man and a foreign woman to each other. If Ezekiel 8 describes abominable behaviour by compromised worshippers at the first temple, Ezra 9 – 10 teaches that past mistakes will be avoided only by uncompromised worshippers at the second temple. Spiritual renewal requires the practice of holiness, which is a disciplined commitment to God's revealed standards of conduct in all areas of life.

Whatever someone today may think about the enforcement of divorce, Ezra 9 and 10 teach that repentance necessitates change and offers hope. Repentance begins with a recognition of wrongdoing, specifically an honest appraisal of how the one repenting has fallen short of God's revealed will. On behalf of those for whom he prays, Ezra admits shame because he realizes and rues the enormity of how generations of Israelites, climaxing in the post-exilic community, have displayed ingratitude for God's goodness by ignoring God's commandments. Agreeing with Ezra's assessment of Israelite history and acknowledging unfaithfulness of contemporary Jews, Shekaniah proposed a covenant with God that tailored change to the specific sin of intermarriage (Ezra 10:2–3). Repentance entails stopping what is wrong in a situation and doing what is right in that same situation. This reversal brings hope not only for the avoidance of full judgment but also for participation in all that God has promised to his people. Ezra feared that Yahweh's anger would consume the offenders. The implication of his prayer and of Shekaniah's covenant is that repentance restores God's favour and brings an open future.

---

40 Blenkinsopp (2009: 196) considers endogamy part of a larger effort by the post-exilic community to preserve its identity in the absence of political autonomy. Other community markers included circumcision, dietary rules and the sabbath.

As mentioned earlier, the members of the post-exilic community struggled to follow Yahweh in the ordinary situations of life. Far from being perfect people, they not only had marital problems but also disagreed on how to resolve them (Ezra 10:15). Ezra 10 may not explain why four individuals, including a Levite, disapproved of the group's decision to break up mixed marriages, but its appreciably honest record of the discordant voices rings true. Church history demonstrates that God's people rarely share the same opinion about any topic. Here, then, is more evidence of the tension between the now and the not yet. For God's people to dwell together harmoniously in the New Jerusalem, God will have to enable them to agree on what his will is and to do it without faltering. How he will do this is indeed a mystery.

Presumably God will remove the ethical conundrums that sometimes lie behind differences of opinion. Such challenges are also part of the tension between the now and not yet. Ezra and Shekaniah had to decide between preserving the religious purity of the group or showing compassion to those affected by inappropriate relationships. The four objectors must have thought that Ezra and Shekaniah chose the wrong solution. Neither option, however, was completely satisfying.[41] Sometimes the best that people can do in this morally complex life is weigh the pros and cons of less than ideal possibilities, pick one and live with the consequences. In so doing, ultimately they leave the resolution of the matter to God. As the redeemer, he can bring good out of bad. No situation exceeds his transforming grace.

One last matter has to do with reading Ezra 9 – 10 in view of 1 Corinthians 7. Whereas the post-exilic men sent their foreign wives away in Ezra 10, Paul instructed Christians to remain married to unbelievers who were willing to stay in the relationship. It may seem as if 1 Corinthians 7 relaxes the standard in Ezra 10. The two cases, however, are not the same. In Ezra, believers who were born into the covenantal community married unbelievers who were never a part of God's people. Shekaniah recommended divorce, and Ezra agreed. In Corinth, two unbelievers were already married at the time that one of them converted to Christianity. Paul says that the believing partner in this instance should stay in the marriage as long as the unbelieving partner remains faithful. If the unbelieving partner is unwilling to preserve the marriage, then divorce

[41] Fyall 2010: 135–137.

may occur. Both passages, however, uphold the same standard for marriage; namely, that believers should not marry unbelievers.

Still, if Ezra thinks that the foreign spouse will have a stronger effect on the Jewish spouse who married for the wrong reason, Paul considers the possibility that the spouse who comes to faith after marrying another unbeliever could have the stronger effect. He says that the believing spouse sanctifies the unbelieving spouse.[42] Perhaps this sanctifying is used of God to convert the unbelieving spouse and/or any children. Perhaps not. The sanctifying may be short-lived for one reason (the unbelieving spouse eventually wants a divorce) or another (the unbelieving spouse eventually weakens the believing spouse's commitment to Jesus). Nevertheless, the unbelieving spouse and any children involved are exposed for a certain length of time to biblical truth.[43] There is mystery here. No one can predict how God may make use of exposure to his Word. Isaiah 55:11 affirms that God's Word accomplishes God's purpose in each situation that the Word is proclaimed. God's purpose in the situations of people's lives may not always be clearly understood (Isa. 55:8–9), but God is working out his purpose nonetheless.

Summary

Ezra 7 – 10 describes the second stage of implementing Cyrus' decree. A new temple required renewed people to worship there. With the king's approval, Ezra taught the post-exilic community how to be prepared for approaching a holy God. Such preparation involved some hard decisions about lifestyle. Being a kingdom of priests before a watching world and a watching God involves the responsibility of behaving circumspectly. Actions must correspond to words. When they do not, repentance can restore both a person's relationship to God and mission to God's world.

[42] For a discussion of the options for understanding sanctification in 1 Cor. 7:14, see Gillihan 2002: 731–741; MacDonald and Vaage 2011: 528–533; Saysell 2012: 182–202.

[43] Fee 1987: 300–302; Blomberg 1994: 135; Hays 1997: 121–122; Gillihan 2002: 716–717; Keener 2009: 43.

6
Rebuilding the wall

Nehemiah 1 – 7 describes Nehemiah's effort to build a literal wall around Jerusalem. The purpose of the wall, however, was not to protect Jerusalem from military invasion by the Persian army. The Jews were already submitting to Persian policy, which had allowed them to rebuild Jerusalem and its temple. Both Ezra and Nehemiah had a good relationship with Artaxerxes, who granted permission first to Ezra to teach the law of Yahweh and second to Nehemiah to build the wall around Jerusalem. A change in Persian attitude towards the Jews did not prompt an interest in building a wall. This third stage of implementing Cyrus' decree involved preserving the sanctity of the temple by promoting the religious and moral holiness of the surrounding city.[1]

Ezra 9:1 likens the people of the land in the post-exilic era to the Canaanites before the monarchy. The Canaanites are said to have committed abominations, which Yahweh long ago had told his people to avoid (Lev. 18:26). They did not obey, and their practice of Canaanite abominations eventually defiled Yahweh's temple (Ezek. 5:11; 8:5–18). When Nehemiah proposed a wall to the residents of Jerusalem (Neh. 2:17), he did not speak of keeping Persians out but of eliminating reproach or shame. In other words, he wanted to prevent the religious mistakes of the past. These mistakes had brought about the defilement of Yahweh's house long before the trampling by Nebuchadnezzar's soldiers. Soon after arriving in Jerusalem, Nehemiah became aware of the potential for more hostility from the people of the land. This threat might have reinforced his decision to build a wall.[2] Even so, he had already made this decision back in Persia. The primary purpose of the wall was to preserve the

1 Eskenazi 1988a: 83–84.

2 For a discussion of the secular purposes of Nehemiah's wall, see Oeming 2012: 135–137, who also argues that the wall had a theological purpose.

sanctity of Yahweh's house by keeping away unholy conduct by Jews and Gentiles.[3] The wall served as a visible reminder of the inviolable space on the other side.[4] This sacred function of the wall explains the priests' consecration of the Sheep Gate (Neh. 3:1) towards the beginning of the project and their purification of the whole wall upon its completion (Neh. 12:30).

Nehemiah's wall recalls the wall around Ezekiel's visionary temple. The enormity of Israel's sin before the exile accounts for the walls, steps and gates of Ezekiel's temple. The outer wall is said to be about 10 feet (3.5 m) high and wide (Ezek. 40:5). Each gate, which is about 36 feet (11 m) wide and 75 feet (23 m) long, has alcoves for six guards. If seven steps lead from the wall to the outer gates and outer court (Ezek. 40:22), eight steps lead from the outer court to the inner gates and inner court (Ezek. 40:31), and ten steps from the inner court to the temple (Ezek. 40:49). Three doorways that become increasingly narrower (about 21, 15 and 9 feet [6.5 m, 4.6 m, 3 m]) control access to the Holy of Holies. The purpose of these steps, gates and doors is to protect, but not necessarily isolate, Yahweh's holiness. Although nobody will rush into his presence, Yahweh has nevertheless maintained availability. Similarly, Nehemiah's wall separated the holy from the unholy. It served as a boundary to define the covenantal community.[5] That said, Nehemiah 3 mentions nine gates or points of entry in Nehemiah's wall, and Ezra 6:21 has already indicated that outsiders could become insiders.

News from 'home'

Nehemiah 2:1 puts most of the events of Nehemiah 1 – 6 in 445 BC, about thirteen years after Ezra's arrival.[6] Although Ezra appears in Nehemiah 8:1 and 12:36, Nehemiah 1 – 6 focuses on the activity of Ezra's contemporary, Nehemiah. Clearly, Ezra–Nehemiah presents a selective account of post-exilic activities. For this reason, it is impossible to know what Ezra

---

[3] Redditt 2014: 223–224.

[4] Redditt (ibid. 239) says that the wall '*demarcated the holy space of the temple*'; emphasis original. See also Wijk-Bos 1998: 58.

[5] Duggan (2001: 66) says that 'the reconstruction of the wall becomes a symbol of the redefinition of the community'.

[6] Because the month Chislev (November–December) in 1:1 was the ninth month of the calendar year, and Nisan (March–April) in 2:1 was the first month, the events of Neh. 1 apparently happened in 446, towards the beginning of Artaxerxes' twentieth regnal year.

did during these years. Presumably, he taught the law of Moses, as he knew it expertly and Artaxerxes wanted him to teach it. There is a lesson here. Ezra laboured faithfully for thirteen years without much fanfare. God's servants face tremendous pressure to be successful outwardly, but they can take comfort in Ezra's ministry. God does not necessarily call his servants to be successful in a grand way; rather, he calls them to be faithful wherever he puts them. Given the people's response to Nehemiah, evidently Ezra had made an impact. As any minister knows, though, that impact did not prevent lapses in faith or obedience. The residents of Nehemiah's Jerusalem remained a 'not yet' fully sanctified people.

Nehemiah 1:2 reports that Hanani, who is called the brother of Nehemiah, travelled from Jerusalem to Susa.[7] The reason for the journey is not given. When Nehemiah asked Hanani about the welfare of the Jews in Jerusalem, Hanani mentioned the wall's state of disrepair, thereby confirming what the reader of Ezra–Nehemiah already knows from Ezra 4:7–23. An earlier attempt to rebuild the wall had met with resistance and come to a halt. The update from Hanani, though, would change Nehemiah's life and bring him into contact with Ezra. Hanani's report awakened a sense of mission in Nehemiah, who decided to trade daily access to the royal court in Susa for serving his God 1,000 miles (1,609 km) away on the western edge of the Persian Empire. That frontier did not have the stability, comforts and splendour of the seat of power. Nevertheless, Nehemiah put the needs of the post-exilic community ahead of whatever personal plans he might have made. How Nehemiah, a cupbearer, gained the skill to oversee the building of a city wall is not explained, but subsequent chapters demonstrate that God had gifted him for this responsibility. Presumably Ezra, the on-site specialist in biblical interpretation, was not the right man for this particular job. What is known is that Nehemiah became aware of a bad situation and could not rest until he had done something about it. That is mission.

Commendably, Nehemiah's immediate reaction was to pray. In fact, Nehemiah 1:4 indicates that Nehemiah prayed persistently. The prayer in Nehemiah 1:5–11 was one of many prayers that shared similar affirmations about God and requests for Jerusalem. This prayer, however, may not initially seem to be consistent logically.[8] Upon hearing that

---

[7] As Nehemiah's brother, Hanani might have been a family member or a fellow Jew.
[8] Laird: 2016: 260–261.

Jerusalem's walls still lay in ruins, Nehemiah confessed the covenantal unfaithfulness of those Jews back in Jerusalem and included himself in their disobedience.[9] Similar to Ezra, Nehemiah as intercessor identified with God's people in their unfaithfulness.[10] Nehemiah most likely prayed this way because Hanani had assessed the dilapidated state of Jerusalem as Haggai had done seventy-five years earlier (Hag. 1:2–6); namely, with reference to Jewish laxity and distraction. Nevertheless, Ezra 4:7–16 attributes the unfinished wall to a letter that complained about an earlier effort to rebuild the wall. In other words, the post-exilic community had tried to make repairs, but opposition forced them to stop. Nehemiah's request for mercy from Artaxerxes (Neh. 1:11) seems to show awareness of the king's reaction to that letter. Because Artaxerxes bore responsibility for the idleness of the Jews in Jerusalem, only his reversal of the earlier ruling could allow them to resume work. So then, the confession of sin against Yahweh and the request for mercy from Artaxerxes do not seem, at first glance, to be logical or obvious corollaries in Nehemiah's prayer.

Recognition of multiple causes of the current state of affairs can ease the perceived dissonance in the prayer. Regarding the confession of sin, Nehemiah might have thought that he and his fellow Jews should have petitioned Artaxerxes earlier to reconsider the labour stoppage. Such a request, though, would have involved greater risk for the residents of Jerusalem, who were already under suspicion and did not know the king as Nehemiah did. It is also possible that Hanani's reference to trouble and shame had in mind the events in Ezra 9 and 10. Wrongful marriages had compromised the holiness of the post-exilic community and therefore jeopardized the sanctity of Yahweh's temple in their midst. If not the mixed marriages, then some other source of trouble or shame (such as the problems discussed in Malachi) might have prompted Nehemiah's confession. Meanwhile, the recollection that 'this man' (Artaxerxes) was still part of the situation necessitated a request for Yahweh to change his heart. So then, the two requests of the prayer can fit together in this context. News from Jerusalem made Nehemiah aware that there was plenty of responsibility to go around and plenty of need for divine

[9] Wijk-Bos (1998: 52) observes, 'Rather than stressing the broken walls, the prayer lifts up the broken commandments.'

[10] Boda 2006: 38–39.

intervention. Nehemiah might not be able to unravel all the strands in order to rectify the situation, but Yahweh was able to do so.

God's people today still receive unsettling news about events near and far. While the initial reaction may be 'I have to do something about this,' Nehemiah models a better approach. Later chapters will demonstrate his skill at making a proposal, organizing a workforce and discerning people's true motives. Even so, four months separate Nehemiah 1:1 and 2:1. During this time, Nehemiah prayed while continuing to perform his duties as cupbearer. There was no sudden action, only seeking the favour of God. In Nehemiah's thinking, a human predicament constituted a divine opportunity. Nehemiah acknowledged God's involvement in this situation and waited on God to work behind the scenes. When Artaxerxes later observed Nehemiah's change of mood and asked about it (Neh. 2:2), Nehemiah had his divinely arranged opportunity to take action. Not just here, but throughout the book of Nehemiah, Nehemiah prays to God. A person with a sense of mission realizes his or her need of God and regularly consults him.

If Nehemiah's prayer in Nehemiah 1:5–11 exemplifies other prayers he uttered during those four months, he did more than confess sin and ask for help. He also reviewed what he knew to be true of God independent of this pressing situation. By calling Israel's God the God of heaven (Neh. 1:5), Nehemiah affirmed that his God was a big God – no less than the ruler of the universe he had made. For an exile whose boss was King Artaxerxes, this was a remarkable claim. Yahweh, despite appearances, was not the minor deity of a subordinate people. Rather, he transcended the physical universe but could intervene in it, even using earthly kings and kingdoms for his purpose. Because of this belief in Yahweh's sovereignty, Nehemiah simply would not concede that the Persian Empire had the upper hand. So, too, God's people today need to remember that their God is big enough to hold the oceans in his hand and weigh the mountains on his scale (Isa. 40:12). A God that immense is not hampered by the problems that beset his people. This is not to say that he does not care, only that he is not restricted.

By contrast, Artaxerxes ('this man') was on earth and therefore subject to the temporal and spatial limitations of all earthlings. Nehemiah recognized that the God of heaven could incorporate him at will into the outworking of his plan for his world. For this reason, he asked Yahweh for success and mercy. Similarly, today's politicians, journalists, professors, employers and others who wield temporal power are mere earthlings. They may make decisions that affect other people, including God's people, but those decisions are not final or irreversible. The God of heaven can always override them in some way. This power to override makes the God of heaven great and awesome. He can surprise like no one else.

Nehemiah also said that his God had redeemed his people (Neh. 1:10) because he had kept his covenant with them (Neh. 1:5). This covenant was based on God's steadfast love. In other words, the God to whom Nehemiah prayed deliberately set his affection on people who had done nothing to merit it. In fact, they were in need of rescue because of their unfaithfulness. Nevertheless, Nehemiah's God remained faithful to his promise to have a people for his name. Keeping this promise involved doing everything necessary to create and even sustain the relationship. Yes, God's people had the responsibility of living as his people by keeping his commandments. Even doing this, though, involved God's great power and strong hand. Humans may not be able to explain how God respects their decisions and yet sanctifies them. Nevertheless, Nehemiah knew that God does not give up on his people – there would be no relationship if he did.

By referring to Yahweh's faithfulness to his covenant (Neh. 1:5), Nehemiah's prayer assumes that God's mission for his people remains incomplete.[11] The covenant might have threatened curses for unfaithfulness (Deut. 28:15–68), and Yahweh might have administered those curses justly. Even so, the covenant also looked beyond the final curse of exile to a restoration (Deut. 30:1–10) that, according to the prophets, included blessing for the nations. Nehemiah's prayer would have no point if he were not aware of Deuteronomy's expected hope for a future beyond the exile. Moreover, Nehemiah, after identifying himself as a servant, refers to the people of Israel as 'your [Yahweh's] servants'. If, as mentioned earlier, Isaiah's prophecies lie behind Ezra's praise in Ezra 7:27, then it is possible that Nehemiah was familiar with them too. While Isaiah 63:17 and 65:9 use the plural form of 'servant' for God's people, the singular form is found in Isaiah 41:8–9. God's people as a group are clearly in view, but are called a servant. The same is true in Isaiah 42:19, which draws attention to how unprofitable God's servant (the group) has become because they would not

---

[11] Breneman (1993: 173) says, 'Nehemiah realized that God had fulfilled much of Deut. 30:1–10; but he was convinced that God's promise included more than the situation in which the Jerusalem community found itself at that moment.'

obey God's law (Isa. 42:24). Meanwhile, Isaiah 42:1 (when read with 42:6a), 49:3 (when read with 49:6a) and 52:13 and 53:11 (when read with 53:8) speak of a servant who seems to identify with the group but, nevertheless, is separate from the group. Whereas the group is an unrighteous and unprofitable servant, the individual is a righteous and profitable servant whose death makes atonement for the group's unrighteousness. Moreover, the redeeming work of this individual enables the group to fulfil its mission to the surrounding nations (Isa. 26:17–18; 42:6b; 49:6b; 54:1–3; 66:7–9). When Nehemiah identifies the people of Israel as 'your servants', he is holding out hope that an unprofitable group of servants will become profitable. They might not have kept Yahweh's commandments (Neh. 1:7) that had to do with performing a mission of being a kingdom of priests, but Nehemiah implicitly implores Yahweh to make his servants able to act as the redeemed people they already are (Neh. 1:10). So then, a redeemed people should resemble their redeemer, and the ethical conduct of a redeemed people is the instrument of their mission on behalf of the redeemer. The surrounding peoples of the land will see the behavioural difference and know who Yahweh is in contrast to their gods. So says the law of Moses (Gen. 18:18–19; Deut. 4:6–8) about which Nehemiah's prayer is so concerned.

Nehemiah admitted that disobedience led to scattering among the nations, and therefore a poor witness to them. Meanwhile, obedience would lead to restoration to the place where God had chosen to put his name. No Old Testament saint after the dedication of Solomon's temple could hear about the place God had chosen and not think of Jerusalem as the centre of God's redemptive programme. God put his people and his temple at the crossroads of the ancient world (Africa to the south-west, Europe to the north-west and Asia to the east) so that they might learn of him and come to faith in him (1 Kgs 8:27–53; Isa. 2:2–3; Ezek. 5:5–8; Mic. 4:1–2). Salvation goes out from the people at the crossroads. By confessing sin and asking for Artaxerxes' change of heart, Nehemiah prayed for the advancement of God's mission. He wanted his God to remove any impediment among and beyond his people. Simply put, God cannot stop now. He has already done too much for the post-exilic community to let the present trouble and shame sabotage his worldwide intention for them.[12]

[12] Holmgren 1987: 92.

Readers of Ezra–Nehemiah should remember what was happening in Greece at this time. Pericles was overseeing the height of Athenian power and culture. While Nehemiah built walls, the Greeks built the Parthenon. The foundations of Western thought and culture were laid in Athens, but Yahweh worked redemptively in the ruins of Jerusalem.[13] The story of biblical religion unfolds in Jerusalem, not Athens, and these ostensibly insignificant events in Ezra–Nehemiah would lead eventually to the death of a Davidic descendant named Jesus who saves his people from sin (Matt. 1:21). These people will come from all parts of the globe (Matt. 28:19; Rev. 7:9–10) over which Jesus has received dominion (Matt. 26:64; 28:18; Acts 2:33–36; Eph. 1:20–23). Nehemiah might not have known as many details about the movement of redemptive history as Christians do today, but his prayer recognized that God had not yet finished his plan for his people and world. Jews had returned to Judea because God wanted to do more through them in that place.

From Susa to Jerusalem

Nehemiah's conversation with Artaxerxes

Nehemiah might have prayed with conviction in chapter 1, but his hesitation in Nehemiah 2:2 is understandable because of how Artaxerxes, after the revolts in Egypt and Syria, reacted to a rumoured rebellion in Judea (Ezra 4:7–23). Ezra 4:12 indicates that work on the Jerusalem walls had begun before Nehemiah's visit to Jerusalem in 445 BC. Artaxerxes, presumably, associated this building project with the earlier uprisings and ordered the work to stop. Meanwhile, Hanani updated Nehemiah on the condition of the walls – evidently news that weighed heavily on Nehemiah's mind. When Artaxerxes enquired about his cupbearer's depressed mood, Nehemiah knew that the walls of Jerusalem were a potentially volatile topic for a Jewish exile to raise. Asking Artaxerxes to reverse an earlier decision could bring a charge of meddling at best or sedition at worst. Either charge would doom Nehemiah.

[13] In the context of discussing the names in Ezra 2, Breneman (1993: 79) says, 'Even though the [post-exilic] community was practically unnoticed in the world at that time, they constituted the center of God's redemptive plan.' Blenkinsopp (2009: 7) adds, 'Socrates was engaged in philosophical debate at the same time that Nehemiah was rebuilding the city wall of Jerusalem.'

It is not immediately clear whetheror not the king's questions in Nehemiah 2:2 demonstrate genuine concern for Nehemiah. Artaxerxes might have been wary of a cupbearer who seemed to be out of sorts, and evidently Nehemiah worried that he had given the king the wrong impression. Still, the close working relationship between these two men – a relationship that involved trust – might have led Artaxerxes at times to relate to Nehemiah more as a fellow human than as a social inferior.[14] This exchange at the beginning of chapter 2 seems to be one of those occasions. Given his ready consent to Nehemiah's request, Artaxerxes seems to have suspected no hidden agenda.[15] Perhaps Nehemiah's respect for his ancestors' graves made Artaxerxes even more aware of their common humanity.[16] The queen's presence might also have contributed to the humaneness.[17]

Even so, Nehemiah offered a quick prayer to God, thereby recognizing that someone else was also a part of this conversation.[18] Nehemiah 'tells us of his praying [here and elsewhere] in order to teach us from his own example that it is prayer that changes things, and that without praying there is no prospering'.[19] Reassured by his appeal to a divine advocate, Nehemiah spoke directly about the cause of his sadness, which was the dishonourable state of his family's homeland. He thereby made Jerusalem a personal place rather than a political hotbed.[20] When the king responded favourably with another question about how to resolve the problem, Nehemiah did not hesitate to list practical steps: leave of absence, guarantee of unhindered passage, provision of building supplies and housing for Nehemiah. His answer indicated prolonged and meticulous thought about what needed to be done. He had prayed fervently and deliberately planned everything. While the recommended solution was by no means cheap, Artaxerxes did not hesitate to make the empire's resources available to his

---

14 For a different perspective, see Nykolaishen 2008: 191–192.

15 Kidner (1979: 81) observes, 'The whole interview gives the impression that it was Nehemiah's personal qualities that won him the right to speak and that gained his point, overriding all the political obstacles.'

16 Williamson (1985: 179) says, 'Respect for ancestral tombs was universal in the Ancient Near East, and especially among the nobility and royalty.' See also Fleishman 2012: 263.

17 The Hebrew word *šēgal*, translated 'queen', is not the usual word for a female monarch. *Malkâ* is the usual word. The verbal root of *šēgal* means 'to lie with' or 'to sleep with', suggesting that the woman with Artaxerxes in Neh. 2:6 was a member of the harem.

18 Brown (1998: 48) says, 'There was hardly time for words; the sigh became a supplication. Between one breath and another, he [Nehemiah] was in the audience chamber of God, assured that he would not lack anything necessary for his daring venture.'

19 Packer 1995: 45.

20 McConville 1985: 79–80; Wijk-Bos 1998: 55.

trusted servant. Of course, politics surely entered into the king's decision. By securing a city on the western edge of his empire, Artaxerxes not only guarded against Egyptian rebellion but also promoted the good will of his Jewish subjects. Nehemiah, no doubt thankful for his boss's generosity, also perceived the silent intervention of his God.[21] His prayer had received the best possible answer. God had mysteriously worked in concert with Nehemiah's careful planning.

The guarantee of unhindered passage included both official letters from the king and an armed guard. Perceptive readers cannot help but notice a difference between Nehemiah and Ezra.[22] Unlike Ezra, who refused an armed guard, Nehemiah accepted a guard. In fact, he probably had no choice in the matter. Ezra, as a religious teacher, wanted to bear witness to his belief in divine protection; therefore, his journey became a lesson in itself. He could hardly travel hundreds of miles to teach about the goodness and power of God (Ezra 8:22) if his manner of travel undercut his message. Nehemiah, however, worked for the king, who would not want any harm to come to his cupbearer. An attack on him was an attack on the king. Moreover, Nehemiah's mission constituted a reversal of the king's earlier edict that had stopped work on the walls. If Nehemiah, who might not have been known outside the palace, travelled to the western edge of the Persian Empire and did not have a convincing show of royal support, the provincial officials along the way would rightly doubt his explanation for his journey and hinder him on the basis of the earlier edict. An appropriate display of pomp and authority was a necessary part of authenticating Nehemiah for the purpose of revising the king's policy.[23] So then, the military escort was hardly evidence of 'Nehemiah's belligerent posture toward the world'.[24]

Nehemiah's arrival in Jerusalem

According to Nehemiah 2:11–12, Nehemiah spent three days in Jerusalem before inspecting the wall at night. He would obviously need to rest and

---

[21] Because Nehemiah as a cupbearer was a slave who received no holidays, Packer (1995: 62) infers, 'For Nehemiah, the royal cupbearer, to be released from his job and dispatched to Jerusalem on a city-building mission would be an unprecedented marvel.'

[22] Ezkenazi's (1988a: 68, 79–81, 136–152) contrast between the self-effacement of Ezra and the self-promotion of Nehemiah interprets the evidence differently and even incorrectly. The author hardly intended a person who prayed like Nehemiah to serve as a foil to Ezra. Moreover, Nehemiah was threatened in ways Ezra was not.

[23] Kidner 1979: 81.

[24] Eskenazi 1988a: 146.

unpack. During this time, he wisely said nothing about his real reason for being there. Nehemiah 2:10 may mention Sanballat and Tobiah, but the reader does not know whether Nehemiah had already encountered these men by the time of his inspection. In fact, Nehemiah 2:19 gives the impression that Sanballat and Tobiah learned about the purpose of Nehemiah's visit after the inspection; that is, at the same time as everyone else in Jerusalem. So then, Nehemiah 2:10, which introduces Sanballat and Tobiah as potential adversaries, does not seem to indicate that these men had already become privy to the content of the king's letters, but only about Nehemiah's arrival from Susa. The arrival of a Jewish man with a military escort was enough to upset these men. Such royal support told them that Nehemiah had come for the benefit of the post-exilic community. A few days later they learned what he wanted to do, with the king's approval.

According to verse 10, Sanballat and Tobiah opposed any effort that promoted the welfare of the people of Israel. Whereas Nehemiah had travelled 1,000 miles (1,609 km) to help a city where he had never lived, Sanballat and Tobiah cared little for neighbours in 'their own backyard'. In other words, they had no regard for the law of Moses that instructed God's people to 'love your neighbour as yourself' (Lev. 19:18). This initial reference to these men, however, does not explain why they were so unfriendly. Nehemiah's arrival signalled that King Artaxerxes, who had already sent Ezra, wanted to help the people of Israel. From a political point of view, Sanballat and Tobiah could deduce that the king did not recognize them as the local leaders of Judea.[25] Whatever power they had in Judea, or hoped to get, was slipping through their fingers, and they were angry about that.[26] From a religious point of view, Nehemiah had come to protect and further establish Ezra's teaching of the law of Moses. Of course, Moses had warned about compromising with people (whether Jew or Gentile) who did not exclusively serve Yahweh in the way Yahweh had prescribed to Moses. Artaxerxes might have cared nothing about Yahweh

[25] A letter among the Elephantine Papyri names a Sanballat as the governor of Samaria about 410 BC (Pritchard 1969: 492). This Sanballat may be Nehemiah's Sanballat, but no independent confirmation exists. If the two Sanballats were the same person, there is no way of knowing whether Sanballat was governor of Samaria when Nehemiah arrived in Jerusalem. Of course, Samaria was once the capital of the northern kingdom. Given the revival of Davidic worship in Ezra 3 and Neh. 12, Sanballat and Tobiah might have wanted to stamp out any loyalty to and hope for David's city and house.

[26] Bright 1981: 382; Brown 1998: 60; Hamilton 2014: 114.

or Moses, but he upheld Cyrus' decree to restore proper worship of Yahweh in Jerusalem (Ezra 6:6–12). In their hostility towards the Jews, Sanballat and Tobiah found themselves on the wrong side of Persian (and Yahweh's) policy.

If Sanballat and Tobiah became upset because Nehemiah 'had come to seek the welfare of the people of Israel', the implication is that these men were not upset before Nehemiah's arrival. Perhaps too few Jews were responding positively to Ezra's teaching, and so the post-exilic community as a whole was not trying to advance Yahweh's purpose for their presence back in the Promised Land. Consequently, they 'were no threat to anyone'.[27] Sanballat and Tobiah would be satisfied to let such a state of affairs continue. Indeed, Hanani had given a discouraging report to Nehemiah. If Malachi ministered during the first half of the fifth century, he also addressed people who had lost a healthy combination of eschatological hope and ethical conduct. Having allowed their circumstances to make them sceptical of God's promises, they held back from obeying his commandments. Disregard for God's will, in turn, prevented any modelling of a redeemed community. The Jerusalem to which Nehemiah travelled might still be situated at the crossroads of the ancient world, but it had no mission to those who passed through it.

Before Nehemiah could tell his fellow Jews why he had come, he had to assess the situation in Jerusalem – a place, presumably, he had never been before then. To be sure, the Jews would hesitate to resume work on the wall without evidence of Artaxerxes' approval, but Nehemiah already had this in the form of letters and soldiers. Even with the king's permission, the Jews would not want to get involved in what many of them would consider a newcomer's unnecessary project. A proposal to construct city walls while being harassed by organized opposition would probably sound naive and unattainable. To be prepared for all questions and objections, Nehemiah did his homework under cover of darkness and with only a few assistants. Nehemiah 2:17–18 then summarizes Nehemiah's meeting with the leaders of the Jerusalem Jews. Nehemiah surely offered practical suggestions for doing the project, but these verses do not mention them except for a vague reference to the king's approval. Instead, they focus on the history that brought Nehemiah and the Jerusalem Jews to this moment. Nehemiah's vision for the future starts with his assessment of the past.

---

[27] Dray 2006b: 67.

The history involves 'disgrace' or 'shame' (*ḥerpâ*). Williamson observes that this word 'is heavy with overtones of the punishment of the exile, behind which lies the disrepute brought upon God's name among the nations by those who should have been his servants'.[28] The appearance of this word in exilic contexts cannot be denied, but Nehemiah uses this word with reference to Jews who were most likely born in the Promised Land several decades after Cyrus' edict. While subservience to Persia and the absence of a Davidic king could suggest the continuation of the exile (Ezra 9:9; Neh. 9:36), Cyrus' edict marked the beginning of restoration – what Isaiah 43:19 calls a new thing and what several prophets (including Jeremiah, who is mentioned in Ezra 1:1) describe as a second exodus. The post-exilic community, despite tension between the now and the not yet, legitimately had a fresh start with an open future. When Nehemiah mentioned their shame, he was not talking only about the failures of their pre-exilic ancestors – he had nearly ninety years of post-exilic failures in mind too. Pre-exilic Israelites and post-exilic Jews had both fallen short of being God's servants, God's kingdom of priests, to the nations. There was more than enough shame and blame to go around.

The history also included unlikely events from a human point of view. The book of Ezra–Nehemiah begins with Cyrus' decree that allowed a captive people to return home and rebuild their temple. Local opposition might have succeeded at stopping the reconstruction more than once, but both Darius and Artaxerxes eventually upheld Cyrus' decree. Each of these rulers made Persian funds available for building supplies. Moreover, Artaxerxes sent Ezra to Jerusalem for the purpose of teaching the law of Moses and gave his cupbearer a leave of absence to rebuild the wall. These surprisingly good developments added up to divine providence. Nehemiah, after reminding the Jerusalem Jews of what God had already done, invited them to participate in God's new work. He offered them a mission bigger than themselves, and they accepted.

Of course, Sanballat, Tobiah and eventually Geshem objected by levelling the charge of sedition. Geshem of Arabia to the south apparently did not want a stronger Persian presence in Jerusalem, which was 'closer to home' than Susa.[29] These three adversaries continued to repeat the

---

[28] Williamson 1985: 191.

[29] Ibid. 192. If Sanballat lived in Samaria to the north, then he, along with Tobiah from Ammon to the east and Geshem from Arabia to the south, had Jerusalem surrounded. Neh. 4:7 adds the men of Ashdod to the west.

unfounded accusation of Jewish rebellion. Apparently they believed that telling a lie long enough was an effective way to revise the truth and win support for their cause. Meanwhile, Nehemiah declared his intention to stay the course by starting the work Artaxerxes had approved and leaving the opposition in God's hands.[30] The implication at the end of Nehemiah 2 is that the Jerusalem Jews shared this intention.

The Christian Bible consistently states that God's people, like Nehemiah, can expect to encounter opposition when they do God's work. Jesus assured his followers of the world's hatred (John 15:18–21), and Paul told new converts that they would enter the kingdom of God through many trials (Acts 14:22). He, of course, had his share (2 Cor. 11:23–28). Peter mentioned a fiery trial (1 Peter 4:12), and John saw the souls of believers who had been slain because of their faithfulness to God's Word (Rev. 6:9). God consistently uses hardship of one type or another to mature his people in humility and trust. This function of hardship (otherwise known as discipline) is somewhat understandable because humans typically learn from sustained effort or from trial and error. Even Jesus in his humanity learned obedience by what he suffered (Heb. 5:8). More mysterious is how God uses hardship to advance his plan of redemption not only in the lives of those who suffer but also in the lives of those who observe. In the case of Job, suffering that he never understood was used of God to make him an intercessor for friends (Job 42:8). The obedience Jesus learned became the basis for his atoning sacrifice on behalf of those he came to save (Heb. 5:9). Perhaps Yahweh, similarly, used Nehemiah's experiences with Sanballat, Tobiah and Geshem to bring some of the so-called people of the land to faith. Nehemiah 10:28 (HB 10:29) suggests this possibility.

As mentioned earlier, many people have read the book of Nehemiah as a leadership manual. Ezra–Nehemiah may be more than a leadership manual, but Nehemiah 2 certainly portrays Nehemiah as an effective leader. His initial actions demonstrated that leadership involves dissatisfaction with what is, dreaming of what can be, identifying concrete steps to get from one to the other and refusing to be deterred by challenges. Moreover, Nehemiah did not ride into town and bark out orders. Rather,

---

30 Smelik (2012: 71) says, 'Nehemiah was merely obeying the king's orders and had therefore nothing to fear. The fact that the king's orders and Nehemiah's longing for a rebuilt Jerusalem concurred assured him that he would remain in the king's favour notwithstanding Sanballat's threats.' This observation may be true so far as it goes, but Nehemiah also confessed his confidence in the God of heaven.

he took time to explain his vision to those who would help him to implement it. He identified with them in their situation, offered an informed way to improve it and provided warrant, both theological and political, for the endeavour. The people's readiness to get involved indicates the trust Nehemiah had established in such a short time. They sensed that his passion for this project grew sincerely out of his care for their home town, which was also 'the city of the Great King' (Ps. 48:2). Nehemiah connected them to the God of the past and of the future. Consequently, they were willing to take a risk in order to solve a problem.

Work on the wall begins

Nehemiah 3 records the names of people who worked on the Jerusalem wall. It further specifies where they worked. Many readers may consider this chapter another uninviting section of the book, and perhaps at first glance it is. Even so, the person responsible for the final form of Ezra–Nehemiah considered it valuable for some reason. So also did the Holy Spirit, who led that person to include this chapter in the book. If Paul later wrote in 2 Timothy 3:16 that all Scripture comes from God and so has value for training in righteousness, then Nehemiah 3 has to be more than a tedious, irrelevant list of names. It has something to say to the post-exilic community and to subsequent generations of God's people.

This chapter emphasizes every-member ministry. The high priest's name may appear first in connection with the Sheep Gate, but he hardly receives credit for the rest of the wall. By the time the reader reaches verse 32, the high priest's name has blended with all the other names to give the impression that the whole community (clergy and laity) took part. Something else to note in this regard is the absence of Nehemiah's name. This chapter does not glorify him either. Chapter 2 may credit him with providing the motivation for the project, but chapter 3 focuses on his team. When chapter 4 brings him back into view, Nehemiah writes not with the first-person singular pronoun, as in chapters 1 and 2, but with the first-person plural pronoun.[31] 'We' are in this project together. No one is more important than another – each person contributes to the final result that glorified God.

[31] In her ongoing effort to contrast the arrogance of Nehemiah with the humility of Ezra, Eskenazi (1988a: 82–83) overlooks Nehemiah's choice to speak in first-person plural.

To press this point further, verse 2 says the men of Jericho worked next to the high priest. A man named Zaccur worked next to them and in close proximity to the high priest. Meanwhile, verse 28 says that other priests worked on the Horse Gate, which was located somewhere else. There does not seem to be any concern for status here. The chapter continues to name people who worked next to one another, but no obvious effort is made to group them by any sociological category – as if some builders did not want to 'rub shoulders' with others. It is true that the chapter mentions goldsmiths, perfumers, leaders and merchants. People in these vocations typically have diverse skills and speak their own technical language. All that these references seem to convey, though, is that the builders came from different walks of life and each shared a commitment to a common task. This unity of purpose – this willingness to work for something bigger than self – is not always seen among God's people, but is a major explanation for the completion of this wall in less than two months.

Nehemiah seemed to let people choose where they wanted to work. That the high priest would take an interest in the Sheep Gate seems obvious enough. Verse 17 says that Hashabiah made repairs for his district, and verse 23 says that Benjamin, Hasshub and Azariah worked near their houses. Meanwhile, those priests who worked on the Horse Gate did so because of its proximity to their houses. In other words, some people worked where their heart was, and Nehemiah did not deter such special interests.[32] Stated differently, he did not try to put square pegs in round holes. God has not made his people all the same, undoubtedly because his kingdom requires a variety of skills and interests. His people can serve him in widely diverse ways and still contribute together to the advancement of his kingdom.[33] Meanwhile, many of the people in Nehemiah 3 seem not to have had any attachment to the section of the wall on which they worked. They simply saw a need and lent a hand. This was their way of promoting Nehemiah's project. Of special note at this point is Malchijah who worked on the Dung Gate (v. 14). If he is the same man mentioned in

---

32 Tollefson and Williamson 1992: 51.

33 DePree (1989: 7) says, 'Understanding and accepting diversity enables us to see that each of us is needed. It also enables us to begin to think about being abandoned to [trusting in] the strengths of others, of admitting that we cannot *know* or *do* everything'; emphases original. He adds, 'The simple act of recognizing diversity in corporate life helps us connect the greater variety of gifts that people bring to the work and service of the organization. Diversity allows each of us to contribute in a special way, to make our special gift a part of the corporate effort.' Using the image of a human body, Paul makes a similar argument in 1 Cor. 12.

verse 31, then he made a living as a goldsmith. In other words, he usually handled materials far more valuable, and cleaner, than what passed through the Dung Gate. Nevertheless, he was not too proud to get involved with what was probably the least desirable part of the project.

The same truth applies to God's people today. The work of God's kingdom requires all the skills of God's people. The preachers might have the most visible position, but nothing would get done if everyone else always listened to sermons. God uses people who work with their hands to build or fix. His church needs people who can work with numbers in order to plan and account. Those who can make music or meals contribute in ways everybody else appreciates. Those who fly aeroplanes, manufacture parts, care for the sick, deliver packages, clean up messes, plan cities, decorate interior spaces, publish reading material, fight crime, and much more, all honour God by doing good to others.

As was said earlier about the names in Ezra 2, most if not all of the names in Nehemiah 3 are unfamiliar. Nothing is known about these people except that they rebuilt Jerusalem's wall. In the book of Ezra–Nehemiah, though, the names in Nehemiah 3 merge with the names in Ezra 2 to become co-participants in the implementation of Cyrus' edict. All of the names in Ezra 2 and Nehemiah 3 reconstructed the new Jerusalem and advanced God's plan of redemption centred there. Meanwhile, the New Testament opens with a genealogy that traces the historical trajectory of God's plan from the patriarchs to the monarchy to the post-exilic community to the intertestamental era to Jesus. The name of Jesus is the last name in the combined genealogies of the Christian Bible. Those who believe in him are said to be in Christ. He, in effect, adds their names to the biblical lists of God's people with the result that they become builders of the New Jerusalem that the new Jerusalem anticipated. Whereas the names in Ezra 2 and Nehemiah 3 are largely unfamiliar, so too are the names of those who are in Christ. Few of God's people achieve fame in their lifetime, let alone in later centuries, but each of God's people is used by God to build the New Jerusalem that the post-exilic Jerusalem anticipated. All of their names blend together into a team that works through the centuries to build God's city and house. In fact, the New Testament says that God's people are his city and house (Eph. 2:19–22; Heb. 11:13–16, 39–40; 12:22–24; 1 Peter 2:4–10). The New Jerusalem is a people more than a place.[34]

[34] Gundry 1987: 254–264.

To recall the earlier discussion of biblical theology, the difference between the new Jerusalem and the New Jerusalem resembles a small acorn and an immense oak tree. At first glance, the two do not seem to be related, but in reality the oak tree grows out of the acorn. There is an organic relationship between seed and mature plant. No other type of organism can grow from an acorn. The same is true for the new Jerusalem and the New Jerusalem. If Jerusalem is the place where God resides among his people and the centre from which his message of redemption goes out to the whole world, then the redeeming activity God began in the new Jerusalem leads to the completion of his redeeming activity in the New Jerusalem. The latter grows out of the former. The seed of redemption God sowed in post-exilic Jerusalem (see Ps. 126; Ezek. 17:22–23) germinated throughout the intertestamental era and grew into a spreading shade tree to which Jesus likened the kingdom of God (Matt. 13:31–32; Mark 4:30–32; Luke 13:18–19). Jesus further said that the birds of the air, or the nations of the world, would find rest in this tree. Ezra, Nehemiah and other members of the post-exilic community might not have had a New Testament perspective on this theme of growth, but Zechariah had already spoken about a day of small beginnings (Zech. 4:10). Moreover, Haggai had promised that the glory of the post-exilic temple would exceed that of Solomon's temple. The post-exilic Jews had enough revelation to know that their work was part of a bigger project of God's. This project had nothing less than the redemptive blessing of the whole world in view.

The same truth, of course, applies to God's people in other times and places. If Hebrews 11 says that Old Testament saints will enter the city of God with New Testament saints, the implication is that no one has yet seen the finished result. Until the second coming of Jesus, all of God's people serve God in faith. Living between the beginning and completion of God's programme for history, God's people may sometimes think, because of favourable circumstances, that the consummation of God's programme is 'just around the corner'. At other times, though, the end may not be anywhere in sight. It is encouraging to know that every generation of God's people is part of a much larger workforce. No generation does all the work alone, and no local setback can stop the progress on God's city. Therefore, members of every generation can persevere with confidence because God will redeem the labour of their hands.

Something else to notice, though, is the candour in Nehemiah 3:5. While many of the residents of Tekoa repaired one section of the wall and then went to work on another (Neh. 3:27), other residents of that town chose not to participate. The stated reason can be understood in more than one way. The Hebrew text says, literally, 'Next to them [the men mentioned in v. 4], the men of Tekoa strengthened [repaired or restored], but their nobles did not bring their neck in service of their lords [supervisors or Lord].' Evidently the leading citizens of Tekoa were not enthusiastic about rebuilding the wall around Jerusalem. Perhaps they considered manual labour beneath their social standing and so refused to lend a hand. Or maybe they did not want to take orders from social inferiors who were acting as foremen for this project. Or maybe they had no interest in volunteering their time and labour for God. Or maybe they did not like Nehemiah. Or maybe they did not like Artaxerxes, whom Nehemiah represented. Or maybe they thought that a wall would send the wrong message to the people of the land. Various English translations favour each of these possibilities.[35] Whatever the Hebrew text intends to say, Nehemiah was trying to mobilize God's people to perform God's mission, but some of them were not cooperating. God's kingdom advances whenever his people 'roll up their sleeves', work as a team and do whatever needs to be done in order to improve a less-than-ideal, even messy, situation. Without this mindset, the status quo tends to prevail, and little progress occurs.

Jesus, of course, prayed that his disciples would be perfectly one (John 17:23). Anyone familiar with church history knows that this prayer has gone unanswered in any universal or enduring sense. Too often, where two or three people gather in Jesus' name, there is disagreement. How, ultimately, God will answer Jesus' prayer for unity remains a mystery, but the overall message of Nehemiah 3 need not be spoiled by the information in verse 5. A majority of the Jerusalem Jews rallied around Nehemiah and worked together on the wall. Despite dissension and threats, they finished the job in a remarkably short amount of time. Observers even concluded that God must have aided the builders (Neh. 6:16). While Ezra–Nehemiah does not say how God was involved, readers of this book should be encouraged in their service to God. Troubles come and go, but the work of God's kingdom continues throughout the generations.

[35] Kidner 1979: 87; Fensham 1982: 174; Williamson 1985: 204; Holmgren 1987: 103–104; Brown 1998: 67.

Opposition from without

One of the verses to the hymn 'Amazing Grace' says, 'Through many dangers, toils and snares, I have already come.' If those who built the wall in Nehemiah 4 and 6 had sung this hymn, they might have thought that John Newton wrote these words about them. Both chapters feature the toil of building a city wall. Whereas chapter 4 emphasizes the danger for the whole crew, chapter 6 describes the snare set for Nehemiah. Meanwhile, chapter 5 mentions another threat: internal oppression. Each of these problems jeopardized the third stage of implementing Cyrus' decree.

When Sanballat and Tobiah first heard Nehemiah's explanation of the purpose of his visit, they falsely accused Nehemiah of rebelling against the king (Neh. 2:19). This tactic, of course, could not succeed because Nehemiah had arrived with an armed Persian guard and letters from the king. There were no greater means of authentication. Shortly thereafter, Sanballat and Tobiah learned that construction had begun, and they adopted a different approach: ridicule (Neh. 4:2–3). When that did not succeed, they tried intimidation (Neh. 4:8) and murderous threat (Neh. 4:11). All three ploys, especially the third, represented a challenge to the king's clear order that Nehemiah, the king's cupbearer, had in hand.[36] Readers of Ezra–Nehemiah will never know if Sanballat and Tobiah would have resorted to killing. They might have intended their rhetoric only to arouse fear and hesitation. Coupled with the exhausting work on the wall (Neh. 4:10), this outside pressure had the potential to cripple the labourers with doubt and discouragement. In fact, Nehemiah 4:10 indicates that the builders began to feel overwhelmed by the magnitude of the task. Meanwhile, friends and family feared for the builders' safety (if not their own) and advised them to come home (Neh. 4:12).

In response to the ridicule, admirably, Nehemiah chose not to counter in public with inflammatory language of his own. Such verbal warfare would have escalated the situation and potentially incited Sanballat and Tobiah to physical violence. Instead, Nehemiah reserved strong words for God in prayer. He asked God not only to do to Sanballat and Tobiah what they wanted to do to God's people but also to withhold forgiveness of their

[36] Readers cannot help but wonder what happened to the armed guard that accompanied Nehemiah to Jerusalem. Neh. 4 never mentions it, but its continuing presence would surely have silenced Sanballat and Tobiah.

sins. Verses 4 and 5 may offend some Christians, who think, on the basis of verses such as Matthew 5:44 and Romans 12:17, that Nehemiah should have prayed for rather than against his enemies.[37] Perhaps, but there is another way of understanding Nehemiah's imprecation.[38]

As in the Psalms, the enemies in Ezra–Nehemiah are God's enemies, who threaten God's mission on earth (Neh. 2:8, 18).[39] It is proper to ask God to eliminate all threats to his mission, which is to establish his righteous kingdom and king. Ultimately, righteousness cannot prevail as long as systemic and organized rebellion exists. The imprecations in the prayers of the psalmist and of Nehemiah are a plea for justice and a cry for help in the face of evil. A desire for justice is hardly wrong or less than Christian. In fact, justice is one of the highest aims in the Bible because justice reflects the character of God. Wanting justice means wanting the full manifestation of God's righteous rule over his world. Imprecations express an awareness that God's world is not yet the righteous way it should be. They inform God of an intolerable situation – one that dishonours him – and call him to act for his honour.[40] In so doing, imprecations also show sensitivity to unjust suffering. Again, it is not wrong or less than Christian to want relief for the oppressed (Prov. 31:9) about whom a righteous God says he cares (Pss 9:9; 10:17–18; 103:6; 146:7). For such relief to happen, though, the oppressor usually has to be removed. Because the one being oppressed is rarely in a position to do that, a prayer for justice goes up to God.

A desire for justice in an unjust situation may be appropriate, but humans cannot always be trusted with restoring justice. Either they

---

37 Kidner 1979: 91; Williamson 1985: 218; Throntveit 1992: 81–82; Packer 1995: 103–104. People who appeal to the supposedly higher ethic of the NT seem to forget about the cry of the martyrs in Rev. 6:10. The martyrs do not feel the insecurity Williamson attributes to Nehemiah.

38 Wijk-Bos 1998: 59–60; Mariottini 2015: 162.

39 Consider the following verses in the book of Psalms: 3:7; 10:15; 17:13; 18:37–42; 28:4–5; 31:17–18; 35:4–8; 41:10–11; 52:5; 56:7; 58:6–12; 59:5; 69:22–28; 70:2–3; 71:13; 74:11; 79:6, 12; 83:9–17; 94:1–2, 22–23; 109:6–15; 137:7–9; 139:19–22; 140:9–11; 143:12; 149:6–9. The point is that the book of Psalms contains not just one or two unfortunate imprecations. Expressions of violence and retribution permeate the laments.

40 Brown (1998: 75) says, 'Nehemiah prayed *realistically*. It would be a mistake to dismiss his vehement prayer as an expression of uncontrolled human indignation. He regards their insults as an offense against God, which indeed they are. They have ridiculed a venture which God inspired and planned. They have not merely reviled God's servants; they have abused God's Name. In calling upon God so passionately, Nehemiah is asking God not to vindicate but to authenticate his truth in the presence of such irreverent and insulting opponents. When God's honour is at stake, it is natural that a man as surrendered and devoted as Nehemiah should be incensed'; emphasis original.

cannot control their anger or an unjust situation has too many variables with too long a history to set right. Imprecatory prayers allow God's people to submit the desire for justice to God.[41] He can be trusted to do what is right with each of the variables. Giving one's rage to God releases the praying person from pettiness and violence, with the result that a legitimate desire is handled in the proper way. In contrast to humans, God can be vengeful in a righteous manner (Deut. 32:35–36; Rom. 12:19). He never loses control of his emotions or overreacts to a situation.

So then, those, such as Nehemiah, who include imprecations in their prayers hold God responsible for his world. Imprecations arise from a conviction that God's justice must prevail, and express a longing that evil conduct and evil people will not have the last word in history. That longing is founded on God's ownership of the world. Evil should not prevail in the world of a righteous God. At the same time, imprecations give the final say to God. The one who prays the imprecations surrenders his or her will to the will of God. He or she acknowledges God's right to judge when and how he sees fit. There are two ways God can answer an imprecatory prayer and eliminate his enemies. The first is conversion, and the second is judgment.[42] Whether the enemies of God and his people repent or not lies beyond the control of the one praying for justice. Even so, Nehemiah's prayers here and elsewhere demonstrate how God's people can fight the good fight against the spiritual forces of evil while maintaining a clear conscience (Eph. 6:12; 1 Tim. 1:18–19).

It is true that God's people should return kindness for unkindness (Exod. 23:4–5; Prov. 25:21–22; Rom. 12:20–21). Nehemiah might not have returned kindness, but he did not retaliate either. His prayer that called for vengeance did not become his deed of vengeance. Instead, Nehemiah stuck to the task that his human boss, Artaxerxes, had given him. As the king's representative, Nehemiah had the responsibility of protecting the empire's resources that had been made available for the project. Once back in Susa, he would have to give an account of his activity in Judea. In other words, Nehemiah had to balance his loyalty to two kingdoms: the eternal kingdom of Yahweh and the temporal kingdom of the Persian

---

[41] Brown (ibid. 74) says, 'Moreover, if fierce anger needs to be released it is far better expressed in prayer than in uncontrolled bitterness toward others.'

[42] Packer 1995: 103; Hamilton 2014: 116.

Empire. In this instance, both kingdoms wanted a finished wall. To complete this task in the face of a serious threat, Nehemiah prayed to God and posted armed guards (Neh. 4:9). Later he armed everyone and devised a warning system (Neh. 4:18–20). He further motivated his crew with the assurance of God's protection (Neh. 4:14, 20) and with their concern for their families' safety (Neh. 4:14). It is hard not to conclude that Nehemiah had a proper understanding of the intersection of the celestial and terrestrial realms. God had his role to play, and the builders had theirs. In the providence of God (Neh. 4:15) and because of Nehemiah's resourcefulness, the human workers were able to do their job without interruption or bloodshed. Both Yahweh and Artaxerxes should have been pleased.

Not to be overlooked is that Nehemiah, like Haggai earlier (Hag. 2:4), encouraged his team of volunteers to work because Yahweh was with them. More specifically, he said Yahweh would fight for them (Neh. 4:20). Both men made the same point; namely, that the covenantal God of the Jews would bless their effort at rebuilding. Of course, God, similarly, had been with Moses (Exod. 3:12), Joshua (Josh. 1:5), Gideon (Judg. 6:16), David (2 Sam. 5:10), Abijah (2 Chr. 13:12), Jehoshaphat (2 Chr. 20:17) and Hezekiah (2 Chr. 32:8). The point for readers of Nehemiah 4 is that God is faithful. He consistently accompanies his people in their service for him. Down through the centuries he has called them to perform tasks on behalf of his redemptive programme and given them the necessary resources. They may do the work, but God does not expect them to labour alone. He reliably, though mysteriously, works behind the scenes to support their effort and incorporate it into his overarching plan. Believing that God acts among his people offers motivation to get started and keep going with ministry.

Trouble from within

Nehemiah's quick thinking in chapter 4 might have enabled the builders to do their work without being interrupted by Sanballat, Tobiah and Geshem, but Nehemiah 5 presents another hindrance to the project: economic hardship among the workers. This distraction seems to have arisen among the Jews independently of the machinations of Sanballat and his cronies. Economic concerns jeopardized not only Nehemiah's mission to build the wall but also the community's mission to model a redeemed lifestyle.[43] What comes to Nehemiah's attention in Nehemiah 5 is more of the trouble and shame Hanani had mentioned.

Because of danger, Nehemiah expected the workers to stay in Jerusalem (Neh. 4:22) for safety. Nehemiah 5:17–18 indicatesthat he provided food for them. While in town, though, they could not tend their fields or work for wages in somebody else's field.[44] Moreover, verse 3 refers to a famine that had caused a food shortage and driven up prices. The famine might have arisen or worsened because of too much attention being paid to the wall and too little to the crops. As a result, some of the builders needed money for their families. Meanwhile, other builders complained about Persia's taxes (Neh. 5:4), which must have put Nehemiah, a Jewish servant of Artaxerxes, in a difficult situation. To get money, they had to take out loans, mortgage land or sell children into slavery. Those who borrowed money risked falling prey to usury. Certain returnees (or descendants of returnees) took advantage of their fellow returnees by charging interest on loans and seizing property from those who defaulted on their loans. Meanwhile, those struggling for economic survival had less time to work on the wall and carry out Cyrus' (and Artaxerxes') decree. Nerves frayed and tempers flared.

Regarding the threat to the community's mission, Nehemiah quickly recognized how internal conflict undermined the Jews' witness to a watching world. In verse 8, he points out how, ironically, Jews who were formerly slaves to Gentiles in Babylon were now slaves to Jews in Judah. In verse 9, he makes the missional application. When those who claim to fear God mistreat each other, outsiders get the wrong message that redeemed people in covenant with Yahweh are no different from anyone else.[45] If God's people lack compassion and if making money by any means takes precedence over love for neighbour, then God's people have nothing to offer outsiders who already live under the other golden rule: whoever has the gold makes the rules.[46] Nehemiah agreed with the outsiders who

---

[43] For a summary of approaches to Neh. 5, see Williams 2002: 57–74. None of the approaches seem to relate Neh. 5 to mission.

[44] Neh. 6:15 says the wall was finished on 25 Elul (2 October 445 BC). Work on the wall began fifty-two days earlier on 4 Ab (12 August 445 BC). Grapes, figs and olives would have ripened during these weeks (Steinmann 2010: 445).

[45] Holmgren 1987: 111; Packer 1995: 121.

[46] Brown 1998: 93–94. Summers (2011: 184) looks at the oppression from an insider's (Jewish) point of view. He says, 'Nehemiah is concerned with the defense of the community against future enemies, and so wants to rebuild the wall around Jerusalem. He is also aware that the defense of the community clearly involves internal values. If the city is a place of

pointed out the hypocrisy and therefore the shame of God's people. Realizing that he and others had presented an inconsistent witness, Nehemiah called for repentance. The builders must live together according to the law of Moses that Ezra had been teaching. That law instructed an already redeemed people how to live as a kingdom of priests and so be a channel of redemptive blessing to the rest of the world. The silence of the listeners in verse 8 was evidence of their conviction: they had forgotten their mission as God's people.

More specifically, Nehemiah appealed to the well-off residents of the post-exilic community to live by what amounted to jubilee theology and immediately return property and payments to their poorer yet rightful owners.[47] The Year of Jubilee, as explained in Leviticus 25, was supposed to happen every fifty years in Israel. For forty-nine years, the Israelites could buy and sell. If bad harvests or poor choices caused a landowner (and every family unit had a patrimony or share of the Promised Land) to suffer an unforeseen setback and become economically distressed, he could mortgage his land until the Year of Jubilee, which would then cancel all remaining debt and return all property to its rightful heir. The Year of Jubilee reminded the Israelites that Yahweh owned the land and gave it to his people for an inheritance. The Israelites were supposed to use their inheritance to live out their covenantal relationship with Yahweh and each other, thereby presenting a distinct witness to the surrounding nations. In other words, the land was the stage on which the Israelites modelled a redeemed community.[48] In Nehemiah 5, Nehemiah realized that he and some of his fellow Jews were hindering some Jews from contributing to

---

exploitation and enslavement of the poor, then there is not much to defend – before God or the enemy.' By mentioning the taunts of the outsiders (their perception of hypocrisy) Nehemiah showed concern not just for defence but also mission (offence). What Summers says appreciably moves in this direction, 'The defense of the community [and of the temple's sanctity] includes the willingness to make all welcome, to offer an opportunity for all to enjoy the blessings of God. Nehemiah is a leader who wants the system to honor God's intentions, and for the community to reflect goodness to the glory of God' (185).

47 Bergsma (2007: 205) says, 'Nehemiah's reform resembles an impromptu proclamation of jubilee, but the jubilee legislation is never mentioned by the text.' He adds that 'the jubilee was the socio-economic expression of the Day of Atonement . . . Just as the Day of Atonement re-establishes wholeness in the cultic and spiritual realm, the jubilee re-establishes it in the social and economic realms' (227). See also Blenkinsopp 1988: 259; Adams 2014: 78–79.

48 McConville (1985: 100) says, 'The brotherhood within Israel is meant to be a showpiece, a model of the potential human society. The nations should look at Israel and see a people harmonious, prosperous and content, and organized so as to be so rather than for the aggrandizement of the few. Israel was to be a radical challenge to the nations, a specimen of love.'

God's mission for his people. To correct this problem, Nehemiah ordered the immediate return of all property and the forgiveness of all loans.

The creditors were to do this out of fear of God and as a witness to the Gentiles. For God's people, fear of God begins with knowledge of his revealed will (Deut. 4:10; Ps. 19:9; Prov. 2:1–6) and then moves to obeying his commands (Deut. 10:12–13; Prov. 3:7). Such obedience, which in the case of debt forgiveness may be countercultural and seem imprudently disadvantageous to one's portfolio, could proceed only from a heart that submitted to God's authority and trusted him to make good on his promises (Deut. 8:7–9; Prov. 15:33; 22:4). God's will, of course, includes treating the less fortunate as graciously as God has treated the redeemed (Lev. 25:35–46; Deut. 15:1–15). One way God's people were supposed to act like God towards one another was the periodic forgiveness of debts for the sake of the communal mission. Although the Old Testament never records the observance of a Year of Jubilee, Nehemiah 5 presents Nehemiah's effort to implement jubilee theology at a moment's notice. He realized that economic callousness by some Jews and economic ruin for other Jews threatened his mission, which in the book of Ezra–Nehemiah constitutes the third stage of implementing Cyrus' decree. This decree was used by Yahweh to advance his redemptive programme after the exile (Ezra 1:1; Isa. 44:24 – 45:7).

Nehemiah 5:12 records the compliance of the creditors. Such compassion towards compatriots in distress would also present a distinct picture of a redeemed community to those observing on the outside. They would see how faith in a covenant-making and covenant-keeping God made a practical difference in daily living. Nehemiah did not forget that those who worked on the wall with him were part of a kingdom of priests to the nations. How they treated one another had as much to do with this mission as carrying out Cyrus' decree. Later Nehemiah 10:31 reports that the post-exilic community, after confessing their history of unfaithfulness, included the observance of sabbatical years among their concrete steps of repentance. Perhaps they also intended to set aside the fiftieth year for a jubilee, but the text is more suggestive than explicit on this matter.[49]

Nehemiah's solution to economic oppression had a precedent in the Pentateuch's provision of jubilee. How much of this jubilee theology

---

[49] Neh. 10:31 mentions debt relief, which was a provision of the Year of Jubilee but not of sabbath years.

affected Nehemiah's decision in Nehemiah 5 is hard to establish, but it seems unlikely that Nehemiah would be ignorant of Israel's story taught by Ezra and the Levites in Nehemiah 8 and then reviewed in the corporate prayer of confession in Nehemiah 9.[50] In fact, Nehemiah's own prayer of confession in Nehemiah 1:5–11 indicates familiarity with that story. Nehemiah understood that love of God entails love of neighbour and that true religion includes justice and compassion.[51] Moreover, Nehemiah was aware of the watching world (Neh. 5:9). The surrounding nations would not be attracted to Israel's God if the people of this God took advantage of one another.[52] This concern for mission explains Nehemiah's unselfish approach to leadership in Nehemiah 5:14–19.[53] During his twelve-year tenure as governor of Judea (Neh. 5:14), he used personal resources, rather than additional taxes, to cover his expenses. If the purpose of the wall was to protect the sanctity of the temple, then love of God at the temple on the sabbath had to lead to love of neighbour in the city during the rest of the week (Isa. 1:10–17). As a holy nation (Exod. 19:6), the Israelites before the exile and the Jews after were supposed to present a distinct witness to the nations. That witness was seen largely in the way they did business with each other and with outsiders. For members of a kingdom of priests, people must come before profit. Fairness, compassion and self-denial should be the bottom line in a redeemed community.

---

50 For Nehemiah's interaction with the Pentateuch, see Berman 2015: 108–110.

51 The NT agrees. See e.g. Matt. 22:36–39; Acts 6:1–6; 1 Tim. 6:6–19; Jas 1:19; 2:14–17; 1 John 3:16–18.

52 Brown (1998: 93) asks, 'If their pagan neighbours saw them behaving cruelly towards their own people, how could they possibly be persuaded of the uniqueness and reality of Israel's distinctive faith? Who would believe that Israel's God was kind, merciful and compassionate when his worshipers were cruel, merciless and mean towards the people he loves?' Dray (2006b: 67) adds, '*A people whose conduct is likely to drive some of its members away and to lead to unbelievers ridiculing its hypocrisy is hardly likely to display God's glory to a needy world*'; emphasis original.

53 Interacting with the writings of Pierre Bourdieu, Laird (2016: 240–244) doubts the purity of Nehemiah's motive. Allegedly Nehemiah pretended to be concerned about the welfare of the whole community but made policy that, in reality and by sinister design, increased his power as leader over oppressors and their victims. In other words, Nehemiah used a crisis for his advantage. The most Laird (2016: 238) can say about Neh. 5:9 is that 'it puts forward other motivations for ceasing these [economically oppressive] actions: "the fear of our God, to prevent the taunts . . . of the nations of our enemies"'. She does not elaborate on the missional intention of these other motivations. Perhaps, though, Nehemiah was sincere. Regarding Nehemiah's prayer of confession in Neh. 1, Laird (2016: 266) says, 'This prayer, on the lips of Nehemiah, adds a level of legitimacy to his actions that later editors [and interpreters] might have felt was absent without the confession.'

First Peter 2 applies this lesson to Christians. Verses 9–10 recall Exodus 19:6 and refer to believers in Jesus as a royal priesthood that has a mission of bearing witness to God's mercy by means of praise. This mercy has rescued believers from darkness (a metaphor for a broken relationship with God because of human sin) and brought them into light (a metaphor for a restored relationship because of God's initiative). Verses 11–12, though, indicate that the verbal witness must be accompanied by behavioural witness. Those who praise God for redeeming them and making them part of his family must act like members of the family. They should avoid conduct contrary to God's character and, instead, live according to his revealed will (righteously). There must be consistency between what is said about divine goodness and what is done in response to it. Otherwise, actions betray words, and the witness is hypocritical and hollow. Like Nehemiah and other members of the post-exilic community, Christians may incur criticism for their 'unusual' lifestyle. They may feel like strangers in God's world, even as Nehemiah and other Jews were unwanted in Judea, which had been part of the Promised Land. Nevertheless, post-exilic Judea and even the whole world belong to God, who is giving his people an inheritance.[54] As God's people show the family resemblance now in adversarial circumstances, they have assurance that God will prevail in the end and thereby vindicate them. The enemies of God and his people will, ultimately, glorify him by receiving appropriate recompense: either judgment for persistent hostility or mercy for eventual repentance.

Personal threat

Nehemiah 6:15 reports that Nehemiah and his crew finished the wall in less than two months: in fifty-two days to be exact. This notice stands out simply because of the magnitude of the project. A group of people who did not make their living at construction accomplished an incredible feat. If nothing else about the situation were known, those who heard about the completion of the wall could wonder how it happened so fast and think that supernatural aid must have been involved. Of course, the builders did not work in unimpeded isolation, and it is the rest of the story that brings even greater glory to Yahweh: he blessed their effort in the midst of danger.

[54] See Josh. 1:6; Heb. 4:8–10; 1 Peter 1:3–4. Canaan was a down payment on the much larger inheritance God has in store for his people.

In addition to the problems mentioned in chapters 4 and 5, chapter 6 adds a vendetta against Nehemiah to the list of challenges that surfaced during those days. Not surprisingly, Sanballat, Tobiah and Geshem were the source. They vaguely invited Nehemiah to meet them at a plain, which would be an out-of-the-way location. When Nehemiah refused because of concern for his safety and commitment to the wall's progress, the conniving triumvirate resorted to another false charge of rebellion and even alleged that Nehemiah wanted to become king. When this tactic failed, they enlisted the help of someone named Shemaiah, who encouraged Nehemiah to hide in the temple, but a layman such as Nehemiah could not go where only the priests entered. Otherwise, he would violate God's presence and be struck down. It seems as if Nehemiah wanted to trust this man as a true prophet and then learned that he, along with others, was a tool of God's enemies (Neh. 6:14). Nehemiah 6:18 also mentions the daughter of Meshullam son of Berekiah. Meshullam was not only one of the builders (Neh. 3:4) but also the father-in-law of Tobiah's son (Neh. 6:18). Apparently Meshullam tried to act as a conciliator between Nehemiah and Tobiah. Because the text does not explain Meshullam's motive, the reader is left in the same position as Nehemiah: unsure of how trustworthy Meshullam or anyone else was. What Nehemiah knew for sure was that Tobiah had personal and commercial relationships with influential members of the post-exilic community and that he used those contacts to his advantage. If people were talking to Tobiah, then Nehemiah had to be careful about what he said to anyone. In the midst of all this scheming, though, Nehemiah and the builders ignored the chatter and did what Artaxerxes had authorized.

Dray says, '*Those in Christian leadership know that spiritual warfare always rages most fiercely around the standard bearer.*'[55] That may be, but a Christian does not have to be highly visible to encounter resistance. Even a person who works quietly behind the scenes can meet with criticism. If someone does not object in principle to what a Christian does, that person may disagree with how the Christian wants to do it. So then, it is not just pastors who are criticized in churches. Anyone who tries to make a contribution can meet with complaints. Nehemiah (whether the book or the man) does not explain how to eliminate conflict or intrigue. Both happen regularly among God's people. Instead, Nehemiah the man modelled perseverance. He stayed true to his mission, did his work with as much

55 Dray 2006b: 68; emphasis original.

integrity and grace as he could and gave the results to God.[56] In the midst of opinions and opposition, God made his presence known (Neh. 6:16). People saw the evidence of his involvement in the completed wall. Whether they liked what they saw is not the issue. Mission happens when the nations learn who Yahweh is and what he has done. God is glorified when he opens mouths to praise or shuts them to stew. Either way, he appears great and awesome (Neh. 1:5).

Like Nehemiah's imprecation in Nehemiah 4:4–5, the prayer in Nehemiah 6:14 may offend certain people (Christians or otherwise) who have learned from the Sermon on the Mount that followers of Jesus should turn the other cheek (Matt. 5:39). In fact, Nehemiah did turn the other check when he did not respond in kind to his enemies. He never escalated the conflict by resorting to their tactics. In other words, he never retaliated by trying to kill them. At the same time, Nehemiah displayed the wisdom or shrewdness of a serpent (Matt. 10:16). He was not naive or gullible. He knew the intention of Sanballat, Tobiah and Geshem. Because they were never going to change, dialogue was futile and trust was out of the question. So then, Nehemiah talked to God and persevered at doing what God (and Artaxerxes) had told him to do. Nothing could be more righteous than asking God to eliminate threats to the advancement of his kingdom and then going about advancing his kingdom according to his revealed will.

For all the saints

At the end of Nehemiah 6, Jerusalem has a completed wall around it, but few residents within it (Neh. 7:4). Even though the first wave of exiles had returned about ninety years earlier, Jerusalem remained something of a ghost town. As such, it was a dangerous place. Moreover, the concluding verses of Nehemiah 6 indicate that Tobiah had strong ties with Jews in the Jerusalem area. Nehemiah clearly did not trust these people to leave Jerusalem alone. Consequently, he posted gatekeepers at the entrances and guards in other strategic locations. These defensive measures would suffice for a while, but they would not be adequate by themselves for long.[57]

---

56 Packer 1995: 131.

57 Steinmann (2010: 498) observes, 'Merely having a wall around the city is not sufficient to make it either secure or prosperous. It needs an adequate population that can mount a defense of the city as well as ensure a thriving economy.' See also Bright 1981: 383; Frevel and Conczorowski 2011: 18.

Jerusalem needed residents who shared the mission of Ezra, Nehemiah and even Artaxerxes. That mission would receive reinforcement from the singers, who led worship, and the Levites, who taught God's Word.[58]

In Nehemiah 7, Nehemiah starts to identify those people by making use of what he calls a book of the genealogy. That book was a copy of the list of names in Ezra 2, which told Nehemiah which Jews had moved back to Judea. Many of their descendants would still be living near Jerusalem. Perhaps some of them had kept their distance from Tobiah because they remembered that their ancestors had returned to the Promised Land as part of a second exodus. Maybe they wanted to be part of the new thing in Isaiah 43:19 or the day of small things in Zechariah 4:10. If so, they would be good candidates for moving into Jerusalem. The occupancy of Jerusalem occurs in Nehemiah 11. Until then, Ezra and Nehemiah had to prepare a holy people to live in a holy city. It is one thing to do a project in less than two months. It is another to engage in service for a lifetime. The new Jerusalem needed the latter level of commitment. How often God's people become engrossed in some major project (such as a building programme or outreach effort) and then suffer a let-down or anticlimax at its 'completion'. Short-term commitment may achieve some positive results, but enduring commitment is needed to sustain progress.

The list of names in Ezra 2 established continuity between post-exilic Jews and pre-exilic Israelites. Like the genealogies in 1 Chronicles 1 – 9, Ezra 2 assured early members of the post-exilic community that they were the heirs of God's promises to Abraham, Moses and David. The exile had not terminated those promises or cut off post-exilic Jews from Yahweh. God still cared about them, and their effort to implement Cyrus' decree contributed to God's plan to have a people for his name. A rebuilt temple symbolized Yahweh's continuing intention to live among his people and bless the world through them (Gen. 12:3; Zech. 2:10–11). The repetition of Ezra 2 in Nehemiah 7 reinforced this continuity for later members of the post-exilic community. Despite challenges, those Jews who finished the wall and later moved into Jerusalem were advancing the mission of Yahweh. They were contributing to something bigger than their personal survival, and had God's approval.

---

[58] Brown (1998: 116) says, 'Nehemiah's appointment of *the gatekeepers and the singers and the Levites* testified to the governor's priorities for body, spirit, and mind. The people needed physical and moral protection, inspiring worship and effective teaching'; emphasis original.

The list of names in Ezra 2 and Nehemiah 7 establishes membership in Yahweh's covenantal community. Those who could not prove their descent (Neh. 7:61, 64) were denied access until they could. The point is that the new Jerusalem was supposed to be home to those who worshipped Yahweh according to the law of Moses that Ezra was teaching. Along with Ezra, Nehemiah was determined to avoid the mistakes and shame of the past. In Nehemiah 8, both Ezra and Nehemiah work together to teach the law of Moses to those who worship at the temple inside the walls.[59] It is their contribution to the realization of Isaiah 2:3 that combines orthodoxy and orthopraxy on the one hand with mission on the other.

Summary

At the end of Nehemiah 6, the post-exilic community has executed Cyrus' decree. The house of Yahweh is ready to be the centre of Jewish religion. Ezra's teaching and Nehemiah's wall, seemingly, should prevent the mistakes of the past. The present situation offers a reason to be optimistic about the Jews' future. Even so, the enemies of the Jews are still alive, and the potential for something to go wrong still exists.

59 Packer (1995: xxvii) says, 'Nehemiah through God built walls; God through Nehemiah built saints.'

7
Reformed and reforming

With the exception of Nehemiah 3, which lists the builders of the wall, Nehemiah speaks in the first person (both singular and plural) in Nehemiah 1:1 – 7:73a. These chapters are often called his memoir. Nehemiah, however, does not speak in Nehemiah 7:73b – 12:26, which refers to him only three times, in the third person (Neh. 8:9; 10:1; 12:26). This section focuses on community renewal by means of reading Scripture, confessing sin, changing behaviour (repenting) and populating Jerusalem. Ezra comes back into view, especially for the reading of Scripture. First-person narrative resumes in Nehemiah 12:31 for the dedication of the wall. Nehemiah is the likely but unnamed speaker.

Nehemiah 7:73b – 13:31 is the third section of Ezra–Nehemiah. While Cyrus' edict has been fully implemented, what Artaxerxes commissioned Ezra to do remained unfinished. Ezra was supposed to teach the law of his God (Ezra 7:25) – a task that never really ends. Both the current generation and generations to come needed instruction about how to apply previous revelation to ever-changing times. More specifically, a holy city (Neh. 11:1) with a protective wall still needed holy people within that wall. People become holy by studying God's Word (Neh. 8), confessing their sin (Neh. 9) and obeying God's commandments (Neh. 10). With its emphasis on the law of Moses, Ezra–Nehemiah does not arouse expectation of continuing revelation. A written text is sufficient to unite the members of the post-exilic community and govern their life together before God. So then, Nehemiah 7:73b – 12:47 describes a society of saints founded on the Word of God. It lives in God's city with the temple at the centre. This holy society, though, is far from utopian.

Scripture

With the infrastructure (temple and wall) in place, Ezra the scholarly priest comes back into view.[1] Ezra began reading the law of Moses on the first day of the seventh month, which was a little more than a month after the completion of the wall (Neh. 6:15). He read for several hours and paused occasionally so that he and the Levites could translate and/or explain the sections of the law. Williamson observes, 'There was to be no place here for a purely liturgical reading that could wash over the consciousness of the congregation.'[2] Both Ezra and the Levites helped the post-exilic listeners to understand how older revelation that might initially have sounded irrelevant applied to a new situation. Without that explanation, the listeners might not have been convicted of their need to make some changes. How much more today do God's people, who are so removed from the ancient world, need assistance with understanding what the biblical text meant to its original recipients and what it means for the contemporary world?

Meanwhile, the body language of the listeners (raising hands, shouting 'Amen' and bowing heads) indicated their eagerness to hear and do what God, Ezra and the Levites had to say. The law of Moses, of course, recounted the history of God's relationship with Abraham's descendants: how God initiated the relationship, how God expected Abraham and his descendants to respond, and how Abraham's descendants struggled to be a blessing to the nations.[3] Just as importantly, the law indicated how a wayward people might go in the right direction.[4] According to verse 9, God's Word caused the listeners to mourn and weep. There was poignant awareness of missed opportunities to act like the people of God and like a kingdom of priests. God's people had not fully performed their mission before the exile or since. Although the original purpose of a section such as Exodus 19 – 23 was to tell an already redeemed people how to live as

---

[1] Wijk-Bos (1998: 71) says, 'Ezra comes back into the picture because his guidance is significant in relation to the law rather than to building programs.'

[2] Williamson 1985: 298; see also 291.

[3] *Tôrâ*, the Hebrew word often translated as 'law', can also mean 'instruction' or 'guidance'.

[4] E.g. the book of Numbers tells the story of two generations. The first generation came out of Egypt, disobeyed Moses and died in the wilderness (Num. 1 – 25). The second generation was born in the wilderness, learned from its parents' mistakes and eventually entered the Promised Land (Num. 26 – 36 and Joshua). See Deut. 1 – 4 for a similar historical review. Deut. 5 – 26 then focuses on a godly lifestyle.

such, what Ezra's listeners knew about the intervening centuries readily convinced these post-exilic Jews that their history was characterized by repeated failure to do what God wanted.[5] Their tears were proof of genuine remorse.

Even so, the leaders told the people to rejoice instead of weep. The order may seem upside down to certain Christians, who are so aware of their unrighteousness that they wallow in their unworthiness. They dare not think that they are anything else but wretched, miserable sinners. Meanwhile, other Christians are so prone to disappointment and depression that they keep rehashing the past, often using the words 'could have', 'should have' and 'would have'. They wish they could turn back time and make different choices. Unable to do so, they feel trapped in a prison of their own making. Before such people can properly address their sin and make changes, they need encouragement. They need to hear that God has already entered the human realm (their world) to introduce redemption. God can forgive and wants to forgive. He can renew and wants to renew. Because an open future is possible with God, people do not have to hang their heads in shame and despair. God is compassionate. That is a reason to be encouraged even at the moment of becoming aware of guilt.[6]

In Nehemiah 8:10, Ezra says the joy of Yahweh is the strength of his people. That joy then takes the form of fine dining and generous sharing. Biblical joy begins with remembering and celebrating God's goodness to undeserving people – what is often called 'grace'. God's Word (whether the five books of Moses or any other portion of the Jewish and Christian Bibles) emphasizes what he has done and what he will yet do to have a people for his name. God must take the initiative to save his people and conform them to his likeness. They are not able to do this for themselves. Even so, God does not give up on those whom he chooses to love. They may disappoint him; they may struggle to be who they already are as God's people; but God perseveres with them, doing whatever is necessary to keep sanctifying them. This divine faithfulness that the Bible trumpets is the source of joy. Joy, then, involves gratitude and confidence that jointly compel (strengthen) God's people to persist in the mission he

---

[5] Boda (2003: 55) says that 'the negative use of the law is essential in Penitential Prayer for the delineation of sin and the explanation of discipline'. The prayer of confession in Neh. 9, of course, follows the reading of the law in Neh. 8.

[6] McConville (1985: 119) says, 'If there is to be a time of rigorous self-examination (chs. 9, 10) let it first be remembered that God is good, and means it well with Israel.'

has given them.[7] They might have failed to act like God's people, but joy allows them to try again. It delivers them from bondage to the past because a forgiving God always wants to do something new.

That something new inevitably will include other people whom God also wants to restore in some way. Why some people in Nehemiah 8:10 were unprepared is not explained, but maybe Nehemiah 5:1–5 holds the answer. What is clear is that God wanted to include them in the celebration. Those who had experienced renewed joy through Ezra's reading of Scripture also wanted to be included. For this reason, they shared what they had with those who had nothing. God continually says throughout the Bible, 'Here is what I have done for you. Now treat others as I have treated you.' Joy is not an exclusive or private reaction to God's goodness. It cannot be contained but has to be shared. Joy is incomplete without mission.

The events of Nehemiah 8 are said to occur during the seventh month of the religious calendar. This month was the high point of the year because three major holy occasions fell in that span of time: the Feast of Trumpets on the first day, the Day of Atonement on the tenth day and the Feast of Tabernacles on days fifteen to twenty-two. The Feast of Trumpets announced not only the arrival of the most special month but also the beginning of the civil (or agricultural) calendar.[8] So then, the first day of the seventh month of the religious year was New Year's Day (Rosh Hashanah or 'head of the year') of the civil year. There was no more fitting way for God's people to start out a new year than to read the law of Moses. Doing so reminded them of how God's people should live as such in response to what he had already done for them.

In Leviticus 23:24, the Feast of Trumpets is said to be a day of rest; that is, a sabbath. This feast might not fall on the seventh day of the week

---

[7] It is possible, of course, to understand 'joy of Yahweh' as a subjective genitive (God's joy because of his people) instead of an objective genitive (the people's joy because of Yahweh). Wong (1995: 384) says, 'Yahweh's joy is the basis of their [his people's] protection from the consequences of their neglect of the law.' This Lutheran understanding of the relationship of joy and law seems to overlook the gracious and missional emphases of the law. Hamilton (2014: 158) also thinks that the joy was Yahweh's, but for a different reason. Because Yahweh had delighted in his people by moving Persian kings to restore them in the Promised Land, his people could know they were safe.

[8] Both New Year's Day and the Feast of Tabernacles occurred during the seventh month. The former marked the beginning of a new growing season, and the latter marked the end of the previous growing season. Winter grain was planted soon after the harvesting of grapes and olives. See Adams 2014: 83–85.

(Saturday), but it was still treated as a sabbath during which God's people were supposed to desist from their normal labour. Sabbath days, especially on the first day of the year, taught Israel that there is more to life than work. The beginning of a new year often makes people pause and number their days. A new year can be a source of anxiety as people consider their limits and realize that time is slipping away. Sabbaths inform people that they are not defined by their work or achievements. Rather than focus on keeping ahead of the competition or realizing self-promoting goals, a person can find contentment in doing work for God's pleasure. With that contentment comes assurance that God will redeem the labour of one's hands for eternity.

Moreover, the Feast of Trumpets is called a memorial. At the start of a new year, God would have his people remember his faithfulness in the past. By looking back and counting their blessings, God's people could then look forward with trust. God who is the same yesterday, today and tomorrow does not fail to keep his word. God's people should never forget that he never forgets. He is always on time with the fulfilment of his promises.

On the day after the Feast of Trumpets (the second day of the seventh month), Ezra and some of the leaders of the post-exilic community continued reading the law and came to the instructions for the Feast of Tabernacles that appear in Leviticus 23:34–43, Numbers 29:12–38 and Deuteronomy 16:9–12 (Neh. 8:13–14). This feast was supposed to begin on the fifteenth day of the seventh month; that is, during the autumn harvest. Farmers would live in temporary shelters so that they could stay out in the fields and harvest as much as possible during the available daylight. They also wanted to guard against theft. God used the shelters as an object lesson to remind his people how he had taken care of them during the wilderness wandering between the exodus and conquest. After settling in the Promised Land, God's people might have had more stability, but this annual feast reinforced a healthy awareness of dependence on God. Even when humans did the hard work of sowing and reaping, God blessed their labour. His goodness should never be taken for granted, nor should anyone come to the point of living as if God is not involved in the events of his world. Even so-called natural occurrences such as planting and harvesting draw attention to divine providence. God sustains the created order and guarantees the regularity of nature that makes agricultural fertility possible (Gen. 8:22).

Not to be forgotten is that Israel's calendar included other feasts besides the feasts of Trumpets and Tabernacles. According to Leviticus 23:2, all of these feasts were appointed times. God, of course, set aside these special occasions that interrupted the business-as-usual of more ordinary days. Israel's calendar taught people that history moves according to God's direction. He superintends whatever comes to pass with the result that there is no random, meaningless succession of days and years. If God is in control, then the events of a person's life do not happen by chance. God is up to something good in them. They are the scene of his blessing.

Nehemiah 8:18 reports that Ezra read more of the law during the week-long Feast of Tabernacles. It seems as if momentum developed. Earlier in the month, the reading of Scripture led to the rediscovery of the Feast of Tabernacles. Now the listeners wanted to hear what else God's Word had to say. True religion and vibrant spirituality start with the Bible. Far from being just a historical artefact, the Bible features the living words of God. God continually meets people in the pages of his Word. When people realize what they have been missing (a personal encounter with a God who wants to talk to them), they cannot get enough of it. Portions long forgotten or never before read speak afresh into people's lives and offer relevant guidance. Consequently, people see themselves, others and the world from a new perspective. Yes, they may be convicted of sins of omission (not doing the right thing) and commission (doing the wrong thing), but they also see how God wants to include them in his grand story of redemption.

Confession

Nehemiah 9 opens with a reference to the twenty-fourth day of the seventh month. The Feast of Tabernacles had ended two days before. This twenty-fourth day began with more reading of Scripture and ended with prayer. For much of the seventh month the post-exilic community had focused on God's law, and all that time in God's Word now climaxed in corporate prayer.[9] The Jews had been humbled by what they heard, and this prayer juxtaposes the twin themes that stood out: God's faithfulness and their unfaithfulness. Not to be missed is that hearing the law of God prompted the post-exilic listeners to take action in the form of speaking (confessing)

[9] Boda (2003: 46) says, 'The law plays an important role within the penitential prayer tradition as the code that defines covenant fidelity.'

and doing (repenting).[10] God's law did not just condemn; it offered hope. The God who gave the law for the sanctification and mission of his people also promised to overcome the failures of his people and give them a future (Lev. 26:44–45; Deut. 30:1–10). That hope provided the impetus for change.[11]

Similar to Psalms 78 and 106, this prayer reviews Old Testament history. After affirming God's creation and sustenance of the world, the prayer narrows its focus to the election and family of Abraham. This narrowing implicitly recalls the worldwide mission God gave to Abraham and his descendants. So far as the Jewish and Christian Bibles are concerned, this mission makes Israel's history important enough to tell and retell. On the one hand, the prayer remembers God's protection of Abraham's descendants and provision of their needs. On the other hand, it documents repeated instances of ingratitude and disobedience. Unfaithfulness occurred after the exodus (vv. 9–21), after the conquest (vv. 22–29) and during the monarchy (vv. 34–35).[12] Meanwhile, God's faithfulness is seen first in his enactment of the covenantal curses in response to his people's sin. Nehemiah 9:33 admits that God righteously subjected his people to hardship. They had reaped what they had sown. Not only had they disregarded God's commandments but they had also ignored his warnings through prophets (Neh. 9:26, 30). Nevertheless, God's faithfulness went beyond a commitment to justice. Second, it was seen in his demonstrations of mercy. Remarkably, all the unfaithfulness of Israel did not result in their annihilation (Neh. 9:19, 27, 31). An entity called Israel is still present at the end of Numbers, at the end of Judges, at the end of Kings, at the end of this prayer and at the end of Ezra–Nehemiah.[13] The only explanation is God's faithfulness not only to his

---

[10] Throntveit 1992: 106; Tollefson and Williamson 1992: 57; Eskenazi 2001: §2.5; Bautch 2003: 122–123.

[11] Laird 2016: 278–280.

[12] The absence of any reference to the transgressions of kings is curious. Redditt (2014: 301) suggests that the people responsible for Ezra–Nehemiah 'did not want to offend and rile their overlords'. Meanwhile, Brueggemann (1991: 136) says that this prayer 'jumped over the monarchic period to find resources in the early sources'. It did this because the post-exilic community lived on the margins of the Persian Empire and so found little encouragement in the memory of the established institutions of kingship and temple. The less stable conditions of post-exilic life more closely resembled the uncertainty of life in Egypt, the wilderness and the settlement. Perhaps, but the covenantal neglect of kings is recalled in vv. 32–34.

[13] Duggan (2001: 239) says that 'the prayer's conceiving of history in terms of successive cycles of rebellion, retribution, mercy, and renewed life ultimately makes sense of the manner in which the book ends – not with a resolution of all tension but with mention of much that still requires amendment'.

justice but also to his grace. This grace in the past implies hope for the present and future.[14] If God did not abandon his people in the past (Neh. 9:17, 19, 31), the present distress (Neh. 9:37) cannot have the last word. God always remains with his people in order to preserve them for the full realization of his promise to Abraham (Neh. 9:8). God remained with his people in Egypt and made a name for himself by delivering them from an external oppressor (Neh. 9:10). The rest of this prayer suggests that God continues to make a name for himself by delivering his people from trouble they bring on themselves by covenantal disobedience. The gracious, sustaining presence of Yahweh is what distinguishes him from false gods all people, including God's people, make for themselves (Neh. 9:18).

God's grace, of course, was linked to his covenants. God swore to Abraham that he would make him into a great nation (Gen. 12:2). God told Moses that the Israelites would be God's inheritance (Exod. 6:7; Deut. 4:20). God promised David he would have a great name (2 Sam. 7:9) and that his throne would last for ever (Ps. 89:36). Moreover, each of these covenants had the welfare of the nations in view (Gen. 12:3; Deut. 4:6; Ps. 72:17). In other words, God's reputation as saviour of his people and of the world was at stake. Abraham, Moses and David might have had feet of clay, but grace by definition overcomes human weakness and unworthiness. Because God had tied his plan of redemption to a people who needed redemption, he had to do for them what they could not do for themselves. Stated differently, God had to meet his people in their imperfection; otherwise, they and everyone else would perish because of well-deserved judgment for sin. Exhibiting genuine sorrow for sin, the prayer in Nehemiah 9 does not try to force God's hand. Nevertheless, it delicately insists that the present distress, however justified, hinders God's objective for his people.[15] Nehemiah 9:32 refers to God's steadfast love, which is not based on the merit of the beloved (Hos. 11:1–9; Zeph. 3:17). Because God's covenantal promises have to do with overcoming human failure, he cannot let his promises fail as a result of human frailty (Ezek. 16:59–63;

---

14 Kugler (2013: 624) says, 'These former incidents [of divine grace] . . . serve here as "objective" grounds guaranteeing the people's continued existence.' See also Japhet 2006: 371–372.

15 Kugler (2013: 615) says that the plea of this prayer 'stems from their [the praying Jews'] conviction that God's nature and past dealings with them will guarantee that He will not allow them to be totally destroyed in their present crisis.'

20:43–44). Consequently, grace and mercy (Neh. 9:31) trump justice in this prayer.[16]

Mission also trumps justice in this prayer, but less directly. As already noted, Nehemiah 9:10 recalls how Yahweh made a name for himself by defeating Pharaoh in the events of the exodus (Exod. 9:16; 14:4).[17] Making a name, however, is not mentioned again in this prayer. Nevertheless, the echo of making a name in Nehemiah 9:10 is heard in verses 36–37, which draw attention to a divine dilemma. God might have linked his holy name with Israel, who had proved to be unholy, but the continuing slavery of the post-exilic Jews (whether in Susa or in Jerusalem) created an intolerable situation. Yahweh's power that was on display during the events of the exodus (Neh. 9:10) is not so evident during the post-exilic period. God's just judgment in the exile, however necessary it might be because of 'our sins' (Neh. 9:37), has now diminished his reputation in the eyes of the nations. He no longer looks like Israel's champion, let alone the creator of heaven and earth and the recipient of heaven's worship (Neh. 9:6). Moreover, Nehemiah 9:34 may mention the unfaithfulness of earlier kings, but the post-exilic community does not have its own king who, as Yahweh's representative, is realizing the ideal of universal dominion in Psalm 72:8–11. Like the prayer in Ezra 9, this prayer in Nehemiah 9 asks God to display his awesome power again by making good on his promises to his people (Neh. 9:32). They missed numerous opportunities to be the kingdom of priests God wanted them to be, but God cannot miss the present opportunity to advance his purpose for them. He will have to find a way not to treat his people as their sins deserve. The New Testament indicates that God has imputed both the unrighteousness of his people to his incarnate Son and the righteousness of the Son to those who trust him for forgiveness.

If this prayer, along with the prayers in Ezra 9 and Nehemiah 1, is read with awareness of Ezra and Nehemiah's concern for mission within the Persian Empire, then, similarly, it combines a more provincial concern with a more global outlook. Members of the post-exilic community in 445 BC recognized that they were part of a history of sin that affected their relationship with Yahweh and impeded their mission to other people.

---

16 Williamson 1985: 312–313, 317, 319.

17 Boda (1999: 44) says, 'A major theme in Penitential Prayer is the appeal to the glorification of Yahweh's name through his redemptive works both in the past and present.'

Individually and corporately they properly wanted to get right with Yahweh in thought, word and deed.[18] At the same time, they also recognized that they, as Abraham's descendants, were involved in Yahweh's restoration of the whole world.[19] Their right relationship with Yahweh advanced his redemptive plan for everyone else. So then, repentance involved both piety and mission. A personal relationship with God spills over into relationships with other people and even the rest of creation. The result of this mission is that the nations no longer taunt (Neh. 5:9). Rather, they know who Yahweh is because they see him in the righteous conduct of his people.

The tension between the justice and grace of God, including in this prayer, is left unresolved throughout the Old Testament. If the prayer emphasizes the justice of Israel's punishment, implicitly it also holds out hope for another manifestation of divine grace. Nehemiah 9:32 pleads with God to consider how much the exile still affects his people in the post-exilic present – though back in the Promised Land, they were not wholly free of foreign control (Neh. 9:36–37). What Persia gave for the support of the temple it took back in the form of taxes.[20] Besides being burdensome, taxes represented servitude. The one who coercively collected the taxes was in control. In some sense, then, Cyrus' decree did not mark the end of the exile.[21] Even so, something salvific did happen in 539 BC. Haggai, Zechariah and the writer of Ezra 1:1 affirmed the renewed activity of God during the post-exilic period. God was neither silent nor distant. He was 'on site' in the post-exilic community to begin the long process of restoring his people and advancing his redemptive plan through them. Faith was required to see the hand of God in these events, but faith and faithfulness are what the post-exilic literature asks of its readers. The plea in this prayer proceeds from faith in God's promises. The declared intention to make specific changes in conduct (Neh. 9:38) demonstrates a desire to be

---

[18] Boda (2015: 154) says that 'the penitential expressions in Ezra and Neh. 9 are clearly communal in orientation, but they lead to agreements focused on individual commitment (Ezra 10; Neh. 10)'.

[19] Boda (2015: 31) says, 'This human–divine relationship will have implications for other relationships, such as with other humans or aspects/members of creation, since the relationship with God is often estranged due to violation of his priorities for human relationships and for the creational order.' See also p. 34.

[20] Wijk-Bos (1998: 63) says, 'Large empires are expensive. All the administrative courts needed to be financed, and large sums had to be raised from the communities in the provinces.'

[21] Boda 2006: 45; Nykolaishen 2008: 197, 199. See also Wright 1992: 268–270; 1996: xvii–xviii, 126–127, 203–204, 248–250; 1999: 258–261.

faithful. The post-exilic community rightly believed that God would respond favourably to their obedience to his law.[22] God's law that they had been reading said so (Exod. 15:26; 23:22; Lev. 26:3–13; Deut. 7:11–16; 28:1–6). So also does the New Testament (Matt. 6:33 with Matt. 5:17–48; Luke 12:31–37; Rom. 13:8–14; 1 Cor. 10:6–13; 2 Thess. 2:15–17; Heb. 11:6; Rev. 22:14). Moreover, the New Testament affirms that God remains with his people and helps them in Jesus (Matt. 1:23; 28:20; Luke 7:11–16; Phil. 1:19; 4:13; 1 Tim. 1:12).

Repentance

Nehemiah 9:38 (HB 10:1) declares the post-exilic community's intention to make a firm commitment to, or a binding agreement with, God (literally, to 'cut a firm pledge'). In Hebrew, a person typically cuts a covenant, but the sense of this unique expression in Nehemiah 9:38 is clear enough.[23] The signatories make a pledge as a vehicle of repentance with regard to an existing covenant. Nehemiah 10:29 further identifies this agreement or pledge as an oath. Those who take the oath promise to keep God's commandments to Moses (Neh. 10:30). Confession of sin in chapter 9 produces amendment of life in chapter 10. God's people say that they want to live as God's people.

Its concreteness

Nehemiah 10:28–39 demonstrates that repentance must be tailored to a person's situation. It is not enough to say, 'I want to do God's will for the advancement of his kingdom.' While commendable, such an affirmation lacks specificity about how to honour God in a specific context. How a person serves God in, say, New York City may not be exactly the same as in Ajo, Arizona, or in Vanderbijlpark, South Africa, or in Kaohsiung, Taiwan. Moreover, how a person serves God in any of these places today will surely look different from what the post-exilic Jews determined to do. Christian readers of this chapter may wonder what shekels, grain and firewood have to do with them. Changes concerning these items were appropriate for the signatories in their context. Their reading of the law

[22] Holmgren 1992: 253.

[23] Gen. 15:10, 17 explains the idiom. When two parties made a covenant, they slew an animal, cut it in half and walked between the pieces. They said, in effect, 'You can kill me if I do not keep my part of the agreement.'

convicted them in these areas, and so they drafted a concrete itemization of repentance.[24] Their list of changes to make may not seem relevant today. For this reason, later readers have to identify the abiding principle behind the laws of Moses and then translate them into contemporary terms in the best possible way.[25] Laws about marriage, money, sabbath, support for the Lord's work and other topics do, in fact, remain concerns of the Christian life.

The first item addressed is the continuing concern about intermarriage. The signatories pledged not to arrange marriages between their children and the children of those who were not part of the covenantal community. The New Testament upholds this pledge. Both Nehemiah 10:30 and 1 Corinthians 7:39 teach, in effect, that God's people should marry someone who shares their commitment to establishing a Christian home. If a married couple do not have similar religious convictions, then they do not agree on the most foundational questions of life. Why are humans here on planet earth? Why is there evil? What can be done about it? How should humans live? What is their hope? And so on. In short, husband and wife do not share the same mission and so will think differently about how to handle conflict, spend money, bring up children, make friends, leave a legacy and so on. God's people in the Old and New Testaments are called a kingdom of priests. Marriage to outsiders who do not share this calling jeopardizes the witness of God's people individually and corporately.[26] Incompatible ideas gradually necessitate compromise that dilutes the purity of belief and practice. Joshua warned of this possibility (Josh. 23:12–13), and the book of Judges confirms it.

Nehemiah 10:31 then discusses a commitment to sabbath days and years. Humans cannot long burn the candle at both ends of a day or week. God has made them to work six days and then rest. God's appointment of the weekly sabbath (Lev. 23:2–3) was designed mercifully to give people an opportunity to step off life's treadmill and catch their breath by remembering in worship who is in control.[27] By counting past blessings, a person

---

[24] Boda (2015: 132) says, 'Repentance [in Ezra–Nehemiah] involves specific, measurable actions to which the people commit themselves under oath in public assembles.'

[25] Even the post-exilic Jews had to do as much with some of the laws of Moses (McConville 1985: 132–134).

[26] Brown 1998: 176–181.

[27] Brown (ibid. 115) adds, 'When people went to the temple, their minds were lifted above those mundane issues which had dominated their minds throughout another week. As they worshiped together, they could reflect on the meaning to life, the confidence of faith, the

receives assurance that God will continue to provide in the present and future. Of course, Genesis 2:2–3 says God rested after creating the universe in six days. God's rest should not be confused with relaxation. God was not tired after the sixth day of creating. Rather, his rest has to do with stability, security and order. Having set boundaries for the water and land (Gen. 1:9), and having filled those spheres with appropriately designed creatures, God is said to rest. The writer of Genesis knew that water was an ANE symbol of chaos. By saying that God rested after creating, Genesis 2:2–3 indicates that there was no threat of chaos because God was in control of his world. So then, the weekly sabbath reminded God's people that he was also in control of their personal worlds, regardless of how hectic and chaotic they might seem. Moreover, the sabbath helps humans to be humane towards each other – always a compelling witness to the difference God can make in a person's life. Love of neighbour includes giving labourers an opportunity to rest, thus affirming their dignity, not perceiving them as constantly producing drones (Deut. 5:14–15) but as creatures made in God's image for his enjoyment and glory. Humans were made to commune with God. When they do not or cannot do this, they 'are not living as God intended and things cannot possibly go right'.[28] Overworked people become resentful that they have no time for other aspects of life (God, family, friends, recreation, service) rightly important to them.

Little evidence exists for the observance of sabbatical years before and after the exile.[29] As already mentioned in the discussion of Nehemiah 5, post-exilic farmers had tax obligations for which their reserves were not always sufficient during non-sabbatical years (years 1–6 of a sabbatical cycle). Persia would certainly require those payments in year 7; consequently, few farmers could afford to stop working for a whole growing season. A sabbatical year seems just as unlikely in the modern, pluralist world. Even so, today's farmers respect the law about sabbath years by rotating crops and allowing portions of fields to lie fallow. By doing so, they recognize at a minimum that the land is not theirs to exploit. The reference to debt seems to combine sabbath years that happened every seven years and jubilee years that happened every fifty years. The original

assurance of forgiveness, the primacy of love, the guarantee of strength, the horizons of hope – treasures not available for purchase in Jerusalem's market places but, in the temple, their reality was confirmed.'

[28] Brown 1998: 114.

[29] Adams 2014: 88–89.

explanations of sabbath years in Exodus 23:10–11 and Leviticus 25:1–7 say nothing about forgiving debt. Meanwhile, the Year of Jubilee allowed normal commerce (with its potential for setbacks because of bad weather and bad decisions) to continue uninterrupted, except for sabbatical years, for forty-nine years (Lev. 25:8–55). During the fiftieth year, all property reverted to its rightful owner so that the owner could again harvest fields he had mortgaged for debt reduction. A jubilee year cancelled any remaining debt and allowed every family unit to start another jubilee cycle with a clean slate. The Year of Jubilee reminded God's people not only that Yahweh owned the land but also that the land was the stage on which a redeemed people, by means of economic activity, performed their mission as a kingdom of priests. People who modelled redemption could not enslave one another for ever. Otherwise, their behaviour would deny their theology.

Whether the post-exilic community declared a year-long jubilee cannot be determined, but they seem to have shared Nehemiah's concern about the deleterious effects of spiralling debt. By forgiving obligations, they put members of the covenantal community ahead of financial portfolios and enabled everyone to remain a participant in the larger mission of the community. Poverty and peasantry could not take hold permanently. There is little evidence, though, that the Israelites before the exile or the Jews after it ever observed the Year of Jubilee. While richer nations in today's world may occasionally talk about forgiving the debts of poorer nations, the jubilee principle does not seem to have much practical application in strictly religious contexts. Instead, it is most often spiritualized as forgiveness of sin. Perhaps the spirit of jubilee theology is maintained by sermons, lessons and policies that warn about debt, teach financial responsibility and advocate generosity to the less fortunate.[30]

Verses 32–39 address the temple. While God's people today may not pay a temple tax or bring produce to church, they may write a cheque for some percentage of their salary and thereby take responsibility for maintaining their local house of worship.[31] Moreover, God's people may no longer have to gather wood for an altar, but they still put their trust in the atoning sacrifice of Jesus, the Lamb of God who takes away the sin of the world. The point is that repentance involves the persistent work of

30 Keller 2015; Nabors 2015.

31 Duggan (2001: 280) notes that in Ezra 1:4, 6:9–10 and 7:21–24 the temple tax replaced the patronage of the Persian kings.

breaking bad habits that neglect God's will and creating new ones that promote his interests on earth. A practical strategy of steps to take in specific situations is necessary for effecting change. Prayer must be combined with deliberate action.

Nehemiah 9 – 10 does not contradict Nehemiah 8:10. Joy cannot come by ignoring sin. Rather, joy starts with an accurate view of self and an awareness of divine grace. It grows with a willingness to repent. Experiencing forgiveness and making specific changes in accordance with God's Word yield gratitude for God's mercy and confidence in his enabling grace. For Christians, the wholly sufficient work of Jesus' righteous life and atoning death is the basis of joy. The absence of joy would seem to betray a misunderstanding of what Jesus has already done for his people.

Its incompleteness

Two other observations arise at this time. They both have to do with perceived omissions from the pledge. In other words, the pledge seems to ignore some issues that have surfaced earlier in the book.

First, the prayer of confession in Nehemiah 9 includes an acknowledgment of the covenantal failure of the kings of Israel and Judah (vv. 32–35), but the steps of repentance in Nehemiah 10:30–39 say nothing about redressing the abuses of the monarchy. The political situation of the post-exilic community could account for the absence of any planned reforms of the monarchy in Nehemiah 10:30–39 or of any messianic zeal surrounding the Davidic descendant Hattush in Ezra 8:2. Though arguably interested in God's promises to David, the post-exilic community did not try to implement the royal eschatology of earlier prophets. It accepted its political reality at the time and focused on other pastoral issues about which something could be done immediately. In the context of demonstrating how Nehemiah, though not a Davidic descendant, resembles an ideal king, Duguid says:

> Certainly there were no overheated messianic hopes, nor incitements to rise up and throw off the Persian yoke, but included in the underlying tone are both gratitude for what God has already done through the Persian authorities in the 'now,' and a patient expectation that there is still more to come in the 'not yet'.[32]

[32] Duguid 2012: 270; see also McConville 1986: 213–214, 223–224.

With or without a Davidic king in Jerusalem, this community recognized its present need to restore its relationship with God, and took concrete steps to do so after receiving instruction from Ezra and the Levites. King Yahweh Is Our Righteousness (Jer. 23:6) would arrive when he arrived. Until then, they would demonstrate their expectation by practising his definition of righteousness.

Second, Ezra–Nehemiah shows some interest in mission. Nehemiah 10, with its application of certain laws to the effort at repentance, may seem to be a likely place for another reference to mission. How could the extensive reading of the law that led to this pledge of change not remind the post-exilic community of its calling as a kingdom of priests (Exod. 19:6)? God's people should treat outsiders as he had treated the Israelite slaves in Egypt (Exod. 22:21; 23:9; Lev. 19:33–34; Deut. 10:19). Nevertheless, Nehemiah 10:30–31 mentions the people of the land only to prohibit marrying them and doing business with them on the sabbath. Refraining from commerce may imply an encouragement or even an invitation to worship Yahweh on the seventh day, but the text is silent on this possibility. Verse 28 even says that those who had separated themselves from the people of the land were participating in this act of repentance. In other words, some outsiders had become insiders.[33] Why not, then, pledge to help other outsiders come to faith in Yahweh? Meanwhile, verses 32–39 discuss support for the temple as the location of Israelite worship and sacrifice. But what about the temple as the centre to which the nations come to hear the law of God (1 Kgs 8:41–43; Isa. 2:3; Mic. 4:1–2)? Artaxerxes had sent Ezra to Jerusalem to teach that law to everyone who did not know it. Ezra, presumably, had asked Artaxerxes for permission to do this (Ezra 7:6). At the critical moment of corporate repentance, though, nothing is said about the law's concern for mission.[34] The signatories had seemingly forgotten the reason for their existence as the people of God. They did not make the connection between keeping the law and being a kingdom of priests. Could it be that this apparent neglect of mission is

[33] Duggan 2001: 268.

[34] Glatt-Gilad (2000: 394) says that the pledge in Neh. 10 'can rightly be seen as the climax of Ezra–Nehemiah, and indeed of the entire restoration period'. If he is correct, then the climax involves disappointment that is typical of life between the now and the not yet. Given the implementation of Cyrus' decree in three stages (building the temple, teaching the people and building the wall), Williamson (1985: 376) seems to be closer to the truth when he identifies the dedication of the wall in Neh. 12 as the climax of the book. Of course, the joy of Neh. 12 is followed by the disappointment of Neh. 13.

partially responsible for the lapse of repentance in Nehemiah 13? When the post-exilic community ignored the missional heart of the law, the signed commitments were not enough to keep them faithful. Rules for the sake of sectarian purity cannot sustain spiritual vitality. People must see how their obedience contributes to the larger story of God's restoration of his world. They cannot just observe change in their life; they have to see it in other people. They need the risk and satisfaction of mission.

Back home in Jerusalem

At the end of Nehemiah 10, spiritually committed people are ready to live in the new Jerusalem. It seems, though, that few people wanted to go there. Nehemiah 7:4 says that there was a housing shortage. Perhaps the residential sections of the city were still in ruins. Chapter 10 ended with an agreement to maintain the temple, and chapter 11 opens with a lottery for the sake of upholding the pledge.[35] Apparently believing that God controlled the outcome of the lot (Prov. 16:33), one out of every ten people agreed to relocate to Jerusalem. Nothing is said about the hardships they encountered when moving from the country where they had grown up to the city where they had no roots. The approbation from those not selected suggests their appreciation of the challenges that lay ahead.

This relocation by lot recalls the settlement of the Promised Land under Joshua (Num. 26:55; Josh. 14:2). In essence, Jerusalem had become something of a new Canaan or holy land. In fact, Nehemiah 11:1 and 11:18 identify Jerusalem as a holy city. The temple and wall had theoretically sanctified the whole city. At this point, it is hard not to recall Ezekiel 48:30–35, where God's city is a square like the Holy of Holies. The name of the city is Yahweh Shammah (Yahweh Is There). Of course, Ezra–Nehemiah never records the return of Yahweh's glory (presence) to the post-exilic temple, and Nehemiah 13 demonstrates that this city is not yet wholly holy. So then, Nehemiah 11 seems to anticipate something else besides this fifth-century repopulation. According to the New Testament, the glory of God returned to the temple in the person of Jesus (John 1:14; 2:13), whose Spirit now lives in Jesus' disciples (1 Cor. 3:16; 6:19). First

---

[35] Eskenazi (1988a: 112) says, 'One must consider Nehemiah 11 as one of the ways the community as a whole implements the immediately preceding pledge. Settling the city constitutes the first step in demonstrating that the people will not forsake the house of God.'

Corinthians 1:26 adds that not many of Jesus' disciples were movers and shakers in the Roman world. Instead, most of the residents of the new/New Jerusalem humbly but devotedly work for the advancement of God's kingdom in their relatively little corner of the world.

Zechariah 4:9–10 referred to the completion of the temple foundation as a small beginning. Nehemiah 11 records another small beginning. Though the kings of Persia had underwritten the cost of rebuilding Yahweh's temple (Isa. 60:5–7) and though God had chosen Jerusalem again (Zech. 1:17), this city was hardly the international centre that unified all humanity in the worship of Yahweh. The 'volunteers' who admirably practised self-denial nevertheless moved into God's city in faith. During their lifetime, they never saw all that the prophets had envisioned for Jerusalem after the exile. They never saw the glory of God in Jesus, who taught at this temple. Nevertheless, they took a holy risk for God.[36] By going beyond conventional wisdom that would advise them to stay put outside the city, they invested in the work of God and left the results to him. Hebrews 11 indicates that God has prepared a better city for them.

The covenant name for God (Yahweh or LORD) may not appear in Nehemiah 11, but it does open the prayer of confession in Nehemiah 9. The Levites called the congregation to bless the 'LORD your God' (Neh. 9:5), and then someone prayed, 'You are the LORD' (Neh. 9:6).[37] Later the congregation pledged to bring the firstfruits of its produce to the house of the Lord (Neh. 10:35). According to Exodus 3:14, God told Moses that his name was 'I am who I am', which is the basis for the covenant name of God.[38] The verbal form of 'I am' allows for the translation 'I will be who I will be'. The present tense emphasizes God's immutability with the result that he will keep his word to Abraham, Isaac and Jacob. The future tense may not deny God's constancy, but it does introduce the reality of relationship. Moses wanted to know who was sending him, and wanted a sign

---

36 What Fried (2015: 288) says in her reflection after Ezra 6 is applicable to Neh. 11: 'Change comes only for those who are willing to step out of their comfort zone and take a chance on God.'

37 The Septuagint attributes the prayer to Ezra. This interpretation seems reasonable in view of Ezra's prayer in Ezra 9 and his presence in Neh. 8. Still, no textual evidence confirms the inference of the translators.

38 In Hebrew, *'ehyeh 'ăšer 'ehyeh*. The verbs are first-person singular. In v. 15, however, Moses is supposed to tell the Israelites in Egypt that 'the LORD . . . has sent me to you'. In Hebrew, *'ehyeh* becomes *yĕhwâ*. This word resembles the third-person singular *yihyeh*, which is then anglicized as Yahweh or Jehovah. So then, 'I am who I am' becomes 'He is'.

or guarantee. God replied, 'I will be who I will be.' In other words, 'Follow me and find out.' The sign of returning to this mountain (Exod. 3:12) will come after Moses trusts this Yahweh and risks his life. So then, Moses' understanding of God will develop as the story unfolds. The implication is that a lifetime is required for getting to know God. In that lifetime, God's people witness his grace in action. They see God's goodness to others and experience it themselves. God's faithfulness to his promises is not an abstract concept. Rather, he proves it over time, and his people become convinced of it in the crucible of life.[39]

The same truth is reinforced in Nehemiah 11. Those who moved into Jerusalem did so on the basis of the law of their covenantal God that they had been reading. Because of the passage of time, they might have known more history of God's relationship with his people than did Moses or the Israelites in Egypt. Nevertheless, they (like Moses and the Israelites in Egypt) had to follow God into an uncertain future and discover his sufficiency for themselves. Every generation of God's people must prove his faithfulness anew. Following God involves more than right belief and conduct. Following God is an adventure that requires trust and risk.

Celebrating the finished project

Nehemiah 12:1–26 lists the names of the religious personnel who ministered at the temple during the nine decades between Cyrus' decree and Nehemiah's labour. The names of Zerubbabel and Jeshua in verse 1 (see Ezra 3:8–9) and Ezra and Nehemiah in verse 26 frame the multigenerational list. These generations of priests indicate continuity throughout the post-exilic era. Like Ezra 2 and Nehemiah 7, Nehemiah 12 makes all the listed names participants in one work of restoration that climaxes in verses 27–47 with jubilant dedication of the finished project.[40] The celebration of the temple's completion and installation of priests in Ezra 6:16–18 anticipates the installation and worship in Nehemiah 12. A continuous line of priests from the exile to the full implementation of Cyrus' decree attests to God's faithful provision of a means of atonement and

[39] For further discussion of the significance of the future sense of God's covenant name, see Wilson 2014: 126–128.

[40] Eskenazi (1988a: 115) says, 'The network of priests and Levites unifies the earlier and later periods into a single, continuous event: the actualization of Cyrus's edict.'

reconciliation for his people. Jerusalem could not have remained a holy city without properly performed sacrifices.[41]

The post-exilic community might have had its struggles and setbacks, but these were not able to stop what God was doing among his people, especially through their performance of Cyrus' decree. Similarly, God's people today can recall high and low moments in church history and see how God has preserved a people for his name. Along with Paul (Rom. 7:15, 19), they are also painfully aware of inconsistency in their lives. The erratic behaviour, though, does not prevent any good behaviour or any good results. God may work through less than fully sanctified saints, but he does work. God's Spirit makes change-for-the-better possible. All believers – past, present and future – will enter the New Jerusalem (Heb. 11:39–40) they have had a hand in building and the new Jerusalem of the post-exilic period anticipated.

Nehemiah 12:27–47 then describes the worship service for the dedication of the wall and the completion of Cyrus' decree. Nothing is said about reading the law or confessing sin. Instead, the emphasis is on giving thanks by means of musical instruments and choral singing. The years Ezra 1–Nehemiah 12 reviews involved some gloomy days that made such a festive occasion seem unlikely. Nevertheless, there were times of rejoicing (Ezra 3, 6; Neh. 8) that offered a foretaste of the finale in Nehemiah 12. It is hard not to imagine that the instrumentalists and singers reached soaring heights that rivalled Handel's *Music for the Royal Fireworks* or performances of the Choir of King's College, Cambridge. Music and lyrics together must have made the worshippers imagine that they had been transported into the presence of God. Indeed, worship can lift people's spirits so that they become more acutely aware of another world beyond the here and now and aspire to promote the full irruption of that world into this present evil age. Of course, the New Testament teaches that Jesus has already entered this present age and inaugurated a new age of salvation. Because the future is now in Christ, Christian worship since New Testament times has jubilantly declared the reality of redemption in a still fallen world. Even so, Nehemiah 12 can teach Christians something about the 'not yet' of the new age. This worship service came at the culmination of a near century of work. Readers of Ezra–Nehemiah should imitate the post-exilic perseverance that made this celebration possible.

---

41 Steinmann 2010: 586.

The service in Nehemiah 12 began with formal purifying or consecrating of those who would live, work and worship within the wall (Neh. 12:30).[42] The worship itself proceeded according to David's instruction (Neh. 12:45–46) but, unlike Ezra 3:11, there is no record of what words of David were sung. As already mentioned, members of the post-exilic community hardly employed the rubrics of Davidic liturgy with no thought of the Davidic theology of the liturgy. Davidic liturgy and Davidic theology cannot be separated. A Davidic descendant might not have revitalized David's kingdom at that time, but the post-exilic community still recalled David in its worship. Gathered together in David's city (Neh. 12:37), these Jews maintained hope for God's eventual fulfilment of his promises to David, which of course had missional significance for the whole world (Ps. 72:17).[43] The worshippers understood their accomplishment of Cyrus' decree as part of God's plan for redemptive history, and were grateful to participate with God's blessing. Nehemiah 12:43 says that people far away could hear the singing. Surely some of them were the so-called people of the land who had tried to thwart the whole project from the beginning. The worship of God's people bore witness to the success God had granted them. Everyone then knew Yahweh was the God who was in Jerusalem (Ezra 1:3).

Nehemiah 12 records the last of several gatherings in the book of Ezra–Nehemiah. These assemblies united members of the post-exilic community in moments of celebration, instruction, repentance and work. The person responsible for the final form of Ezra–Nehemiah obviously thought that communal activities benefited the growth of individual believers and the corporate mission of these believers. God's people cannot be what God wants them to be, and do what God wants them to do, in isolation. They need one another for encouragement, correction, inspiration and motivation. This emphasis on community in Ezra–Nehemiah carries over to the New Testament. Jesus called and trained twelve disciples to be the foundation of his church. Hebrews 10:23–25 urges Christians as the heirs of apostolic teaching to keep gathering together for the purpose of

---

[42] Eskenazi (ibid. 120) says, 'In Neh 12:30, priests and Levites purify not only themselves, the wall, and the gates, but the people as well, hence broadening the realm of the sacred. The wall in Ezra–Nehemiah encloses a sacred space, one that is dedicated to God and requires special purification upon entering. Only after the purification can the procession begin. The purified people now enter the house of God, whose perimeters have also been duly purified.'

[43] Japhet (2006: 222) observes that Davidic kingship preceded the construction of the first temple but would, according to Haggai, follow the construction of the second temple.

remaining hopeful, encouraging one other and doing good deeds. Other New Testament letters have 'one another' sayings that promote fraternal bonds. If Cain asked, '[A]m I my brother's keeper?' (Gen. 4:9), the 'one another' sayings of the New Testament provide an affirmative answer. From beginning to end, the Christian Bible considers the gathering of God's people to be a healthy and necessary part of an individual's relationship and service to God. Such gatherings foreshadow the future assembly of God's perfected people around his throne (Rev. 7:9–12; 21:1–4).

Not yet the way it should be

Perhaps the theological affirmations of the worship shaped daily behaviour (ethics) more than Ezra–Nehemiah reports. Nehemiah 12:47 indicates attention to the earlier pledge (Neh. 10:37) to care for the needs of the temple workers. Even so, Nehemiah 13 brings the book to an unsatisfactory, though realistic, close. Post-exilic Jews struggled to live in view of God's promises to David. Of course, even David fell short of practising his ideals of kingship in Psalm 72.[44] So also did his son (1 Kgs 11:1–8; Neh. 13:26). So then, Nehemiah 13 resembles a splash of cold water in the face. The temple did not remain wholly set apart for the worship of Yahweh, and the new David had not come. Instead, problems beset the new Jerusalem. Apparently these problems arose while Nehemiah was away in Susa (Neh. 13:6). One cannot help but wonder where Ezra was. It seems as if the community could have benefited from his expertise in the law of Moses. When Nehemiah later returned to Jerusalem, quite a religious and social mess was waiting for him.

According to Nehemiah 13:1–3, the post-exilic Jews continued reading the law, and specifically Deuteronomy 23:2–6. These verses prohibit Ammonites and Moabites from entering the assembly of Yahweh because of their refusal to assist the Israelites after the exodus. It is not clear whether this assembly, as understood by Moses, refers more narrowly to religious services at the temple or more broadly to quotidian activities in

44 Ps. 72:20 attributes Ps. 72 to David. The psalm's title, which can be translated 'for Solomon' or 'about Solomon', suggests that David wrote this prayer for the occasion of his son's coronation. Evidently he hoped that Solomon's reign would promote God's mission more than his had. Neh. 13:26 indicates that the tension between the now and the not yet also characterized Solomon's reign.

the Promised Land. Who did the reading in Nehemiah 13:1 is not specified, but the listeners concluded that they should ban all foreigners from not only the temple but also the city. Even if the wall now made this city a Holy of Holies, this decision exceeded what Deuteronomy required and so violated the law's interest in mission (Exod. 19:6; Deut. 23:7–8). At this point it is hard not to recall the story of Ruth. On the basis of her evident faith in Yahweh, the Moabitess Ruth was welcomed into the social community of God's people and presumably granted access to religious gatherings. God blessed the marriage of Ruth to Boaz with the birth of Obed (Ruth 4:13), who was David's great-grandfather. So then, the exclusion of foreigners in Nehemiah 13:3 misread Deuteronomy 23, ignored Ruth and forgot about the inclusion of outsiders (who had become insiders by profession of faith) at the Passover after the completion of the temple's foundation (Ezra 6:21).

If some Jews went too far in the direction of exclusion, others were too inclusive. Nehemiah 13:4 says a priest named Eliashib (presumably the high priest of Nehemiah 3:1 and 13:28) allowed Tobiah to use a room in the temple. The book of Nehemiah does not explain why Tobiah wanted the room or how he and Eliashib became so friendly. Nevertheless, Eliashib showed poor judgment in allowing an ill-advised relationship to compromise his priestly responsibility. Perhaps he had never fully supported Nehemiah's leadership. Even so, Tobiah and his associates had demonstrated their resistance to the edicts of Cyrus and Artaxerxes. Clearly, they were not committed to the law of Moses that Ezra was authorized to teach. Moreover, Tobiah, who was an Ammonite, did not come from a priestly family of the tribe of Levi. He had no right to be in the temple, and no priest should have become so careless as to let Tobiah defile holy space. Maybe Tobiah was not struck dead because the glory of Yahweh had not yet returned to the temple. Even so, history seemed to be repeating itself. The priests were enabling covenantal infidelity (Hos. 4:4–6).

An extra room might have been available in the temple because of the information given in Nehemiah 13:10. The rest of the Jews were not tithing, with the result that the priests and Levites were not being paid. Without support, they took up farming in order to provide for their needs. Not so long before, these Jews had pledged to provide for the needs of the Levites. Now they had reneged on this promise to God and forced their Levitical brethren out of the ministry. In addition to manifesting lack of interest in God's purpose in human history, failure to support the Lord's work probably indicated a lack of trust in God to provide for their needs. Similar to the pre-exilic Israelites (Zeph. 1:12), many of the post-exilic Jews had become practical atheists. God was not active in their lives.

When the prophet Malachi told the post-exilic community to test Yahweh's provision of needs by means of tithing (Mal. 3:10), he might have been addressing this situation in Nehemiah 13.[45] God's people then and now were and are tempted to be ruled by their circumstances and make financial decisions according to conventional wisdom. Malachi reminded God's people to recognize their dependence on God and put their trust in him. Trusting God with money began with tithing, which affirmed God's ownership of everything and his beneficence towards the one giving back. To many people from the post-exilic era to the present, the command to tithe sounds undoable. Why would anyone give 10 per cent of his or her money to God when there never seems to be enough to go around? Malachi promised that God would pour out blessing, and tithing tangibly evidenced trust in that promise. To be clear, Malachi never said that God's people should trust God to give them what they wanted; otherwise, potentially God becomes a servant of idolatrous cravings. Trusting God has to do with wanting his will to be done on earth. Of course, God's will takes into account the needs of his people. Therefore, his people should cheerfully do what he has told them to do and trust him to take care of the rest for his glory and their benefit.

The Jews also failed to keep the sabbath. Business-as-usual continued seven days a week in violation of Nehemiah 10:31. Here was the worship of the 'Almighty Dollar'. People were preoccupied with their needs and wants. Maybe they did not trust God to provide for their needs and relied instead on their own efforts for security. Maybe they understood their self-worth in terms of accomplishments and earnings. Whatever the reason, they deprived themselves (and their workers) of God's appointed rest at the end of each week and set themselves up for exhaustion. Not to be missed is how Nehemiah's closure of the gates promoted mission. By shutting down Jerusalem for business on Saturday, Nehemiah encouraged public worship at the temple. These weekly services were a means by which

[45] As mentioned earlier, the exact time when Malachi ministered during the post-exilic period is not known. He might have ministered in Jerusalem before Ezra's arrival in 458 BC or during Nehemiah's absence after 433 BC (Neh. 13:6). Artaxerxes later allowed Nehemiah to return to Jerusalem, but Neh. 13 does not record the year. The conditions Nehemiah found in Jerusalem resemble the problems Malachi addressed.

the surrounding merchants witnessed the Jews' faith in Yahweh. The clear message of Nehemiah's sabbatarian policy was that Yahweh could be trusted to provide for the needs of his people. He was mightier than the 'Almighty Dollar'. Nehemiah 13:19–22 does not explain why guarding the gates on the sabbath required some of Nehemiah's servants (and even Levites) in addition to the gatekeepers appointed in Nehemiah 7:1. Perhaps Nehemiah did not think that the gatekeepers were spiritually mature enough to resist the solicitations of the merchants.

The problem of intermarriage occurred again, thus illustrating the incomplete sanctification of the members of the post-exilic community and reinforcing the ongoing tension between the now and the not yet in the post-exilic period and throughout redemptive history.[46] This disregard of Ezra's earlier policy also violated the pledge in Nehemiah 10:30. Although not mentioned in Ezra 10, a concern for the covenantal education of children surfaced in Nehemiah 13. More specifically, the children were not learning Hebrew, which was the language of the law of Moses.[47] If the children could not understand the law, they would not know about their divine calling to a distinct mission. Before long they would blend with the people of the land around them instead of modelling a redeemed lifestyle.[48] In this regard they would imitate Solomon, who became apostate because of his marriages (Neh. 13:26), many of which sealed

46 McConville (1986: 211–212) says that 'the compiler of Ezra–Nehemiah intended to end his work with the rather depressing re-emergence of problems which had beset the community, marital abuse in the centre. It is evident that Neh. xiii represents a low note, despite Nehemiah's claims to have set the problem to right. There is something akin to desperation in the account, together perhaps with a tiredness reflected in his closing words: "Remember me, O my God, for good" (v. 21; cf. v. 14). The clear implication is that, were the story of the post-exilic community to be protracted, it would continue to follow the same chequered course that it has throughout our books.'

47 Modern readers need to remember that a plethora of Bible translations was not available in post-exilic times.

48 Packer (1995: 192) adds that these children 'would not be able to pass on Israel's faith to the children that they themselves would have in due course, so that the future spiritual unity of the nation would be at risk'. See also Rothenbusch (2011: 62–63), who considers speaking the language of Judea to be a marker of ethnic identity. A common language may promote a group's cohesiveness, but the post-exilic community in Ezra–Nehemiah had a Hebrew text, consisting of the Law and the Prophets, that united them in the mission of making their God known to the rest of the world. A Gentile king had commissioned Ezra to teach this text to everyone in the western part of the Persian Empire (Ezra 7:25), and that same king was still ruling during the events of Neh. 13 (Neh. 13:6–7). Some members of the post-exilic community might have forgotten or ignored Artaxerxes' approval of Ezra's burden to teach the law of Moses (Ezra 7:6), but Ezra's mission remained sanctioned by the Persian government throughout Artaxerxes' reign. So then, Hebrew was more than an identity marker.

political alliances that further compromised the mission of a kingdom of priests. Solomon's kingdom did not fail because of invasion from without but because of unfaithfulness from within, and a repetition of Solomon's unfaithfulness clearly worried Nehemiah.

Solomon, of course, was said to be the wisest man in the ancient world (1 Kgs 4:30), but the overall impression of his wisdom is that it was a gracious gift to an inadequate man. Although brought up in economic and religious privilege, he chose to ignore God's covenant and so failed to live up to his potential. He died a fool, not heeding his own instruction in Proverbs 19:27. He might have brought Israel to the zenith of their national history, but in doing so he also sowed the seeds of Israel's ruin. His policies divided the country (1 Kgs 12:4). Like other Old Testament characters, Solomon was seriously flawed. As a character in God's story, he leaves the reader longing for something and someone better – someone whose character and conduct match his charismatic endowment (Luke 2:40, 52). In this regard, Solomon anticipated the ending of Ezra–Nehemiah, which also leaves the reader with disappointment.

The children who did not know Hebrew in Nehemiah's Jerusalem did not enjoy the privileges of Solomon's upbringing and so were even more likely to go the wrong way. In a section on 'guardians of the city' that was more at risk from internal failures than external foes, Wilson says:

> In short, for the rabbis [the Jewish heirs of Ezra's teaching ministry], the antidote to moral decay and corruption is education in Scripture. It is the spiritual and ethical values of Hebraic heritage that have given inward strength to and sustained the people of God over centuries. Through study of the Scriptures, the Jewish people realized they must commit themselves to be empowered within. The rabbis believed that internal strength of character, developed through religious textual edification guided by dedicated teachers, brought about the best spiritual fortification to meet, resist, and survive any attack in life.[49]

The same can be said about Christian families and churches. By means of individual, familial and ecclesiastical instruction, God's Word moves from the eyes and ears to the heart and then to the mouth, hands and feet.

[49] Wilson 2014: 267.

It changes people from the inside out with the result of increasing personal integrity and public righteousness.

Sadly, Nehemiah 13:28 reports that the high priest's grandson had married Sanballat's daughter. Sanballat is identified as a Horonite, a term that could refer to a family or to a place. It is not certain whether Sanballat was Jewish or not. This marriage might have violated Nehemiah 10:30, which forbade intermarriage in general, and Leviticus 21:14, which specifically forbade marriage of the high priest to a Gentile. If Sanballat's daughter was Jewish, the decision of Eliashib's grandson still showed disregard for God's law and Nehemiah's rightful authority. The grandson's father-in-law was no friend of Ezra and Nehemiah's orthodoxy. Anyone, especially Nehemiah, could see that more trouble loomed ahead. The issue was not whether Sanballat would cause more unrest but when he would do so. Nehemiah's reaction in 13:28 is not so different from Jesus' instruction in Matthew 5:29–30. Extreme measures are sometimes needed for the health of a person and community, but there was only so much Nehemiah could do. He could not make people want to be righteous.

Another extreme measure is mentioned in Nehemiah 13:25, which says that Nehemiah, in response to learning of intermarriage, cursed people, beat them and pulled out their hair. Ezra 9:3 reports that Ezra, after hearing of the same problem, pulled out his own hair without any violence towards others. Whether Ezra and Nehemiah literally pulled out hair (or merely pulled at it) is hard to know. Nehemiah's reaction, however, seems to be excessive. The biblical writers often narrate events without editorial comment, thus allowing the reader to ponder the lesson to be learned. With the exception of Jesus, the biblical characters are not perfect examples of righteousness but a mixed bag of virtue and vice. Nehemiah's heart might have been in the right place, but his emotions wrongly got the better of him in this instance. His prayers in chapter 13 and elsewhere demonstrate a better way to handle justifiable indignation.

Three times in Nehemiah 13 (vv. 14, 22, 29) Nehemiah shows his frustration by asking God to remember him. This community for which Nehemiah had risked his life still struggled with sin. In fact, they fell into the same nagging sins. God's people never arrive at perfection in this life. Here, then, is the lot of anyone who endeavours to serve God by serving his people. Significant strides may occur, but the highs of revivals do not last for more than a short while. A person's resolve to change for the better usually encounters resistance almost immediately, and then fickleness often surfaces. Where once there was regular reading of the Bible, a person might stop consulting God's Word for lifestyle choices. There is always more work to be done in the messiness of daily life. Sanctification is a lifelong process with ups and downs.

This process can adversely affect those who do God's mission. Being a religious leader is not like being a contractor or professor. A contractor finishes a job and collects his or her fee. A professor usually attends the graduation of students within a few years of their matriculation. Religious leaders, especially pastors, rarely see such closure. So then, readers of Ezra–Nehemiah should not mistake Nehemiah's prayers for arrogance or self-congratulation.[50] He appealed to God for closure. He asked God in private to redeem the labour of his hands by bringing some good out of seeming bad. That was his only hope, and it is the only hope of Christian servants who can identify with Nehemiah.

In this regard, Ezra–Nehemiah ends unsatisfactorily, but any other ending would deny what later readers of this book know to be true about the Jewish community in later centuries. During the centuries after Ezra and Nehemiah, Jerusalem and its temple remained works in progress. While the post-exilic community had carried out Cyrus' decree to rebuild God's city and house, time did not stand still. Later generations saw changes and made changes to Jerusalem and the second temple. Some of these new developments were welcomed by the residents of Jerusalem and Judea, and others were not. To be more accurate, some residents of Jerusalem and Judea appreciated the changes, and other residents opposed them. These developments caused no small amount of trouble, and some changes came as a result of war. Pagan rulers wreaked havoc on God's city, God's house and God's people. Moreover, some members of the people of God behaved badly towards one another and towards the Gentiles. God's people often did not look like a kingdom of priests to the nations. People laboured with different motives to the glory of God and to the benefit of themselves. God's people have always faced the tension between the now and the not yet.

That tension may go unresolved in Ezra–Nehemiah, but Ezra 1:1, which recalls Jeremiah's expectation of restoration, should not be forgotten. Jeremiah announced on two occasions (25:11; 29:10) that the exile would last seventy years. Then Yahweh would restore his people to the Promised

[50] Eskenazi 1988a: 144–147; Packer 1995: 31–32, 35–36, 183–185; Schnittjer 2016: 53–54.

Land. Ezra–Nehemiah knows about this restoration and honestly describes its ups and downs. Nevertheless, Yahweh's promise to give his people a future (Jer. 29:10) still stands. That future includes the promise of a new heart (Jer. 24:7) undivided in its loyalty and conduct (Jer. 32:39). To make this heart possible, Yahweh will write his law on the heart (Jer. 31:33). In other words, he will bring about the internalization of the law that changes people from the inside out. Jeremiah might have told his listeners to return to Yahweh (Jer. 3:12–14, 22), but he also assured them that Yahweh would graciously enable their return. Jeremiah might not fully explain the relationship between the human and divine roles in repentance. Moreover, the placement of the narratives in Jeremiah 34 – 43 after the oracles of restoration in Jeremiah 31 – 33 informs the reader that the fullness of the new covenant is not experienced all at once. Tension between the now and not yet requires walking by faith, as illustrated by the Rechabites (Jer. 35), Ebed-melech (Jer. 38:7–13; 39:15–18), Gedaliah (Jer. 40:7–12) and, of course, Jeremiah. The person(s) responsible for the final form of Ezra–Nehemiah considered the post-exilic community part of the restoration Jeremiah announced.[51] Though aware of this community's struggles, the writer of Ezra 1:1 set the community's story in the eschatological hope of Jeremiah. Yahweh had worked through Persian policy to begin giving his people the transformative future that would, according to Jeremiah, follow the return from exile.

Summary

The person responsible for the final form of Ezra–Nehemiah might have wished that he could have ended the book at Nehemiah 12:47. This stopping point would say, in effect, that the post-exilic community continued to praise God according to David's design and evidence the fruit of repentance. But Ezra–Nehemiah does not end with Nehemiah 12. Ezra–Nehemiah also has Nehemiah 13. The joy of Nehemiah 12 is not the last word in the book. The upsetting conclusion of this book offers insight into the reason for the book's composition.[52] The writer did not consider the

---

[51] For verbal and thematic parallels between Ezra and Jeremiah, see McConville 1986: 214–218. For consideration of what version of Jeremiah was available to those responsible for the final form of Ezra–Nehemiah, see Ulrich 2015: 15–21.

[52] McConville (1985: 146) says, 'This warning about defection from the ideal thus becomes one of the key points of the combined work.'

realization of Cyrus' decree the climax of redemptive history. The decree might have been a significant moment, but it did not signal the consummation of God's purpose for history. Instead, the ending suggests the writer's reaffirmation of the prayer in Nehemiah 9. He hoped that God would graciously give his people what they do not deserve (a future) and mercifully not give them what they do deserve (judgment). Jeremiah's oracles of well-being were the stated basis of that hope.

8
Conclusion

Ezra–Nehemiah begins by saying that God moved Cyrus to issue a decree that allowed his exiled people to go home for the purpose of rebuilding the temple. God is also credited with moving some of his people to act on Cyrus' policy. Other verses (Ezra 5:5; 6:22; 7:27–28; 8:18; 9:9; Neh. 2:8, 12, 18; 6:16; 7:5) similarly assign developments to the intervention of God. Quite clearly, the events recorded in Ezra–Nehemiah do not occur only because of Persian or Jewish initiative. Even so, Ezra–Nehemiah does not record any miracles. Restoration, reformation and revitalization may permeate Ezra–Nehemiah, but God is said to initiate these by moving internally on the hearts of people. God worked through faith, prayer and awareness of providence to accomplish his will. Moreover, the community discerned God's will through Ezra's teaching of Scripture. God was in control through less overtly supernatural means. Godliness grew as people attended to the ordinary means of grace.[1] The post-exilic community might not have achieved perfection (Who does in this lifetime?), but progress occurred. Ezra–Nehemiah clearly attributes the progress to God's blessing.

Ezra–Nehemiah may begin well, but ends with disappointment. Over the course of a century, it became painfully obvious that the exile had not changed the hearts of God's people. After the exile they looked like God's people before the exile. They struggled with the same sins and made the same mistakes. Nehemiah 13 demonstrates how the post-exilic community failed to make good on its pledge of repentance in Nehemiah 10. Though Ezra tried so valiantly to prepare a holy people to live in a holy city and worship in a Davidic way at a new temple, he would surely share

[1] Fyall (2010: 44) says, 'Ezra often fails to charm at a first reading, largely because it often seems so low-key and factual. Yet as we look at what is happening and catch the echoes of earlier Scriptures and see the book in the overall biblical picture we realize that God is working his purpose out.' This observation can also apply to Nehemiah.

Nehemiah's frustration and prayer in Nehemiah 13:14, 22, 29 and 31. For everything the descendants of those listed in Ezra 2 and Nehemiah 7 had accomplished (And who cannot marvel at what God did through these ordinary people?), they did not build the New Jerusalem. Zechariah 4:10 refers to this beginning as a day of small things. Those who lived in Ezra–Nehemiah's Jerusalem might have sampled a preview of the city of God (the 'now'), but fell short of the eventual perfection of the inhabitants of the New Jerusalem (the 'not yet').[2] They even went so far as to defile Yahweh's temple yet again by allowing Tobiah, the enemy, to live within God's house (Neh. 13:9). Moreover, Nehemiah 13:26 records how the post-exilic community repeated its earlier sin of intermarriage, which the writer of Ezra–Nehemiah compares to the disastrous marriages of Solomon and thereby recalls the failures of Davidic kingship. Who could imagine that all the pure joy of Nehemiah 12 could be spoiled so quickly by the relapses of Nehemiah 13? What is more, the disappointment in Nehemiah 13 was not a momentary setback. It continued into the intertestamental period and prompted the founding of diverse communities, such as the Qumran sectarians. Later Luke's account of John the Baptist's ministry in the first century AD drew attention to continuing economic oppression (Luke 3:12–14). Of course, both John and Jesus condemned religiosity devoid of love for God and neighbour.

As Zechariah opened his book with a call to repentance and so recognized the inability of the exile to change the human heart, so Ezra–Nehemiah closes not with utopia but with prayer in the face of bitter reality. More than the implementation of Davidic worship would be needed to answer Nehemiah's prayer. If Ezra–Nehemiah begins with a reference to Jeremiah, then Jeremiah's new David, whose name is Yahweh Is Our Righteousness (Jer. 23:6; 33:16), will have to implement a new covenant that changes the heart and makes lasting righteousness possible. Only then will the jubilant worship of Nehemiah 12 become an uninterrupted practice.

What is curious, though, is that the New Jerusalem, according to Revelation 21:22, has no temple. This observation may seem to belittle the efforts of the post-exilic community, but not really. According to John 1:14, the glory of God took up residence in Jesus, who visited the second temple during his first coming. Because God was present in the person of

[2] See Throntveit 1992: 126; Bergsma 2008: 60–61; Boda 2015: 160.

Jesus, Jesus was and is the ultimate temple. Moreover, those who trust Jesus for forgiveness of sins, become the residence of the Spirit of Jesus. For this reason, Paul calls Christians God's temple (1 Cor. 3:16–17; 6:19). Paul, of course, was aware that Christians (including himself) were still prone to sin in this present evil age, but he also expected God to finish the good work of redemption he had begun in his people. As a result, believers in Jesus would eventually become as perfect as Jesus, in his humanity, is perfect. Such perfection would allow humans to have immediate access to God's presence. No temple with its division into a court of the Gentiles, a court of the Jews, a holy place and a most holy place would be necessary. God will live among humans in unimpeded communion. The 'not yet' of the present will give way to an eternal 'now'.

Bibliography

Ackroyd, P. R. (1987), *Studies in the Religious Tradition of the Old Testament*, London: SCM Press.

Adams, S. L. (2014), *Social and Economic Life in Second Temple Judea*, Louisville: Westminster John Knox.

Angel, H. (2007), 'The Literary Significance of the Name Lists in Ezra–Nehemiah', *JBQ* 35: 143–152.

Applegate, J. (1997), 'Jeremiah and the Seventy Years in the Hebrew Bible: Inner-Biblical Reflections on the Prophet and His Prophecy', in A. H. W. Curtis and T. Römer (eds.), *The Book of Jeremiah and Its Reception*, BETL 128, Leuven: Leuven University Press, 91–110.

Arnold, B. T., and B. E. Beyer (2008), *Encountering the Old Testament: A Christian Survey*, 2nd edn, EBS, Grand Rapids: Baker Academic.

Bauckham, R. J. (2003), *Bible and Mission: Christian Witness in a Postmodern World*, Carlisle: Paternoster; Grand Rapids: Baker.

Bautch, R. J. (2003), *Developments in Genre Between Post-Exilic Penitential Prayers and the Psalms of Communal Lament*, SBLAB 7, Atlanta: Society of Biblical Literature.

Beale, G. K. (2011), *A New Testament Biblical Theology: The Unfolding of the Old Testament in the New*, Grand Rapids: Baker.

Becking, B. (2011), *Ezra, Nehemiah, and the Construction of Early Jewish Identity*, FAT 80, Tübingen: Mohr Siebeck.

Beckwith, R. T. (2001), *Calendar and Chronology, Jewish and Christian: Biblical, Intertestamental, and Patristic Studies*, Boston: Brill.

Bedford, P. R. (2002), 'Diaspora: Homeland Relations in Ezra–Nehemiah', *VT* 52: 147–165.

Bergsma, J. S. (2007), *The Jubilee from Leviticus to Qumran: A History of Interpretation*, VTSup 115, Leiden: Brill.

—— (2008), 'The Persian Period as Penitential Era: The "Exegetical Logic" of Daniel 9.1–27', in G. N. Knoppers, L. L. Grabbe and D. N. Fulton (eds.), *Exile and Restoration Revisited: Essays on the Babylonian and Persian Periods in Memory of Peter R. Ackroyd*, LSTS 73, New York: T&T Clark, 50–64.

Berman, J. (2007), 'The Narratological Purpose of Aramaic Prose in Ezra 4:8–6:18', *ARST* 5: 165–191.

—— (2015), 'The Legal Blend in Biblical Narrative (Joshua 20:1–9, Judges 6:25–31, 1 Samuel 15:2, 28:3–25, 2 Kings 4:1–7, Jeremiah 34:12–17, Nehemiah 5:1–12)', *JBL* 134: 105–125.

Blenkinsopp, J. (1988), *Ezra–Nehemiah: A Commentary*, OTL, Philadelphia: Westminster.

—— (2009), *Judaism: The First Phase*, Grand Rapids: Eerdmans.

—— (2013), *David Remembered: Kingship and National Identity in Ancient Israel*, Grand Rapids: Eerdmans.

Block, D. I. (2010), 'Transformation of Royal Ideology in Ezekiel', in W. A. Tooman and M. A. Lyons (eds.), *Transforming Visions: Transformations of Text, Tradition, and Theology in Ezekiel*, PTMS 127, Eugene: Pickwick, 208–246.

Blomberg, C. L. (1994), *1 Corinthians*, NIVAC, Grand Rapids: Zondervan.

Boda, M. J. (1999), *Praying the Tradition: The Origin and Use of Tradition in Nehemiah 9*, BZAW 277, Berlin: de Gruyter.

—— (2003), 'The Priceless Gain of Penitence: From Communal Lament to Penitential Prayer in the "Exilic" Liturgy of Israel', *HBT* 25: 51–75.

—— (2006), 'Confession as Theological Expression: Ideological Origins of Penitential Prayer', in M. J. Boda, D. K. Falk and R. A. Werline (eds.), *Seeking the Favor of God*, vol 1: *The Origins of Penitential Prayer in Second Temple Judaism*, Society of Biblical Literature Early Judaism and Its Literature 21, Atlanta: Society of Biblical Literature, 21–50.

—— (2015), *'Return to Me': A Biblical Theology of Repentance*, NSBT 35, Nottingham: Apollos; Downers Grove: InterVarsity Press.

Breneman, M. (1993), *Ezra, Nehemiah, Esther*, NAC, Nashville: Broadman & Holman.

Bright, J. (1975), *The Authority of the Old Testament*, Twin Brooks Series, Grand Rapids: Baker.

—— (1981), *A History of Israel*, 3rd edn, Philadelphia: Westminster.

Brown II, A. P. (2005), 'The Problem of Mixed Marriages in Ezra 9–10', *BSac* 162: 437–458.

Brown, R. (1998), *The Message of Nehemiah: God's Servant in a Time of Change*, BST, Leicester: Inter-Varsity Press; Downers Grove: InterVarsity Press.

Brueggemann, W. (1991), 'Rethinking Church Models Through Scripture', *ThTo* 48: 128–138.

Brueggemann, W., and T. Linafelt (2012), *An Introduction to the Old Testament: The Canon and Christian Imagination*, 2nd edn, Louisville: Westminster John Knox.

Butler, T. C. (1978), 'A Forgotten Passage from a Forgotten Era (1 Chr. XVI 8–36)', *VT* 23: 142–150.

Byun, P. (2019), 'A Paradoxical Situation and God's Righteousness in Ezra 9:15', *ZAW* 131: 467–473.

Calvin, J. (1981a), *Commentaries on the Book of the Prophet Jeremiah and the Lamentations*, vol. 4, Grand Rapids: Baker

—— (1981b), *Commentaries on the Twelve Minor Prophets*, vol. 4, Grand Rapids: Baker.

Campbell, G. Van Pelt (2017), 'Structure, Themes, and Theology in Ezra–Nehemiah', *BSac* 174: 394–411.

Childs, B. S. (1979), *Introduction to the Old Testament as Scripture*, Philadelphia: Fortress.

Cogan, M. (2000), 'Cyrus Cylinder', in W. W. Hallo and K. Lawson Younger Jr, *The Context of Scripture*, vol. 2: *Monumental Inscriptions from the Biblical World*, Leiden: Brill, 314–316.

Conczorowski, B. J. (2011), 'All the Same as Ezra? Conceptual Differences Between the Texts on Intermarriage in Genesis, Deuteronomy 7, and Ezra', in C. Frevel (ed.), *Mixed Marriages: Intermarriage and Group Identity in the Second Temple Period*, New York: T&T Clark, 89–108.

DePree, M. (1989), *Leadership Is an Art*, New York: Doubleday.

Douglas, M. (2002), 'Responding to Ezra: The Priests and the Foreign Wives', *BibInt* 10: 1–23.

Dray, S. (2006a), 'Ezra: An Applied Overview', *Evangel* 24: 34–37.

—— (2006b), 'Nehemiah: An Applied Overview', *Evangel* 24: 66–70.

Duggan, M. W. (2001), *The Covenant Renewal in Ezra–Nehemiah (Neh 7:72B–10:40): An Exegetical, Literary, and Theological Study*, SBLDS 164, Atlanta: Society of Biblical Literature.

—— (2006), 'Ezra 9:6–15: A Penitential Prayer Within Its Literary Setting', in M. J. Boda, D. K. Falk and R. A. Werline (eds.), *Seeking the Favor of God*, vol. 1: *The Origins of Penitential Prayer in Second Temple Judaism*, SBLEJL 21, Atlanta: Society of Biblical Literature, 165–180.

Duguid, I. (2012), 'Nehemiah–The Best King Judah Never Had', in I. Provan and M. J. Boda (eds.), *Let Us Go Up to Zion: Essays in Honour of H. G. M. Williamson on the Occasion of His Sixty-fifth Birthday*, VTSup 153, Leiden: Brill, 261–271.

Dumbrell, W. J. (1976), 'Malachi and the Ezra–Nehemiah Reforms', *RTR* 35: 42–52.

Edelman, D. V. (2005), *The Origins of the 'Second' Temple: Persian Imperial Policy and the Rebuilding of Jerusalem*, London: Equinox.

Eichrodt, W. (1961), *Theology of the Old Testament*, vol. 1, tr. J. A. Baker, Philadelphia: Westminster.

Enns, P. (2003), 'Apostolic Hermeneutics and an Evangelical Doctrine of Scripture: Moving Beyond a Modernist Impasse', *WTJ* 65: 263–287.

Eskenazi, T. C. (1988a), *In an Age of Prose: A Literary Approach to Ezra–Nehemiah*, SBLMS 36, Atlanta: Scholars Press.

—— (1988b), 'The Structure of Ezra–Nehemiah and the Integrity of the Book', *JBL* 107: 641–656.

—— (2001), 'Nehemiah 9–10: Structure and Significance', *JHS* 3: article 9. Online: <www.jhsonline.org>.

—— (2006), 'The Missions of Ezra and Nehemiah', in O. Lipschits and M. Oeming (eds.), *Judah and the Judeans in the Persian Period*, Winona Lake: Eisenbrauns, 509–529.

—— (2008), 'Unity and Disunity in Ezra–Nehemiah: Responses and Reflections', in M. J. Boda and P. L. Redditt (eds.), *Unity and Disunity in Ezra–Nehemiah: Redaction, Rhetoric, and Reader*, HBM 17, Sheffield: Sheffield Phoenix, 315–328.

Fee, G. D. (1987), *The First Epistle to the Corinthians*, NICNT, Grand Rapids: Eerdmans.

Fensham, F. C. (1982), *The Books of Ezra and Nehemiah*, NICOT, Grand Rapids: Eerdmans.

Fishbane, M. (1985), *Biblical Interpretation in Ancient Israel*, Oxford: Oxford University Press.

Fleishman, J. (2012), 'Nehemiah's Request on Behalf of Jerusalem', in I. Kalimi (ed.), *New Perspectives on Ezra–Nehemiah: History and Historiography, Text, Literature, and Interpretation*, Winona Lake: Eisenbrauns, 241–266.

Frevel, C., and B. J. Conczorowski (2011), 'Deepening the Water: First Steps to a Diachronic Approach on Intermarriage in the Hebrew

Bible', in C. Frevel (ed.), *Mixed Marriages: Intermarriage and Group Identity in the Second Temple Period*, New York: T&T Clark, 15–45.

Fried, L. S. (2003), 'The Land Lay Desolate: Conquest and Restoration in the Ancient Near East', in O. Lipschits and J. Blenkinsopp (eds.), *Judah and the Judeans in the Neo-Babylonian Period*, Winona Lake: Eisenbrauns, 21–54.

—— (2008), 'Who Wrote Ezra–Nehemiah – And Why Did They?', in M. J. Boda and Paul L. Redditt (eds.), *Unity and Disunity in Ezra–Nehemiah: Redaction, Rhetoric, and Reader*, HBM 17, Sheffield: Sheffield Phoenix, 75–97.

—— (2015), *Ezra: A Commentary*, Sheffield: Sheffield Phoenix.

Fyall, R. (2010), *The Message of Ezra and Haggai: Building for God*, BST, Nottingham: Inter-Varsity Press; Downers Grove: InterVarsity Press.

Gaffin Jr, R. B. (1988), 'The New Testament as Canon', in H. M. Conn (ed.), *Inerrancy and Hermeneutic: A Tradition, a Challenge, a Debate*, Grand Rapids: Baker, 165–183.

Germar, A. (2008), *Roots of Theological Anti-Semitism: German Biblical Interpretation and the Jews, from Herder and Semler to Kittel and Bultmann*, SJHC 20, Leiden: Brill.

Getz, G. A. (1995), *Nehemiah: Becoming a Disciplined Leader*, Men of Character, Nashville: Broadman & Holman.

Gillihan, Y. M. (2002), 'Jewish Laws on Illicit Marriage, the Defilement of Offspring, and the Holiness of the Temple: A New Halakic Interpretation of 1 Corinthians 7:14', *JBL* 121: 711–744.

Glatt-Gilad, D. A. (2000), 'Reflections on the Structure and Significance of the *ʾ*ᵃ*mānāh* (Neh 10:29–40)', *ZAW* 112: 386–395.

Glover, N. (2009), 'Your People, My People: An Exploration of Ethnicity in Ruth', *JSOT* 33: 293–313.

Goldingay, J. E. (1990), *Approaches to Old Testament Interpretation*, updated edn, Leicester: Apollos; Downers Grove: InterVarsity Press.

—— (1994), *Models for Scripture*, Grand Rapids: Eerdmans; Carlisle: Paternoster.

Goswell, G. (2010), 'The Handling of Time in the Book of Ezra–Nehemiah', *TJ* 31: 187–203.

—— (2012), 'The Absence of a Davidic Hope in Ezra–Nehemiah', *TJ* 33: 19–31.

Grabbe, L. L. (2001), 'The Law of Moses in the Ezra Tradition: More Virtual Than Real?', in J. W. Watts (ed.), *Persia and Torah: The Theory of Imperial Authorization of the Pentateuch*, SBLSS 17, Atlanta: Society of Biblical Literature, 91–113.

Green, D. (1993), 'Ezra–Nehemiah', in L. Ryken and T. Longman III (eds.), *A Complete Literary Guide to the Bible*, Grand Rapids: Zondervan, 206–215.

Greidanus, S. (1999), *Preaching Christ from the Old Testament: A Contemporary Hermeneutical Method*, Grand Rapids: Eerdmans.

Gundry, R. H. (1987), 'The New Jerusalem: People as Place, Not Place for People', *NovT* 29: 254–264.

Hagner, D. A. (2012), *The New Testament: A Historical and Theological Introduction*, Grand Rapids: Baker Academic.

Hamilton Jr, J. M. (2014), *Exalting Jesus in Ezra and Nehemiah*, Christ-Centered Exposition Commentary, Nashville: Broadman & Holman.

Harrington, H. K. (2008), 'Holiness and Purity in Ezra–Nehemiah', in M. J. Boda and P. L. Redditt (eds.), *Unity and Disunity in Ezra–Nehemiah: Redaction, Rhetoric, and Reader*, HBM 17, Sheffield: Sheffield Phoenix, 98–116.

—— (2011), 'Intermarriage in Qumran Texts: The Legacy of Ezra–Nehemiah', in C. Frevel (ed.), *Mixed Marriages: Intermarriage and Group Identity in the Second Temple Period*, New York: T&T Clark, 251–279.

Hayes, C. (1999), 'Intermarriage and Impurity in Ancient Jewish Sources', *HTR* 92: 3–36.

Hays, R. B. (1997), *First Corinthians*, Interpretation, Louisville: John Knox.

—— (2002), 'Can the Gospels Teach Us How to Read the Old Testament?' *Pro Ecclesia* 11: 402–418.

Hill, A. E. (1998), *Malachi: A New Translation with Introduction and Commentary*, AB 25D, New York: Doubleday.

Holmgren, F. C. (1987), *Israel Alive Again: A Commentary on the Books of Ezra and Nehemiah*, ITC, Grand Rapids: Eerdmans; Edinburgh: Handsel.

—— (1992), 'Faithful Abraham and the *ʾămānā* Covenant: Nehemiah 9:6–10:1', *ZAW* 104: 249–254.

Janzen, D. (2008), 'The Cries of Jerusalem: Ethnic, Cultic, Legal, and Geographic Boundaries in Ezra–Nehemiah', in M. J. Boda and P. L. Redditt (eds.), *Unity and Disunity in Ezra–Nehemiah: Redaction, Rhetoric, and Reader*, HBM 17, Sheffield: Sheffield Phoenix, 117–135.

Japhet, S. (2006), *From the Rivers of Babylon to the Highlands of Judah: Collected Studies on the Restoration Period*, Winona Lake: Eisenbrauns.

Johnson, W. M. (2011), *The Holy Seed Has Been Defiled: The Interethnic Marriage Dilemma in Ezra 9–10*, HBM 33, Sheffield: Sheffield Phoenix.

Karrer-Grube, C. (2008), 'Scrutinizing the Conceptual Unity of Ezra and Nehemiah', in M. J. Boda and P. L. Redditt (eds.), *Unity and Disunity in Ezra–Nehemiah: Redaction, Rhetoric, and Reader*, HBM 17, Sheffield: Sheffield Phoenix, 136–159.

Keener, C. S. (2009), 'Interethnic Marriages in the New Testament (Matt 1:3–6; Acts 7:29; 16:1–3; Cf. 1 Cor 7:14)', *CTR* 6: 25–43.

Keller, T. (2015), *Ministries of Mercy: The Call of the Jericho Road*, 3rd edn, Phillipsburg, N.J.: P&R.

Kennedy, J. (2008), *The Recapitulation of Israel: Use of Israel's History in Matthew 1:1–4:11*, WUNT 2/257, Tübingen: Mohr Siebeck.

Kidner, D. (1979), *Ezra and Nehemiah: An Introduction and Commentary*, TOTC, Leicester: Inter-Varsity Press; Downers Grove: InterVarsity Press.

Kissling, P. J. (2014), 'The So-Called "Post-Exilic" Return: Already-But-Not-Yet in Ezra–Nehemiah', *Stone-Campbell Journal* 17: 207–220.

Klement, H. H. (2011), 'Rhetorical, Theological, and Chronological Features of Ezra–Nehemiah', in J. A. Grant, A. Lo and G. J. Wenham (eds.), *A God of Faithfulness: Essays in Honour of J. Gordon McConville on His Sixtieth Birthday*, Library of Hebrew Bible/Old Testament Studies 538, New York: T&T Clark International, 61–78.

Knowles, M. D. (2004), 'Pilgrimage Imagery in the Returns in Ezra', *JBL* 123: 57–74.

Koch, K. (1974), 'Ezra and the Origins of Judaism', *JSS* 19: 173–197.

Kugel, J. L. (2007), *How to Read the Bible: A Guide to Scripture, Then and Now*, New York: Free.

Kugler, G. (2013), 'Present Affliction Affects the Representation of the Past: An Alternative Dating of the Levitical Prayer in Nehemiah 9', *VT* 63: 605–626.

Kuruvilla, A. (2009), *Text to Praxis: Hermeneutics and Homiletics in Dialogue*, LNTS 393, New York: T&T Clark International.

Laird, D. J. (2011), 'The Temple Building Account in Ezra 1–6: Refracting the Social World', *Conversations with the Biblical World* 31: 95–114.

—— (2016), *Negotiating Power in Ezra-Nehemiah*, Ancient Israel and Its Literature 26, Atlanta: SBL.

LaSor, W. S., D. A. Hubbard and F. W. Bush (1996), *Old Testament Survey: The Message, Form, and Background of the Old Testament*, 2nd edn, Grand Rapids: Eerdmans.

Lau, P. H. W. (2009), 'Gentile Incorporation into Israel in Ezra–Nehemiah?', *Bib* 90: 356–373.

Levenson, J. D. (1993), *The Hebrew Bible, the Old Testament, and Historical Criticism: Jews and Christians in Biblical Studies*, Louisville: Westminster John Knox.

Levering, M. (2007), *Ezra & Nehemiah*, BTCB, Grand Rapids: Brazos.

Longman III, T., and R. B. Dillard (2006), *An Introduction to the Old Testament*, 2nd edn, Grand Rapids: Zondervan.

Lubeck, R. (2010), 'Ezra–Nehemiah Reconsidered: Aiming the Canon at "Godly Leaders"', Paper presented at the annual meeting of the Evangelical Theological Society, Atlanta: November 17, 2010.

McConville, J. G. (1985), *Ezra, Nehemiah, and Esther*, DSB, Philadelphia: Westminster.

—— (1986), 'Ezra–Nehemiah and the Fulfillment of Prophecy', *VT* 36: 204–224.

MacDonald, M. Y., and L. E. Vaage (2011), 'Unclean but Holy Children: Paul's Everyday Quandary in 1 Corinthians 7:14c', *CBQ* 73: 526–546.

McEntire, M. (2012), 'Portraits of a Mature God: What Would a Theology of the Hebrew Scriptures Look Like if Ezra–Nehemiah Was at the Center of the Discussion?', *PRSt* 39: 113–124.

Maciariello, J. (2003), 'Lessons in Leadership and Management from Nehemiah', *ThTo* 60: 397–407.

Mariottini, C. (2015), 'Prayer in 1–2 Chronicles, Ezra, and Nehemiah', in P. G. Camp and T. Longman III (eds.), *Praying with Ancient Israel: Exploring the Theology of Prayer in Ancient Israel*, Abilene: Abilene Christian University Press, 151–156.

Miller, J. M., and J. H. Hayes (2006), *A History of Ancient Israel and Judah*, 2nd edn, Louisville: Westminster John Knox.

Miller, J. V. (1983), 'The Time of the Crucifixion', *JETS* 26: 157–166.

Min, K.-j. (2008), 'Nehemiah Without Ezra?', in M. J. Boda and P. L. Redditt (eds.), *Unity and Disunity in Ezra–Nehemiah: Redaction, Rhetoric, and Reader*, HBM 17, Sheffield: Sheffield Phoenix, 160–175.

Moberly, R. W. L. (2000), *The Bible, Theology, and Faith: A Study of Abraham and Jesus*, Cambridge Studies in Christian Doctrine, Cambridge: Cambridge University Press.

—— (2013), *Old Testament Theology: Reading the Hebrew Bible as Christian Scripture*, Grand Rapids: Baker Academic.

Moffat, D. P. (2013), *Ezra's Social Drama: Identity Formation, Marriage, and Social Conflict in Ezra 9 and 10*, Library of Hebrew Bible/Old Testament Studies 579, New York: T&T Clark.

Moore, G. F. (1962), *Judaism in the First Centuries of the Christian Era*, vol. 1, Cambridge, Mass.: Harvard University Press.

Nabors, R. (2015), *Merciful: The Opportunity and Challenge of Discipling the Poor Out of Poverty*, North Charleston: CreateSpace Independent Publishing Platform.

Noth, M. (1967), *The Laws in the Pentateuch and Other Studies*, tr. D. R. Ap-Thomas, Philadelphia: Fortress.

Nykolaishen, D. J. E. (2008), 'The Restoration of Israel by God's Word in Three Episodes from Ezra–Nehemiah', in M. J. Boda and P. L. Redditt (eds.), *Unity and Disunity in Ezra–Nehemiah: Redaction, Rhetoric, and Reader*, HBM 17, Sheffield: Sheffield Phoenix, 176–199.

Oeming, M. (2012), 'The Real History: The Theological Ideas Behind Nehemiah's Wall', in I. Kalimi (ed.), *New Perspectives on Ezra–Nehemiah: History and Historiography, Text, Literature, and Interpretation*, Winona Lake: Eisenbrauns, 131–149.

Oswalt, J. N. (2009), *The Bible Among the Myths: Unique Revelation or Just Ancient Literature?*, Grand Rapids: Zondervan.

Packer, J. I. (1995), *A Passion for Faithfulness: Wisdom from the Book of Nehemiah*, Wheaton: Crossway.

Pakkala, J. (2008), 'Disunity of Ezra–Nehemiah', in M. J. Boda and P. L. Redditt (eds.), *Unity and Disunity in Ezra–Nehemiah: Redaction, Rhetoric, and Reader*, HBM 17, Sheffield: Sheffield Phoenix, 200–215.

—— (2011), 'Intermarriage and Group Identity in the Ezra Tradition (Ezra 7–10 and Nehemiah 8)', in C. Frevel (ed.), *Mixed Marriages: Intermarriage and Group Identity in the Second Temple Period*, New York: T&T Clark, 78–88.

Pritchard, J. B. (ed.) (1969), *Ancient Near Eastern Texts Relating to the Old Testament*, 3rd edn, Princeton: Princeton University Press.

Rad, G. von (1962), *Old Testament Theology*, vol. 1, tr. D. M. G. Stalker, New York: Harper & Row.

—— (1963), 'Typological Interpretation of the Old Testament', in J. L. Mays (ed.), *Essays on Old Testament Hermeneutics*, Richmond: John Knox, 17–39.

—— (1965), *Old Testament Theology*, vol. 2, tr. D. M. G. Stalker, New York: Harper & Row.

Redditt, P. L. (2008), 'The Dependence of Ezra–Nehemiah on 1 and 2 Chronicles', in M. J. Boda and P. L. Redditt (eds.), *Unity and Disunity in Ezra–Nehemiah: Redaction, Rhetoric, and Reader*, HBM 17, Sheffield: Sheffield Phoenix, 216–239.

—— (2012), 'The Census List in Ezra 2 and Nehemiah 7: A Suggestion', in I. Kalimi (ed.), *New Perspectives on Ezra–Nehemiah: History and Historiography, Text, Literature, and Interpretation*, Winona Lake: Eisenbrauns, 223–240.

—— (2014), *Ezra–Nehemiah*, SHBC, Macon: Smyth & Helwys.

Reinmuth, T. (2008), 'Nehemiah 8 and the Authority of Torah in Ezra–Nehemiah', in M. J. Boda and P. L. Redditt (eds.), *Unity and Disunity in Ezra–Nehemiah: Redaction, Rhetoric, and Reader*, HBM 17, Sheffield: Sheffield Phoenix, 241–262.

Ridderbos, H. (1982), *When the Time Had Fully Come: Studies in New Testament Theology*, Jordan Station, Ont.: Paideia.

Rosner, B. S. (2000), 'Biblical Theology', in B. S. Rosner, T. D. Alexander, G. Goldsworthy and D. A. Carson (eds.), *New Dictionary of Biblical Theology*, Leicester: Inter-Varsity Press; Downers Grove: InterVarsity Press, 3–11.

Rothenbusch, R. (2011), 'The Question of Mixed Marriages Between the Poles of Diaspora and Homeland: Observations in Ezra–Nehemiah', in C. Frevel (ed.), *Mixed Marriages: Intermarriage and Group Identity in the Second Temple Period*, New York: T&T Clark, 60–77.

Sanders, E. P. (1977), *Paul and Palestinian Judaism*, Philadelphia: Fortress.

Satterthwaite, P. E., and J. G. McConville (2007), *Exploring the Old Testament*, vol. 2: *A Guide to the Historical Books*, Downers Grove: InterVarsity Press.

Saysell, C. (2012), *According to the Law: Reading Ezra 9–10 as Christian Scripture*, JTISup 4, Winona Lake: Eisenbrauns.

Schnittjer, G. E. (2016), 'The Bad Ending of Ezra–Nehemiah', *BSac* 173: 32–56.

Segal, M. (2002), 'Numerical Discrepancies in the List of Vessels in Ezra I 9–11', *VT* 52: 122–129.

Smelik, K. A. D. (2012), 'Nehemiah as a "Court Jew"', in I. Kalimi (ed.), *New Perspectives on Ezra–Nehemiah: History and Historiography, Text, Literature, and Interpretation*, Winona Lake: Eisenbrauns, 61–72.

Smith, B. D. (1991), 'The Chronology of the Last Supper', *WTJ* 53: 29–45.

Southwood, K. (2011), 'An Ethnic Affair? Ezra's Intermarriage Crisis Against a Context of "Self-Ascription" and "Ascription of Others"', in C. Frevel (ed.), *Mixed Marriages: Intermarriage and Group Identity in the Second Temple Period*, New York: T&T Clark, 46–59.

Steinmann, A. E. (2008), 'A Chronological Note: The Return of the Exiles under Sheshbazzar and Zerubbabel (Ezra-2)', *JETS* 51: 513–522.

—— (2010), *Ezra and Nehemiah*, Concordia Commentary, St. Louis: Concordia.

Stuhlmacher, P. (1995), *How to Do Biblical Theology*, PTMS 38, Allison Park: Pickwick.

—— (2002), 'My Experience with Biblical Theology', in S. Hafemann (ed.), *Biblical Theology: Retrospect and Prospect*, Leicester: Apollos; Downers Grove: InterVarsity Press, 174–191.

Summers, C. (2011), 'Nehemiah 5:1–13', *Int* 65: 184–185.

Swindoll, C. R. (1998), *Hand Me Another Brick: How Effective Leaders Motivate Themselves and Others*, rev. edn, Nashville: Thomas Nelson.

Tacitus, C. (1970), *The Agricola and the Germania*, tr. H. Mattingly and S. A. Handford, Penguin Classics, New York: Penguin.

Thiessen, M. (2009), 'The Function of a Conjunction: Inclusivist or Exclusivist Strategies in Ezra 6.19–21 and Nehemiah 10.29–30?', *JSOT* 34: 63–79.

Throntveit, M. A. (1992), *Ezra–Nehemiah*, Interpretation, Louisville: John Knox.

Tollefson, K. D., and H. G. M. Williamson (1992), 'Nehemiah as Cultural Revitalization: An Anthropological Perspective', *JSOT* 56: 41–68.

Ulrich, D. R. (2015), *The Antiochene Crisis and Jubilee Theology in Daniel's Seventy Sevens*, OtSt 66, Leiden: Brill.

—— (2016), 'David in Ezra–Nehemiah', *WTJ* 78: 49–64.

Usue, E. O., (2012), 'Is the Expulsion of Women as Foreigners in Ezra 9–10 Justifiably Covenantal?', *AcT* 32: 158–169.

Vanhoozer, K. J. (2000), 'Exegesis and Hermeneutics', in B. S. Rosner, T. D. Alexander, G. Goldsworthy and D. A. Carson (eds.), *New Dictionary of Biblical Theology*, Leicester: Inter-Varsity Press; Downers Grove: InterVarsity Press, 52–64.

Venema, G. J. (2004), *Reading Scripture in the Old Testament: Deuteronomy 9–10, 31; 2 Kings 22–23; Jeremiah 36; Nehemiah 8*, OtSt 48, Leiden: Brill.

Verhoef, P. A. (1987), *The Books of Haggai and Malachi*, NICOT, Grand Rapids: Eerdmans.

Vos, G. (1948), *Biblical Theology: Old and New Testaments*, Grand Rapids: Eerdmans.

—— (1980), 'The Idea of Biblical Theology as a Science and as a Theological Discipline', in R. B. Gaffin Jr (ed.), *Redemptive History and Biblical Interpretation: The Shorter Writings of Geerhardus Vos*, Phillipsburg: P&R, 3–24.

Waltke, B. K., and C. J. Fredricks (2001), *Genesis: A Commentary*, Grand Rapids: Zondervan.

Waltke, B. K., and C. Yu (2007), *An Old Testament Theology: An Exegetical, Canonical, and Thematic Approach*, Grand Rapids: Zondervan.

Walton, J. H. (2006), *Ancient Near Eastern Thought and the Old Testament: Introducing the Conceptual World of the Hebrew Bible*, Grand Rapids: Baker.

Wellhausen, J. (1957), *Prolegomena to the History of Ancient Israel*, Cleveland: World.

Werline, R. A. (1998), *Penitential Prayer in Second Temple Judaism: The Development of a Religious Institution*, SBLEJL 13, Atlanta: Scholars Press.

Wielenga, B. (2013), 'Renewal and Reconstruction: Holy Writ in Ezra–Nehemiah – A Missional Reading', *In die Skriflig* 47, art. 72.

Wijk-Bos, J. van (1998), *Ezra, Nehemiah, and Esther*, Westminster Bible Companion, Louisville: Westminster John Knox.

Williams, G. R. (2002), 'Contextual Influences in Readings of Nehemiah 5: A Case Study', *TynB* 53: 57–74.

Williamson, H. G. M. (1982), *1 and 2 Chronicles*, NCB, Grand Rapids: Eerdmans.

—— (1985), *Ezra, Nehemiah*, WBC 16, Waco: Word.

—— (2008), 'More Unity than Diversity', in M. J. Boda and P. L. Redditt (eds.), *Unity and Disunity in Ezra–Nehemiah: Redaction, Rhetoric, and Reader*, HBM 17, Sheffield: Sheffield Phoenix, 329–343.

Wilson, M. R. (1989), *Our Father Abraham: Jewish Roots of the Christian Faith*, Grand Rapids: Eerdmans; Dayton: Center for Judaic-Christian Studies.

—— (2014), *Exploring Our Hebraic Heritage: A Christian Theology of Roots and Renewal*, Grand Rapids: Eerdmans.

Wong, G. C. I. (1995), 'A Note on Joy in Nehemiah VIII 10', *VT* 45: 383–386.

Wright, C. J. H. (2006), *The Mission of God: Unlocking the Bible's Grand Narrative*, Nottingham: Inter-Varsity Press; Downers Grove: InterVarsity Press.

Wright, N. T. (1992), *The New Testament and the People of God*, Christian Origins and the Question of God 1, Minneapolis: Fortress.

—— (1996), *Jesus and the Victory of God*, Christian Origins and the Question of God 2, Minneapolis: Fortress.

—— (1999), 'In Grateful Dialogue: A Response', in C. C. Newman (ed.), *Jesus and the Restoration of Israel*, Downers Grove: InterVarsity Press, 244–277.

—— (2012), *How God Became King: The Forgotten Story of the Gospels*, New York: HarperOne.

Index of authors

Index of Scripture references

Titles in this series:

1 *Possessed by God*, David Peterson
2 *God's Unfaithful Wife*, Raymond C. Ortlund Jr
3 *Jesus and the Logic of History*, Paul W. Barnett
4 *Hear, My Son*, Daniel J. Estes
5 *Original Sin*, Henri Blocher
6 *Now Choose Life*, J. Gary Millar
7 *Neither Poverty Nor Riches*, Craig L. Blomberg
8 *Slave of Christ*, Murray J. Harris
9 *Christ, Our Righteousness*, Mark A. Seifrid
10 *Five Festal Garments*, Barry G. Webb
12 *Now My Eyes Have Seen You*, Robert S. Fyall
13 *Thanksgiving*, David W. Pao
14 *From Every People and Nation*, J. Daniel Hays
15 *Dominion and Dynasty*, Stephen G. Dempster
16 *Hearing God's Words*, Peter Adam
17 *The Temple and the Church's Mission*, G. K. Beale
18 *The Cross from a Distance*, Peter G. Bolt
19 *Contagious Holiness*, Craig L. Blomberg
20 *Shepherds After My Own Heart*, Timothy S. Laniak
21 *A Clear and Present Word*, Mark D. Thompson
22 *Adopted into God's Family*, Trevor J. Burke
23 *Sealed with an Oath*, Paul R. Williamson
24 *Father, Son and Spirit*, Andreas J. Köstenberger and Scott R. Swain
25 *God the Peacemaker*, Graham A. Cole
26 *A Gracious and Compassionate God*, Daniel C. Timmer
27 *The Acts of the Risen Lord Jesus*, Alan J. Thompson
28 *The God Who Makes Himself Known*, W. Ross Blackburn
29 *A Mouth Full of Fire*, Andrew G. Shead
30 *The God Who Became Human*, Graham A. Cole
31 *Paul and the Law*, Brian S. Rosner
32 *With the Clouds of Heaven*, James M. Hamilton Jr
33 *Covenant and Commandment*, Bradley G. Green

34 *Bound for the Promised Land*, Oren R. Martin
35 *'Return to Me'*, Mark J. Boda
36 *Identity and Idolatry*, Richard Lints
37 *Who Shall Ascend the Mountain of the Lord?*, L. Michael Morales
38 *Calling on the Name of the Lord*, J. Gary Millar
40 *The Book of Isaiah and God's Kingdom*, Andrew T. Abernethy
41 *Unceasing Kindness*, Peter H. W. Lau and Gregory Goswell
42 *Preaching in the New Testament*, Jonathan I. Griffiths
43 *God's Mediators*, Andrew S. Malone
44 *Death and the Afterlife*, Paul R. Williamson
45 *Righteous by Promise*, Karl Deenick
46 *Finding Favour in the Sight of God*, Richard P. Belcher Jr
47 *Exalted Above the Heavens*, Peter C. Orr
48 *All Things New*, Brian J. Tabb
49 *The Feasts of Repentance*, Michael J. Ovey
50 *Including the Stranger*, David G. Firth
51 *Canon, Covenant and Christology*, Matthew Barrett
52 *Biblical Theology According to the Apostles*, Chris Bruno, Jared Compton and Kevin McFadden
53 *Salvation to the Ends of the Earth* (2nd edn), Andreas J. Köstenberger with T. Desmond Alexander
54 *The Servant of the Lord and His Servant People*, Matthew S. Harmon
55 *Changed into His Likeness*, J. Gary Millar
56 *Piercing Leviathan*, Eric Ortlund
57 *Now and Not Yet*, Dean R. Ulrich

An index of Scripture references for all the volumes may be found at http://www.thegospelcoalition.org/resources/nsbt.